Raised in Captivity

Raised in Captivity:

Why Does America Fail Its Children?

LUCIA HODGSON

GRAYWOLF PRESS

Publication of this volume is made possible in part by a grant provided by the Minnesota State Arts Board through an appropriation by the Minnesota State Legislature, and by a grant from the National Endowment for the Arts. Significant additional support has been provided by the Andrew W. Mellon Foundation, the Lila Wallace-Reader's Digest Fund, the McKnight Foundation, and other generous contributions from foundations, corporations, and individuals. To these organizations and individuals who make our work possible, we offer heartfelt thanks.

Published by Graywolf Press
2402 University Avenue, Suite 203
Saint Paul, Minnesota 55114
All rights reserved.
www.graywolfpress.org
Published in the United States of America

ISBN 1-55597-261-6
2 4 6 8 9 7 5 3 1

First Graywolf Printing, 1997
Library of Congress Catalog Card Number: 97-70215

Cover design: A N D
Cover photograph: Kritina Lee Knief/Photonica

Acknowledgments

I would not have written this book without the encouragement and support of the people around me. I would like to thank, in order of appearance, Jack Olsen for politicizing me; Jane Brown for conceiving of the notion that I could and should write a book; Fiona McCrae for seeing the book's shape long before I did and extracting it from me; Nicole Aragi and the Watkins Loomis Agency for taking a chance on me; Wendy Martin and The Claremont Graduate School for providing me with academic support; Mary Askew and the Harvard Project on Schooling and Children for giving me a sense of my own worth; members of the Graywolf staff for their intelligence and commitment; and Paul Cummins and the Crossroads School for Arts & Sciences for giving me the opportunity to transform theory into practice.

I would also like to express my gratitude to the members of my family: To Mom and Dad for teaching me how to read; to Emily, Molly, Nick, and Hannibal for loving and appreciating me; and to Dr. Lunt for helping me to make my life worth living.

Raised in Captivity

To Nick

Raised in Captivity

Children in an Adult World

When I discovered children's issues as a college senior, I knew immediately that I had found my life's calling. All my interests—in cultural policy, in identity politics, in literary theory, and in the well-being of humanity—converged in the study of children and their issues in popular culture. I believe that I was attracted to children's issues, first and foremost, because I identified strongly with the children involved in the social conflicts I observed in the media—whether against their parents or the state or both. And I felt, in case after case, that the adults involved were not sufficiently sensitive to the children's plight, and that the media implicitly adopted an adult perspective.

In fact, I began to notice attitudes in adults and the media that I hadn't expected, including hostility toward children, distortion of their natures and needs, exasperation at their traumas, confusion about their degree of responsibility for their difficult situations, and even occasional ridicule and denigration of their personalities and predicaments. These attitudes surprised me, not because I am naive about the existence of ignorance and cruelty in our culture, but because I observed them alongside pro-child sentiment and genuine concern about the state of children's welfare in the United States. I have since learned that the aspects of child advocacy which make it appear at first to be the most straightforward turn out to be the ones that make it the most politically, culturally, and rhetorically challenging.

For example, child advocates do not, for the most part, have to battle blatant anti-child groups or policies. No group that I am aware of organizes on a platform of antipathy for children (as the KKK does for African Americans or the religious right for feminists). In fact, the situation vis-à-vis children is quite the opposite. Most Americans view children as a national resource, an essential, positive element of cultural well-being. A 1996 *Time*/CNN poll found that nearly three-quarters of those surveyed supported increased funding for government programs aimed at young people. Yet our government is cutting funding for children's services with unprecedented vigor. Individually and collectively, American adults, despite their stated intentions, cause children to experience a great deal of preventable suffering.

The forces working against children's interests are subtle and disguised to the point of being practically invisible; they are rooted less in conscious antagonism than in unconscious conceptual frameworks. The disconnect between our apparently child-centered culture and our treatment of individual children stems in part from the fact that we do not see children as a social group with a distinct political status. Our culture categorizes young people into our own children, other people's children, ourselves as children, good children, bad children, etc. I have found that our culture has a great deal of difficulty consolidating these views into an assessment of how we actually treat human beings under the age of eighteen. And any attempt at such an assessment collides with our conviction that we care about children and that we want what's best for them. As one magazine article put it: "Americans cherish the notion that they cherish their children, but there's woeful evidence to the contrary."

Another factor of child advocacy that I thought could easily be used to its advantage was universality: Every adult has been a child; many adults are raising or have raised children. Theoretically, children have a larger potential organic constituency than all other special interest groups combined. Yet, I have been taken aback again and again by the relative lack of interest in children that I have encountered in various social circles. Acquaintances who are raising children have a great deal to say about them, but surprisingly little knowledge of how other children live. Acquaintances who don't spend time with children show little curiosity about their welfare.

I have struggled to understand why I don't come across more people lamenting the decrepit, overcrowded schools in which so many children are forced to spend thirteen years of their lives, or criticizing the owners of the expensive cars cruising their local red-light district for teenagers desperate to turn a trick. I have come to believe that, for the most part, adults do not empathize with children—certainly not to the degree that they identify with their own adult peers. Most adults don't even seem to have the capacity or the inclination to relate to the children they themselves once were. It's as if most adults, having endured childhood, want nothing more to do with it until they can enforce its constraints on their own children in their own way. Even though we have all been children, as adults we do not, as a rule, remember clearly the feelings associated with that stage of our lives or empathize with young people currently undergoing that stage. As adults, we assume a different mind-set—we stop examining constraints and we start rationalizing them.

This collective adult disassociation from the state of

childhood has profound implications for the politics of child advocacy. To begin with, our social policies are driven much more by the stories we tell ourselves as adults about childhood than by its actual conditions. We maintain a number of deeply held myths about childhood and its relationship to adulthood and to adult policies. Operating within the context of a great deal of ambivalence about the importance of children and childhood in our society, these myths obscure the actual relationship between adults and children in America and distract us from the kinds of observations that make good policy probable, if not possible.

Adult disassociation from childhood contributes to an irrational conceptual disconnect between children and adults—between what children experience and what kinds of adults they become. In order to mobilize against preventable childhood hardship and trauma, we need to be able to do two things: to identify with mistreated children (which I have already shown to be problematic) and to believe in the negative consequences of their suffering for them and for society as a whole. Our culture also has difficulty with this latter requirement.

If we truly believed that many children were mistreated, and that this mistreatment was damaging, we would expect the adolescents and adults they become to be troubled and dysfunctional to varying degrees. Yet, in general, we are not sympathetic toward troubled, dysfunctional adults. I am perpetually fascinated by the disparaging attitude many adults have toward their peers involved in the recovery movement. The specter of millions of adults acknowledging publicly that they feel their childhoods were unjustifiably difficult, inadequate, abusive, and damaging has incited society to reply: Stop your whining! Who cares about your past? Buck up and cope with the present.

Adults who spend time and energy trying to sort through their childhood experiences and to understand how the resulting feelings have shaped them are accused of being self-obsessed, immature, and pathetic. Wendy Kaminer echoes this attitude in her best-selling attack on the recovery movement, *I'm Dysfunctional, You're Dysfunctional: The Recovery Movement and Other Selp-Help Fashions.* She argues further that the recovery movement is unempowering and apolitical. "It is meanness to exaggerate the emotional problems of middle-class adults in the name of helping victims of child abuse," she writes, "while ignoring the growing numbers of poor children and the crisis in foster care." Kaminer does not consider the possibility that our neglect of poor children stems in part from our refusal, and therefore her refusal, to acknowledge the association between childhood experience and adulthood dysfunction.

If it doesn't really matter how difficult someone's childhood is, give or take infanticide, then why should we care about children in poverty? If we don't believe that childhood poverty causes adult dysfunction, what's wrong with it? When poor children grow up to be mothers on welfare and career criminals (as they are statistically more likely than their middle- and upper-class counterparts), we can simply blame them for lacking character and values. I agree with Kaminer when she writes, "Somewhere along the line we still become accountable for ourselves," regardless of our childhood, but I disagree with her that as a result "the factors that shaped us are moot." Taking accountability for our actions and recognizing the role of childhood circumstances are not mutually exclusive; in fact, they are mutually interdependent, particularly from a political perspective.

American society can't improve children's lives until it takes some responsibility for the adults they become. Yet, our society is currently pushing the notion of individual accountability to absurd extremes by, for example, trying juvenile delinquents as adult criminals. Notions of individual responsibility are of limited use to contemporary social policy debates because they preclude progressive reform. If we dismiss the forces that to a great extent determine who we are, then the concepts of prevention and therefore reform surely are moot. Holding children entirely responsible for their dysfunction highlights the limitations of personal responsibility politics. Refusing to hold social systems like the family, the community, the government, and the corporation partially accountable for individual dysfunction makes true individual accountability impossible. On a societal level, public outcries for more personal accountability in fact constitute an evasion of collective responsibility.

My observations over the past several years about the challenges faced by child advocacy led me to write this book. I believe that rhetorical frameworks, and the myths and conceptual blind spots they perpetuate, pose a much greater obstacle to reform than diminished material resources, a weakened faith in government, a dearth of good intentions, or any of the other usual suspects. This book is an attempt to expose, and ultimately to transform these frameworks through a focus on the rhetorical attributes of specific children's issues as debated in popular culture.

ONE

Cruel to Be Kind

The notion that young people even have rights comes as a shock to many parents . . . . [M]ost people believe kids do belong to their parents, body and soul. As a practical matter, the courts have tended to uphold that view.

PAT WINGERT AND ELOISE SALHOLZ

Our culture regards having children as an act of altruism. Parents, according to this view, are people who have put self-interest aside to serve the interests of their offspring. Even though raising children requires a great deal of time, money, and energy, parents presumably don't expect any payback other than the health and happiness of their children. Theoretically, the well-being of children becomes the goal, and therefore the predominant self-interest of the adults raising them. Cultural sayings support this notion that parents will do whatever it takes to meet their children's needs, even if it entails material and emotional sacrifices. For example, most Americans are familiar with the image of a father, belt in hand, who approaches his terrified child and says ominously: "This is going to hurt me more than it's going to hurt you."

In this scene, the father chooses to do something he finds painful for the good of his child. And the child submits because he knows the dreaded punishment is for his own good; he has to "take his medicine." This idea that the interests of adults and children converge in the act of child

9

rearing facilitates the cultural conviction that the parent-child relationship is free from inherent conflicts. Certainly, children may balk at having to do what's best for them, just as parents sometimes recoil at the prospect of having to mete out disciplinary measures. But, deep down, according to our culture, the good of the child dictates all parental behavior; what adults do and what children need are one and the same. Parents, according to conventional wisdom, just want what's best for their children.

Historically, however, parenting has not been socially constructed as an altruistic endeavor. American common law clearly states that adults reap certain benefits from child rearing. In exchange for meeting their obligation to sustain and manage their children, parents accrue authority over their children, and the rights necessary to exercise that authority. In his *Commentaries on American Law*, written in the 1820s, James Kent wrote, "The rights of parents result from their duties," and called the right to control and discipline children "the true foundation of parental power." Most legal challenges to parental authority originate from the state on behalf of children in cases where parents fail to maintain or severely harm their children.

As our society has begun to recognize children as autonomous individuals with their own rights, the injustice of the deal struck between parents and the state has become more apparent. Contrary to cultural beliefs, what a parent wants for her child or thinks is best does not necessarily correspond to her child's needs. Unfortunately, many of the ways that parents exercise their rights actually compromise their children's well-being. In addition, a parent's right to control his child and a child's right to control his own life often conflict. Traditionally, the courts have automatically sided with parents against their children in legal disputes over whose rights should prevail. Parent-child conflicts of interest have been the rule, not the exception; they simply haven't been recognized. But if children are citizens, not chattel, then their rights cannot be bartered. A parent can't nullify those rights in exchange for the costs of maintenance. As our legal system recognizes children's human rights, the question becomes: How can we balance a child's need to be maintained, educated, and protected with her right to self-determination appropriate to her developmental level?

In order to answer this question, our culture has to rethink the relationships among parents, their children, and the state, and to determine what role parental rights have to play in a system designed to meet the needs of children, not those of adults. If the purpose of our legal system is to ensure that children have the opportunity to become healthy, happy adults and to protect their civil rights, then laws affecting minors should be evaluated by their effectiveness at meeting those goals. Yet our culture adamantly resists debate about children's rights and privileges, let alone reform. We persist in the notion that adults, on the whole, have children's best interests at heart, and that they will act on behalf of those interests. We avoid the reality that both parents and the state often put their own interests first and neglect those of children, especially when the two sets of interests conflict. As a result, children remain inadequately equipped to be protected or to protect themselves from arbitrary and unjust adult authority.

When a variety of news organizations stepped forward to defend Hillary Rodham Clinton, wife of presidential candidate Governor Bill Clinton, during the pre-election mudslinging in 1992, it appeared, at first, that the politically motivated distortion of children's rights issues would finally be checked. Critics of the Clintons had attacked several progressive legal articles that Hillary Rodham Clinton, a lawyer, had written in the seventies. She had argued that children should have a substantial set of both protective and civil rights. Media efforts at clarifying her writings on children's legal rights came on the heels of several inflammatory remarks made by prominent Republican politicians. Richard N. Bond, chairman of the Republican National Committee, stirred audience members in a preconvention speech in Houston by saying that Hillary Rodham Clinton "has likened marriage and the family to slavery. She has referred to the family as a dependency relationship that deprives people of their rights."

In response to these remarks and others like them, Eleanor Clift wrote in *Newsweek*, "What Hillary Clinton actually believes bears little resemblance to the caricature drawn by the Republicans." In general, Clinton's allies took issue with the conservative claim that her views challenged parental authority and traditional family values. They represented their concerted effort as a nonpartisan attempt to set the record straight on behalf of Clinton and of American children. While this defense of Clinton may have served her and children in this country well in so far as it aided the success of her husband's presidential campaign, it did not correct the popular portrayal of her views. Instead, it muffled the most salient aspects of her legal arguments, stifling what could have been an exciting and important cultural debate. Whether or not it was politically motivated, Hillary Rodham Clinton's defense reflected our culture's general tendency to avoid straight, comprehensive debates about children's rights.

Conservatives did distort Hillary Rodham Clinton's written views about children's rights during the 1992 presidential race, however, not in the way that the media claimed. For example, her defenders denied the accusation that Clinton's views on children's rights were radical. Yet, to the extent that "radical" means extreme or significantly different from the norm, Republicans were not wrong in casting her views in that light. In her 1973 article, "Children under the Law," Clinton proposed that, at birth, children acquire all the rights of an adult. She recommended that we presume that people under eighteen, like people over eighteen, "are capable of exercising rights and assuming responsibilities until it is proven otherwise," proposing that the courts shift the burden of proof to those who want to deny children a right, rather than leaving the burden where it still is today, on the shoulders of those who want to increase children's limited stock. In theory, then, children as a class, particularly older children, would only be denied constitutional rights based on "supportable findings about needs and capacities at various ages." And, of course, children could take their grievances to court if they felt that they were being unfairly denied a right.

As the law stands today, children are summarily denied a wide range of legal rights automatically accorded to adults. Children do not have the right to decide where they want to live, where they want to go to school, with whom they want to associate, or what religion they want to practice. In most states, children do not have the right to consent to medical treatment, including abortion, without parental involvement, and do not have the right to have a say in custody and visitation disputes that involve them. As one article summarized, "[M]any states have expanded the legal rights of children . . . . But the law continues to hold that in most situations, children derive their legal rights through their parents or, when parents are missing or abusive, through the state."

The case of Kimberly Mays illustrates both the current limits of children's rights and the arbitrary and excessive power parents can wield over their biological offspring. When Mays was ten years old, her biological parents, the Twiggs, whom she had never met, wanted her "back." Due to a hospital mix-up, she had been sent home with another couple just after her birth—an error that was only discovered a decade later. Even though the Twiggs were complete strangers to Kimberly and were told that Kimberly did not want to meet them, they had a strong case and they went ahead with it. After a legal struggle, Kimberly's father settled with the Twiggs, yielding them visitation rights.

Although the Twiggs' right to Kimberly meant that the young girl had to spend time in a strange household against her will, as a minor, Kimberly had no right to assert her desires and needs. After five upsetting visits with the Twiggs, Kimberly took the highly unusual step of petitioning the court for the legal standing necessary to be heard on the issue of her custody. Fortunately, the judge of the local circuit court found that the Twiggs had "no legal interest in or right to Kimberly Mays," and that her demand never to see them again had to be met. However, due to the unique and extreme circumstances of the case, legal analysts predicted that the decision would have little effect on future decisions. Kimberly was, according to one article, "uniquely lucky" in convincing a judge that her interests should prevail over those of her biological parents.

The views that Hillary Rodham Clinton expressed in her writings in the seventies would, if implemented, accord children a great deal more power than they currently enjoy, which would, as conservatives correctly fear, dramatically lessen parental authority. To the extent then that the word "family" currently refers to a grouping of adults and minors in which the adults have a disproportionate amount of unmitigated and arbitrary power, Clinton's detractors were also right to call her anti-family. As the late conservative critic, Christopher Lasch, wrote in *Harper's Magazine*: "Instead of assuming that parents know best, Hillary Rodham Clinton has argued that "[w]e should recognize [children's] competence to make their own decisions."

Clinton moderated the implications of her views when she added that parental rights should prevail "[i]f the consequences [of parental action or inaction] seem reversible or insubstantial." However, Clinton's writings, if realized, would fundamentally transform the family dynamic. Many parents need the law behind them because they enforce an authority that is intolerable to their children. According to Shere Hite, author of *The Hite Report on the Family: Growing Up under Patriarchy*, parental power, as opposed to mutual respect, is intrinsic to the contemporary American family, especially the traditional one:

> [P]ower and love are combined in the family structure: in order to receive love, most children have to humiliate themselves, over and over again, before power.

> In our society, parents have complete legal, economic, and social "right" to control children's lives. Parents' exclusive power over children creates obedience. Children are likely to take on authoritarian (or obedient) emotional, psychological, and sexual patterns, and see power as one of the central categories of existence.

Granting children the presumption of competence to enjoy all legal rights afforded adults, as Clinton has proposed, would alter the status of children in families. It would lessen the authoritarian nature of the family and increase its democratic character. It would also pave the way for a reconsideration of the notion of parental rights.

In a legal article entitled "Parents' Religion and Children's Welfare: Debunking the Doctrine of Parents' Rights," author James Dwyer argues that "the claim that parents should have child-rearing rights—rather than simply being permitted to perform parental duties and to make certain decisions on a child's behalf in accordance with the child's rights—is inconsistent with principles deeply embedded in our law and morality." He proposes instead that adults who decide to raise children gain a "child-rearing privilege" that authorizes them to make decisions in their child's best interests. Paternalism, then, would be justifiable only to the extent that it respected the child's welfare and self-determination rights. And it would lessen as the child developed.

Clinton's recommendations, if implemented, would undermine parental authority. However, an increase in children's rights would not lead to a unilateral shift of power over children from parents to the state, as some conservatives have claimed. An editorial in *National Review* complained, "On [Clinton's] principles, the state could decide that parents violate their children's 'rights' by keeping them out of public schools, or deny them 'equal protection of the laws' when they forbid them to do whatever liberal judges think they should be allowed to do." In this case of conservative distortion, Clinton's defenders generally failed to speak up. They did not emphasize enough that children's rights would empower children against both parents *and* the state. Children could decide that their parents had violated their rights by keeping them out of public school, and children could decide that the state had violated their rights by, for example, forcing them to attend a dangerous or educationally inadequate school. Children's rights, in theory, would check the arbitrary and unjust authority exercised by *any* adult force in the child's life—parent, teacher, neighbor, social worker, or faceless bureaucracy.

The 1992 case of Gregory Kingsley, a twelve-year-old boy who petitioned the court to grant him say in the decision about his custody, illustrates the ways in which parental rights currently work against children's welfare and the extent to which children need more legal power. In theory, the child-protection system exists to meet children's need to have an appropriate, safe, and stable living environment. When parents are found to be abusive and neglectful, the state has the authority and the obligation to intervene to protect the interests of the child. In Gregory's case, the child-protection system did not perform as it was supposed to. At the time of his widely publicized trial, the twelve-year-old had spent two and a half years in various foster-care families and residential centers. He might have remained in limbo even longer had he not taken his case to court.

Yet even if the system had worked perfectly, Gregory

could legally have spent eighteen months in foster care without knowing where he would end up at the end of his sentence. As many child-protection experts argue, the system prioritizes parental rights over children's welfare. It provides abusive and neglectful parents with countless opportunities to remedy their situation, and to fail at that remediation. As a result, many children experience "years of foster care . . . , repeated episodes of abuse when they are returned, and, finally, permanent emotional damage."

In addition, the state places the burden of proof for terminating parental custody and rights on child-protection agencies, rather than requiring parents to prove they are fit to continue or resume their child-rearing responsibilities. This dynamic reflects the fact that the Supreme Court "framed termination as a contest between the parents and the state, and was thus willing to err in the parents' favor," according to an article by the associate director for the American Bar Association National Legal Resource Center for Child Advocacy and Protection. "The child, unfortunately, was not considered, nor the consequences to the child when termination does not occur."

The state's criteria for rights termination require an overwhelming amount of absolutely incontrovertible "clear and compelling" proof of continued abuse, neglect, or abandonment. Because agencies are overwhelmed, children languish in foster care while workers struggle to gather evidence. Because emotional abuse and neglect are so difficult to prove, social workers "often have to wait until the child suffers concrete physical damage even though in many cases . . . the emotional damage is far more scarring and permanent."

Even when workers make compelling cases to terminate parental rights, they face an uphill battle. Judges often resist such termination proceedings. Even after Gregory had spent thirty months in the system, hadn't been contacted by his mother in over two years, and had found a foster-care family willing to adopt him, the agency charged with his care refused to recommend that his biological mother's rights be terminated. To compound matters, the more poorly the system functions, the more likely judges are to resist termination. According to a staff attorney at the National Center for Youth Law in San Francisco, "When the proposed cut-off date comes . . . judges are reluctant to terminate parental rights, in consideration that the parents never got any help from the agency or never had a fair chance." Agencies that are too overwhelmed to provide families with rehabilitative services extend children's stays in foster care to buy time to deliver those services. The result is the "use of perpetual foster care to mask a failure to provide preventive services to families in crisis." In sum, children's interests are sacrificed to both parental and state interests.

At first it appeared that media pundits and cultural commentators would take advantage of Gregory Kingsley's case to examine how parental rights often prevail at the expense of children's well-being. The *New York Times* declared that Gregory's trial "could substantially alter the legal rights of children and broaden the debate over the structure of contemporary American families." However, the debate that occurred ended up doing almost the opposite. It became an opportunity for the liberal media to rationalize the status quo by arguing that children in the nineties have most of the legal rights they need, and that the current problem with children's status "reflects the breakdown of the social welfare system," not a lack of legal standing.

While coverage acknowledged that the state had failed to protect Gregory, and fails to protect hundreds of thousands of children every year, it did not force the issue of giving children the legal standing they need to challenge or even to influence rulings concerning an abusive parent or an abusive agency. Many children in the system are assigned a guardian ad litem, an attorney whose charge is "to confer with the child, present the child's concerns and desires during formal proceedings and then express [his or her] own opinion about the best solution." However, children are rarely allowed to speak directly to the judge about their situations, and if the child's sense of her own best interests conflicts with the guardian ad litem's determination, the child does not even have direct representation in court.

To make matters worse, many courts "simply ignore" laws requiring the appointment of a guardian ad litem, or overload attorneys who perform this role with unmanageable caseloads. Gregory Kingsley never had a chance to meet or speak with the attorney he had been assigned for over two years. What made Gregory's case unique was that he was granted independent legal status to seek the termination of his mother's parental rights so that he could free himself for adoption. In most states, any interested party can petition for termination proceedings, including a foster parent, an agency, or even a judge.

However, before Gregory Kingsley, no child had ever been allowed to petition the court on his own behalf, i.e., to be an interested party in his own life. Even though Gregory Kingsley was only one of thousands of children failed by state child-protection departments in the early nineties, coverage continued to stress that children should have the right to petition for termination of rights only "as a last resort." Just as we require that children be severely injured before they can be freed for adoption from dangerously inadequate parents, we want them to be egregiously wronged by state departments before they can have a significant say in their own placement. Gregory Kingsley may have found a "place to be" at last, but it took him twelve miserable years.

Coverage further obscured the issue of children's legal standing by emphasizing the struggle between Gregory Kingsley and his mother over the one between young Kingsley and the state. The *Newsweek* cover story featured the headline, "Mom, I Want a Divorce," and was accompanied by a photo of Gregory and his biological mother cut down the middle, separated by a jagged line. However, Gregory was in state custody at the time of his trial. He hadn't lived with his mother for more than eight months in the past eight years. He petitioned the court to force the state to do its job, not his mother. As one advocate pointed out, Gregory went to court primarily "to fight the government bureaucracy" and "to seek his freedom from state government control." As a foster child, Gregory could not legally run away from his placements, nor could he control them. He needed a legal "divorce" not so much from his mother, as from Florida's Department of Health and Rehabilitative Services.

The media's take on the Gregory Kingsley case actually worked against the children's rights movement by allowing conservatives to set the terms of the debate. The conservative media trotted out what they saw as the foreboding consequences of the ruling to give Gregory Kingsley standing in court. They focused on what they viewed as the dangers of giving children the voice and power to contest their living situations. What the conservatives saw as their most politically lethal weapon against Hillary Rodham Clinton and her sympathizers was the threat that the Kingsley ruling could "unleash a flood of frivolous litigation by willful children against their parents," or, as a more liberal spin would have it, that "a nation of youngsters [would drag] their parents into court for being crummy moms and dads." The underlying anxiety to all the apocalyptic prophecies revolved around the potential ability of children to challenge parental control. In other words, conservatives feared that if children had the power to contest or escape their parents' rule, they would do so in a heartbeat—by the thousands.

Ultimately, the media did the opposite of enriching the debate: By referring to the case as a "divorce," it inflamed anxieties that had been generated by the opposition, and then it bent over backward to placate them. The word "divorce" aggravated conservative warnings of further family breakdown as a consequence of increased rights. *Newsweek* even postulated, "If Gregory's story contains a moral, it is how deeply fractured the American family has become." The media repeated conservative threats of mass suings by minors, and then completely dismissed them. The *New York Times* editorialized that the ruling "need not and almost assuredly will not lead to a flood tide of suits by children seeking to 'divorce' their parents." In a particularly stark example of liberal backsliding, Hillary Rodham Clinton told the *New Republic*: "I never meant the presumption of competence to be anything other than a thought-provoking idea."

In many ways, the press was even more at fault for what it didn't do, than what it did. It didn't question the appropriate role, if any, of parental rights, particularly those that conflict with children's interests and rights. It didn't publish any polls about how many children would take their parents to court if they could, or about what allegations they would make. And it didn't wonder out loud what conservative fears said about families. What does it mean that parents all over the country fear, perhaps justifiably, that their children would run away from them if they could? What does the conservative fear about children stampeding the local courthouse, if justified, say about how children are doing and feeling in today's families? Shouldn't our society be concerned about children if so many are so unhappy that they would take their parents to court to get away from them? And if they are so unhappy, what is going on in their homes? And shouldn't they be allowed to leave if they want to so desperately? The media didn't ask these important questions. It simply absorbed and perpetuated the two fundamental implications of the conservative charges.

First, the media promulgated the widely held stereotype that children as a group are much less judicious than adults about the crucial issues of their lives. Coverage reaffirmed the notion that, in general, children of all ages lack the capacity to make reasonable petitions regarding their living arrangements. An editorial in the *Chicago Tribune* stated bluntly, "Most children are not yet capable of understanding and acting in their own long-range interests." Other articles referred to the serious, articulate Gregory Kingsley as if he were exceptional. A *New York Times* article described him as "[e]xhibiting a presence and sophistication unusual for a boy his age." Typically, the press showed no compunction about making these unsubstantiated generalizations about children, despite the fact that they failed to differentiate between children's average competence at different ages.

Second, the media advocated the myth that most American children suffer nothing worse at the hands of their parents than having to eat cruciferous vegetables with dinner.

According to legal aid offices, minors seek lawyers when their welfare is at stake, when, for example, they are being forced to live with an abusive parent, being forced to carry an unwanted pregnancy to term, being institutionalized by a parent against their will, being denied vital medical care due to their parents' religious beliefs, being denied mental health counseling because they lack parental consent, or being denied the right to visit siblings because of parental custody disputes. As the director of Legal Services for Children, a San Francisco law firm that provides free attorneys to children, put it: "We've been here for 17 years and I have yet to have a kid call up and say I want to leave my parents' home because they didn't buy me a Nintendo."

In other words, the media's response perpetuated the stereotype that children are too incompetent to have power, and not oppressed enough, as a group, to benefit from more constitutional rights. The press almost unanimously adopted the position that children, including Gregory Kingsley, would not need expanded rights if the child-protection system functioned as designed. It thereby deflected several crucial arguments about the current system: that even if it functioned perfectly, the system would retain its intrinsic bias in favor of parental rights over children's rights; that it will never function perfectly, although we can hope it will function much better; and that it has never, even in theory, adequately incorporated children's perspectives on issues like family setting that affect them so profoundly.

Any increase in children's legal empowerment faces opposition from adults who jealously guard their prerogative to control their offspring—current or potential. As an article in the *Los Angeles Times* summarized, children's rights over the past decades "have been lurching forward and backward in a tug of war with grown-ups who don't want to concede any more parental authority." Jane Carey, the attorney for Gregory Kingsley's biological mother, summed up the prevailing cultural stance. "[T]here must be recognition of the constitutional rights of parents," she wrote in an article on the case. "Parental rights must supersede any asserted liberty or interests of children." Yet our culture tends to sidestep the reality that an increase in children's rights is tantamount to a decrease in parental rights and vice versa. The children's rights that adults are most vociferously opposed to involve a direct challenge to adult rights over their offspring. In 1994, *Ladies' Home Journal* published an article entitled "Know Your Children's Rights." It argued, "For parents, knowing where the law stands has never been more important," and ten of the fifteen rights discussed directly affected parental rights.

Advocates, like Hillary Rodham Clinton, may have played down the issue of children taking legal action against parents or the state for a good reason—to further their cause. However, the long-term effects of their strategy may prove to undermine any short-term gains. A parental rights backlash that began to gain national momentum in 1995 threatens to set children's rights back in an insidious and profound way. And our culture has failed to identify it as a threat, let alone hone a rhetorical defense. The backlash consists of "pro-family" groups, religious right groups, and parent groups pushing for legislation that holds, "The right of parents to direct the upbringing and education of their children shall not be infringed." The federal version, entitled the Parental Rights and Responsibility Act, prohibits the government from "interfering with or usurping the right of a parent to govern the upbringing of a child" without proof of compelling state interest.

Proponents of parental rights legislation insist that their goal is to establish a definitive answer to the question: "Who decides what's in the best interests of the child—the parent or the government and its institutions?" They want to reassert their "fundamental rights" over their children's upbringing, rights "that traditionally and properly are theirs." They argue that they want to shift control over children "from the education bureaucracy and special interests back to parents" in order to "raise children without government intrusion."

When children are mentioned at all by advocates of parental rights legislation, they are portrayed as the passive, vulnerable victims of a skirmish among adults over the definition of their best interests. And in the rare event that children's rights are mentioned, it is only to assert that they have very little to do with the issue. Proponents argue defensively that the legislation is not meant to address or even recognize conflicts between parents and children. "This is not a dispute between parents and children with the government as referee," a director of legal policy for the Family Research Council told *Christianity Today*. "It's a dispute between parents and government over who is going to be the custodian of children's rights."

In their opposition, children's advocates and the media have by and large mimicked the conservative spin on parental rights legislation. Their criticisms reflect the proponents' framework of parents versus the government. They fall into two main categories: negative effect on the (government-run) education system and negative effect on the (government-run) child-protection system. Regarding schools, opponents argue that the legislation will "dismantle the effectiveness of public education" because it will "produce excessive litigation for schools" and encourage parents "to veto courses and curriculum plans." At the same time, opponents worry that the legislation will "hamper the ability of social service agencies to investigate allegations of child abuse," and cause social service workers to deny treatment to abused children "lest they be seen as interfering with child rearing."

Opponents who see a more sinister agenda on the part of parental rights groups suggest that the "real intent" is "to impose their brand of morality on school curriculums" in order to "dictate a point of view they possess to the rest of us." When opponents mention children, they too portray them as passive vessels whose educational or safety needs might not get met if the legislation passes. The primary problem with the laws, according to a vice president for legislation with the National Parent Teachers Association, is "that they address the rights of parents without considering the needs of children." Perhaps for strategic reasons, advocates steered clear of discussing the role of children's rights in the debate, and reporters neglected to report on it.

However, the children's rights movement has clearly played a seminal role in the development and momentum of parental rights legislation. Groups on both sides of the issue readily agree on the movement's impetus: the increasing dissemination in the schools of information and services related to adolescent sexuality. Parent groups pushing for parental rights legislation began forming in response to children's exposure in school to discussions about contraception, safe sex, masturbation, sexually transmitted diseases, abortion, and homosexuality, and their access to condoms and counseling. In other words, these groups were motivated by their opposition to the implementation of children's right to privacy in matters of sexuality and reproduction.

Most of the core issues of the parental rights movement

have little to do with governmental control over children. For example, the movement supports mandatory parental involvement in a teenager's decision to have an abortion. Supporters of notification and consent clauses want to take the right to choose an abortion away from teen women and hand it over to their parents. The ostensible reason for such clauses—to ensure that young girls have guidance while they deal with a difficult event—does not hold up under scrutiny. Teens with caring, competent, and present parents will not need to be compelled by a law to approach them with their problems. Teens without such parents will in all likelihood not benefit from forced communication. "If teenagers have a history of comfortable verbal give-and-take with their parents, they will be willing to share even unpleasant information with them and will expect to receive reassurance and support," according to David Elkind, author of *The Ties That Stress: The New Family Imbalance*. And, "Those teenagers who have had little or no history of open communication with their parents feel the strongest need to guard their privacy."

However, advocates of notification and consent clauses want parents to have the right to know if their child is seeking an abortion, whether or not they have earned that knowledge through competent parenting, and whether or not their knowing does their child any good. In Minnesota vs. Hodgson, Minnesota made the argument in its brief that "the presumptive right and duty to raise children and be involved in their lives and decisions rightfully belongs to parents." As a *New York Review of Books* article on teen abortions pointed out, this language signals "a sense of parenthood as a property right." It substitutes legal rights for quality parenting.

The parental rights movement also supports the use of corporal punishment that, like notification and consent clauses, conflicts with children's rights and substitutes for quality parenting. Parental rights advocates have framed the issue of corporal punishment as one of government versus parents. Many parents "believe that spanking is a form of discipline and a lifestyle issue that comes out of their faith," the director of the North Dakota Family Alliance and a supporter of the Parental Rights Amendment told the *New York Times*. "With this amendment, the state would have to show a really compelling interest to intervene. Where it is simply a lifestyle issue, they would have to stay out." However, when a parent uses corporal punishment, it is a rights issue, not simply a "lifestyle" issue.

Murray Straus, author of *Beating the Devil Out of Them: Corporal Punishment in American Families*, defines corporal punishment as "the use of physical force with the intention of causing a child to experience pain, but not injury, for the purpose of correction or control of the child's behavior." Exempting parents who use physical force against their children from assault laws is often rationalized by defining such punishment as in children's best interests. However, the vast majority of child-development experts advise against the use of physical punishment. Beyond being ineffective, it is, according to Straus, "*deeply traumatic for young* children," and "*inconsistent with humane* values."

Parents who use corporal punishment do so despite the fact that it is an unjustifiable infringement on children's human rights and harmful to their development. Parents who use corporal punishment substitute power for communication and teaching. Physical punishment may achieve immediate, short-term "results," but it "does nothing to further the long-term goal of successful parenting: raising happy, well-socialized adults." Corporal punishment is, however, consistent with conservative religious beliefs which hold that parental authority over children is absolute and that the "primary responsibility of children is to obey parental directives."

Parental rights groups don't want children to have the opportunity or the resources to exercise their rights, hence their battle against "government interference." As a consequence of their opposition to children's rights, they oppose the state's role in facilitating those rights. The parental rights movement is about parents' control over their children, and regardless of what services the government provides, children, not the government, are the greatest threat to this control. Adults who rely on legal dominance to parent—as opposed to mutual respect, communication, and caring—are particularly vulnerable to an increase in children's rights, and particularly opposed.

Conservatives have acknowledged their opposition to an increase in children's power in their criticism of the United Nations Convention on the Rights of the Child. The Convention contains over fifty articles that outline "the civil and political rights of children as well as their social, economic and cultural rights." According to the late Michael John Jupp, former executive director of the Washington-based Defense for Children International, U.S.A., the Convention is driven by several fundamental principles, including "that in all actions concerning children it is the best interests of the child that must prevail," and that "where a child is capable of forming his or her own views, due weight must be given them." It also emphasizes the state's "direct obligation to the individual child and not to the child, indirectly, as part of a family." Conservatives are opposed to ratifying the Convention precisely because it restructures the relationship between parent and child, allowing children to have a direct relationship with the state, "entitled both to make claims upon the community and to be claimed by the community." Conservatives are opposed to legislation that "treats children as government constituents" instead of as subjects of their parents, indirectly affected by rights and services.

By characterizing the parental rights movement as a battle between parents and the state, parents have inevitably come to be seen as David fighting an impersonal, bureaucratic, yet powerful Goliath. This positioning has displaced children who are the true underdogs. Children's civil rights are being assaulted by a powerful contingent of parents groups, religious groups, and conservative political groups, and few organizations are coming to their defense. Our apathy reflects both our rhetorical approach to children's rights, and our wishful thinking about parent-child relations. We want to believe that parents will do what is best for their children, and that children with parents don't need their own rights.

We are especially anxious to believe that those parents who fight to strengthen their rights over their children are caring and competent. A *Newsweek* story on the parental rights movement concluded that the proposed legislation was "attempting to accommodate the needs of two entirely different types of families." The article described one type as the kind that "demands the legal right to raise their children by their own lights," and the other as the kind that "left alone might place their own kids at risk." The implication is that parents who demand rights do not put their children at risk. Yet parents who fight for the right to control their children are the very ones who fear what their children will do if they have civil rights: run away, inform themselves about safe sex, etc. And they are the parents who feel they need legal authority in order to control their children, as opposed to being able to rely on a healthy, open, communicative relationship.

Parents who invoke the law to assert authority over their children tend to be unilaterally regarded by our culture as devoted to their children's best interests. For example, after several children died during their "treatment" in so-called wilderness-therapy camps, both *Time* and *U.S. News & World Report* published articles on the subject that included profiles of parents who claimed to be well meaning, truly concerned about their children, and faced with adolescents so out-of-control that they needed to be forcibly detained. One story identified a teenage girl as "one of the growing ranks of troubled teens who have been packed off to wilderness-therapy camps by their desperate parents in the hope that the experience will turn their lives around."

The portraits of the parents never implied that they might be in any way responsible for their children's problems, or that they might be exaggerating those problems in order to justify the extreme measures they took. One mother, whose son died during a sixty-three-day grueling wilderness-survival course, was described as having "decided to take action" in response to her son's behavior. She was quoted as saying that she imagined her son "sitting around campfires, being nurtured by nature. . . . I thought I was sending him to a little slice of heaven." In another article, a mother, Marianna, attributed her son's behavior to his learning problem and his unusual size for his age. Several examples involved parents who had looked on helplessly as their children were taken over by drugs, gangs, and violence. A sidebar on child-escort companies that abduct children and deliver them to camps for a fee perpetuated the image of caring parents at their wit's end desperate to help save straying children.

Typically, articles about the camps glossed over the issue of children's rights, portraying both the children and their parents as victims of greed-driven businesses or lax governmental regulations. They didn't consider the possibility that parents might have been depriving their children of their civil liberties without just cause. While there are no doubt many parents who really want to help their children when they have them abducted and forced to undergo "wilderness therapy," some may well be incompetent to make such a decision, and still others may be motivated primarily by their desire to assert their control. They may be punishing their child for not becoming what they want, e.g., heterosexual, religious, sexually abstinent, obedient, etc. Certainly, the fact that these parents have embraced the philosophy of these camps should raise a red flag. Many of the programs boast about breaking children's wills, making them subsist on minimal rations, exposing them to the elements, and subjecting them to "physical hardship" so that counselors can "establish control" over them. Some parents hire professional kidnappers to escort their children to the camps, kidnappers who admit to using pepper spray, choke holds, and hog-tying to restrain the teens they abduct.

Even though articles acknowledge that parents are often misinformed and/or exploited by child-escort companies and wilderness camps, they don't consider that parents' rights to commit their children to such treatment should be mitigated. While proponents of parental rights persist in emphasizing that they are in conflict with the government over the rearing of their children, parents and other authorities often *agree* about what should happen to a child. And when they do, children are particularly at risk. In the case of Gregory Kingsley, his parents and the state agreed that he should forgo adoption and remain in foster care indefinitely to give his mother even more time to get her act together. In the case of wilderness camps, parents and the state agree that adolescents can be held against their will in unlicensed programs without the involvement of a social service agency to determine the appropriateness and safety of the treatment.

Our culture's inability to mitigate parental rights hurts children, yet we find it extremely difficult to debate children's rights in a reasonable and comprehensive manner. If we did, we would have to face a painful realization whose implications we would evidently rather avoid: Parents' desires and their children's needs are inherently in conflict. Most parents want to determine what kind of people their children will become. They have children, in part, to mold them, to dictate their religion, their sexual orientation, their professional aspirations, and their cultural predilections. Yet children have their own ideas about who they are that do not necessarily, if ever, meet with their parents' approval. Should the family as a social institution cater to parents' desires to have particular types of children, or should it provide a forum in which children can discover and become who they want to be?

Currently, our culture has organized the family to meet

parents' interests at the expense of children's, even though, in the long run, parents rarely end up getting what they want. Our culture resists empowering children with rights, not only because it would allow them to challenge arbitrary and unjust parental control, but also because it would make it less likely that they would turn out the way their parents wish. In the 1995 version of *Village of the Damned*, directed by John Carpenter, a small town turns on a group of eight unusual children born at the same time to different families. The adults hate the powerful, half-alien children because they defend themselves against adult abuse, maiming and killing those who hurt them, but also because the children show no interest in being humans like their parents. The scientist studying them characterizes their existence as "implantation," which she defines as, "the production of an offspring unlike that of the parent or should I say host."

In general, adults don't want to make the sacrifices necessary to raise children only to play the role of "hosts." In exchange for supporting their children, they expect control over their behavior and the authority needed to enforce that control. In order to yield to children comprehensive protective and civil rights, our culture has to view child rearing differently, as a privilege bestowed on adults for the sake of their children, not the other way around. As it stands, adults and children need very different things from the parent-child relationship. Our cultural myths can obscure this conflict of interests, but they can't resolve it.

TWO

Self-Centered

━━━━━━

The idea that children do better with their birth parents is indeed a cherished value and belief in our society, but it is not a belief that rests on much scientific evidence.

RICHARD J. GELLES

Americans tend to see themselves as sympathetic to children's needs, and their country as essentially child centered. The expression, "best interests of the child," has become a staple in discussions concerning custody issues. The best-interests standard dictates that children's psychological needs, not their biological backgrounds, determine their placement in families. When biology and psychology mandate different placements, as when a child is placed in a foster-care family at birth only to be reclaimed by his biological parents several years later, our society believes that psychology should prevail. A child-centered society means, by definition, not an adult-centered one. Therefore, even if a child's claim to a psychologically appropriate placement conflicts with an adult's genetic claim, the child should triumph.

Yet, our society often rejects child-centered custody decisions. Despite our child-centered philosophy, our legal system and our cultural attitudes toward childbearing generally favor adult biological rights. Presumably, instances in which adult prerogatives clearly prevail over children's best interests would force us to acknowledge this contradiction.

However, our culture believes that children win out over adults, and this belief compromises our ability to recognize contrary societal patterns. Our culture does champion the interests of children in certain high-profile cases in which adults have prevailed, but our attention deflects potential momentum for reform. The cases are characterized as exceptions to a child-centered norm, or are reconfigured to appear child centered.

The case of Jessica Anne DeBoer illustrates our culture's defective approach to the adult-oriented bias in custody decisions. The night after the U.S. Supreme Court ruled that it would not grant the DeBoers a stay while it decided whether or not it would hear their case, Jan and Robby knew that they had to give up the fight. In two weeks, Jessica would have to be permanently separated from the life the three had created together in order to live as a different person in a different world with two adults with whom she shared a genetic background, but had met only a handful of times.

On 2 August 1993, two-and-a-half-year-old Jessica was transferred from the DeBoers in Michigan to the Schmidts in Iowa. Her anguish at being separated from her psychological parents was captured on film and broadcast around the world. Her private tragedy became a public spectacle, preserved in magazine photos that show a frightened toddler, strapped in a car seat, looking desperately, disbelievingly out the window in a futile attempt to find her mother and father. Jan and Robby DeBoer had remained in the house. As Jessica was carried away, they had "tried through their tears to explain that they still loved her, that none of this was her fault," but they couldn't stand watching her cry as she was driven away.

In her book *Losing Jessica*, Robby DeBoer describes the scene in which she told her daughter what was going to happen:

> As we snuggled in bed that night I told Jessi of our love for her. . . . Then I told her she would be going away, to stay with Dan and Cara, that the court had made up its mind that she would live there. . . .
>
> She began screaming, "No, I don't want to go to Iowa!" I held her close to my chest, as she clung to me, not wanting me to let go of her. I'll never forget the look of terror in her eyes as she screamed. I held her, rocking back and forth, trying to reassure her, telling her that Mommy and Daddy didn't want her to go, that we loved her, and this was not her fault. . . .
>
> "I'll be back, I'll be back," she kept saying.

Given the obvious acute pain caused to Jessica DeBoer by being wrenched from her parents to be transported to the two biological progenitors she did not know, the public opposition to her move seemed to reveal a pro-child streak in our culture. A survey of reader opinions conducted by *Glamour* magazine found that 87 percent of respondents did not think "the courts were right to send Jessica DeBoer back to the Schmidts," and 95 percent felt that the child's best interests "should count for more in the rulings on adoption disputes." *People* magazine reported that the cover story it published on the DeBoer case attracted one of the largest responses in the magazine's history. "Overwhelmingly," according to the magazine, "correspondents expressed their outrage over the court's decision to return Jessica to her birth parents."

Even mainstream coverage of the case, particularly of the fateful day of the transfer, reflected what appeared to be a pro-Jessica, pro-child bias. Reporters and photographers focused on Jan, Robby, and Jessica DeBoer's pain at the moment of separation, but not at all on the Schmidts' presumable elation upon receiving the little girl they had fought to acquire for over two years. Even an article that agreed with the courts' decision to hand Jessica over to the Schmidts found coverage of the separation scene to be "searing and even horrifying." For the reporter, it raised the question: "What monsters would inflict such torment on a child?" A *Time* cover story announced that the courts had treated Jessica "more as property than as a person"; a *Newsweek* story entitled "Who's Looking After the Interests of Children?" proclaimed that the case "highlights the need for child-friendly custody laws"; and *Parents Magazine* ran a story entitled "The Baby Jessica Story: Why the Court Was Wrong."

However, the outcome of the case troubles the image of our culture as pro-child, fighting for children's best interests in the face of cruel, antiquated laws and judicial rulings. If our culture is "overwhelmingly" on the side of the child's best interests, why don't our laws reflect this? Why did the courts rule in favor of the Schmidts? Why did the U.S. Supreme Court refuse to grant the DeBoers a stay, and Jessica a reprieve, while it decided whether or not it would hear the case? As Elizabeth Bartholet, Harvard law professor and author of *Family Bonds: Adoption and the Politics of Parenting*, pointed out in an opinion piece, "While many have expressed outrage at Jessica's plight, the law that her case reflects is, tragically, consistent with the law of the land."

Every major article on the case told readers that our legal system is currently organized to rule in favor of biological parents regardless of the best interests of the children involved. For example, in the context of the DeBoer case, an article in *McCall's* stated that, in general, the law sides with "the property right of the birth parents against the psychological needs of the child." Only one of the major magazine articles on the case indexed in the *Readers' Guide to Periodicals* made a reference to how our laws are created, and what it would take to change them. *Time* quoted Howard Davidson, director of the American Bar Association Center on Children and the Law: "If the law works to the disadvantage of children, it's incumbent upon the legislatures to change the law. The courts can't change the law."

Despite the fact that it is common knowledge that our legal system does not privilege the needs of children over the rights of adults, the coverage of the Jessica DeBoer case did not generate a widespread call for reform of this aspect of our laws. It did not demand that our laws prioritize the right of children to have their interests served by the courts over the right of adults to acquire or maintain custody of their biological offspring. It did not challenge the "biological bias" which, according to Elizabeth Bartholet, who was frequently quoted in articles on the DeBoer case, "explains why the courts so often award children to birth parents, regardless of psychological and emotional bonds built through years of nurturing." And it did not explain why the public that so wholeheartedly championed the right of Jessica DeBoer to a permanent, loving family did not champion the same right for all of America's children.

Although coverage of the DeBoer case did not work to children's advantage, it was consistent with the prevailing belief that our culture is child centered. Media coverage shielded us from the knowledge that we often don't put children first, and protected us from the imperative to change our laws. It allowed us to engage in a public debate that emphasized tangential issues, displacing the crucial ones, and adopted a cultural template that could only lead to fundamentally irrelevant observations and solutions. In addition, coverage diluted and finally dismissed the negative consequences for the child involved, voiding the case of its tragic dimension, and thus of its potential positive impact on child-centered reform efforts. Coverage allowed us to lose our way and the momentum for meaningful reform to fade like the "searing" image of a devastated toddler named Jessica DeBoer.

One of the most powerful editorializing strains of magazine articles, and one of the most accepted even in so-called "objective" reporting, is the association of the subject of an article with a broader social issue. Editors and/or reporters characterize the subject as being representative of another more general issue. They use the subject as a "window" on a supposedly more substantial, less anecdotal, trend. Specific cases become opportunities for more general social commentaries. While early articles on a subject may result in several different associations, later coverage reflects a surprising degree of homogeneity. The characteristics and parameters of a dominant association are established early on, and most future articles follow suit. Homogenous coverage creates a closed circuit in which every article simply recycles a small, predetermined set of associations, questions, and possibilities.

The Jessica DeBoer case could easily have been associated with the children's rights movement. It could have been framed as a case that symbolized the need for the children's best-interests standard to prevail in all custody disputes, in all states. Her case suited this association particularly well *because her best interests were never in question.* As Elizabeth Bartholet told the *New York Times*:

> The courts in both Iowa and Michigan have clearly stated that if they were looking at the best interests of the child, there's at least a good chance that the DeBoers would retain custody. . . . But what they've made clear is that they aren't looking at the best interests of the child and they don't think they are allowed to.

The question posed by the circumstances of the case was not: Where would Jessica be better off—with the DeBoers or with the Schmidts? It was: Whose rights should prevail—Jessica's or her biological father's? In Michigan, where the best-interests standard is decisive, the courts ruled in favor of the DeBoers. In Iowa, where the biological rights of parents are preeminent, the courts ruled in favor of the Schmidts. While both courts agreed that Jessica would be better off with the DeBoers, they also agreed that Iowa had final jurisdiction over the case.

The Jessica DeBoer case could have been used as an opportunity to publicize several existing proposals to reform our legal system so that it better serves the needs of children. Reform goals include placing "a higher value on nurturing than on procreation"; resolving all custody disputes "with a determination of the child's best interests"; and recognizing "children's liberty interest in familial relationships," replacing a "parent-centered" approach with a "child-centered" one. However, out of the hundreds of mainstream magazine articles written about the Baby Jessica case, as it came to be called, only a handful associated the case with the larger issue of children's rights. And the majority of those did nothing more than make the association. They didn't follow through and discuss the implications of the case for that area of law. For example, the *Time* cover story argued in its subtitle that the case "challenges . . . the rights of children" but hardly elaborated on which rights or how they were challenged.

One of the *People* magazine articles also incorporated the issue of rights into its subtitle, saying the case "raised the issue of children's rights—or lack of them," and also did not follow through in the article itself. An article in *McCall's* stated, "To make the often-invoked phrase 'the best interests of children' mean something, [one] organization proposes amending the Constitution to finally give children rights as people," but quickly veered in another direction by adding, "While protecting adoptees in custody disputes is essential, the major cause for the turmoil in adoption lies in the fact that each of the fifty states has its own laws about how parents surrender parental rights."

Instead of exploring the rights issue, the vast majority of articles written about the Jessica DeBoer case focused on the narrower issue of adoption law. In *Newsweek,* "Jessica symbolized every adoptive parent's nightmare," and "the case has come to symbolize the perils and fears of modern adoption." According to *U.S. News & World Report,* "For the practice of adoption, these are troubled times. And nothing has tarnished it more than the unfolding nightmare of Baby Jessica." In *McCall's,* "The Baby Jessica case illustrates how adoption has become an emotional and legal battleground." Although a few of the early *New York Times* articles emphasized the children's rights aspect of the case, later articles mimicked the adoption association. For example, one article stated, "The emotionally wrenching case . . . underscores . . .

the pressing need to revise adoption laws in this country." And later spin-off articles focused exclusively on adoption policy, including "Adoption Is Getting Some Harder Looks," and "The Strain on the Bonds of Adoption."

The linking of the Baby Jessica case with the broader social issue of adoption law was the single most important factor in determining how the social problem "represented" by the case would be constructed, and therefore what solutions and reforms could be envisioned. It opened up the door to one particular avenue of cultural inquiry, while it shut many others. As the Baby Jessica case came to be seen as "the impetus to improve the way courts handle adoption," coverage focused on "the circumstances under which a birth mother gives an irrevocable consent to adoption" and the "clarification of the rights of fathers," shifting emphasis toward parental rights, and further away from children's rights. As one delegate to the National Conference of Commissions on Uniform State [adoption] Laws was quoted as saying: "The basic thrust of adoption-law reform is to guarantee fairness to the biological parents and certainty to the adoptive parents."

Reporters interviewed family-law experts who specialized in adoption law as if they were leading readers to the source of Baby Jessica's problems. If only Cara Clausen had been given a few more hours and some counseling before giving up her baby. . . . If only Dan Schmidt had either somehow been notified right away of his pending offspring, or had his rights automatically terminated after a certain period of time. . . . If only the DeBoers had recognized that they would eventually lose in court and had let go of Jessica as soon as they could. . . .

Once coverage had organized the Baby Jessica case around

clarifying and reinforcing parents' rights, the "true" origin of Baby Jessica's problem could easily be located in the individual adults involved and outside of our cultural policies regarding child-custody decisions. Some articles preferred to paint the DeBoers as desperate, baby-obsessed, scheming people who dragged out the legal battle in order to establish a relationship with Jessica. Then, according to one article, they "used this fait accompli—together with the claim that disrupting the bond would damage Jessica emotionally—to argue that, legal issues aside, they should be allowed to keep her." Others considered Cara Clausen, "the architect of this entire tragic mess." But most agreed that Jessica's problems began when she was born, not before, and that ultimately her "tragic mess" originated with incompetent individuals, not flawed social and legal systems. As one article put it: "The makings of a custody nightmare began within hours of the baby's birth . . . when the child's unmarried mother . . . named the wrong man as the baby's father and got his consent for the adoption rather than that of Mr. Schmidt."

While coverage reassured readers that reformed adoption laws would prevent future Baby Jessica sagas, only a few mentioned in passing that they probably would not have helped Baby Jessica herself. The Jessica DeBoer case was not at all typical of most adoptions, or even of most problem adoptions since Cara lied about the identity of Jessica's father. As a result, two adults did sign away parental rights, but one turned out not to be biologically related. Dan Schmidt's rights had never legally been severed, and in a court system that favors biological parental rights, he would have had a case no matter how much time had passed.

Associating the Baby Jessica case with adoption-law reform had the effect of distracting readers from the children's rights issues involved. The way in which coverage of the case was structured also had a similar impact. Most articles built their coverage of the Jessica DeBoer story in such a way as to dissipate the harm that came to the little girl at the hands of our culture. Articles shifted emphasis away from the best interests of Jessica to the interests of the adults vying for her custody. They structured the story as a conflict between two sets of adults: the adoptive parents vs. the biological parents. The *New York Times* stated that the "case has become a rallying cry for groups representing adoptive families and those fighting for the rights of biological parents," and that it "turned on several tangled and agonizing legal questions, including how to weigh the rights of Mr. Schmidt as the biological father against those of the DeBoers, who by all accounts adopted the child in good faith." This structure evaded the fundamental question of why our culture refused to do what was best for Jessica, elucidating an adult-centered perspective, while obscuring a child-centered one.

People magazine narrowed the question posed by the case down to the following: "Which parents were entitled to this little girl: those whose blood flowed in her veins or those who had nursed her through the darkest nights of early childhood?" By characterizing the Baby Jessica case as a "struggle over parental power," coverage conflated the interests of Jessica with one or another set of parents, and deviated from the crucial issue of the relationship between American children's interests and the law. As a result, Jessica was reduced to the victim of a struggle between adults, rather than of larger anti-child cultural forces such as parental rights and biological bias in custody-dispute rulings.

To some extent, the shift to adult interests allowed an

idealized adoptive parent to displace Jessica as the true victim of her case. Article after article called attention to the pain of adoptive parents, rather than adopted children or children besides Jessica whose best interests had not been served by the courts. *People* wrote that "Jessica's story wreaked havoc on the peace of mind of adoptive parents everywhere." *Newsweek* proclaimed that "Jessica became the symbol of every adoptive couple's nightmare—that biological parents will show up one day to take back their child." *Time* wrote that the custody ruling which transferred ownership of Jessica to her biological parents "sent shudders throughout the nation's adoption community" and conjured the image of adoptive parents who "go to sleep wondering whether their precious child will stay *their* child."

The DeBoers vs. Schmidts framework also had the effect of presenting the Jessica case as if it had two comparable sides—as if the appropriate solution to the custody dispute weren't obvious and straightforward. In the context of the case, the *New York Times* wrote that "there are few ideas that seem so obvious, and in practice prove so elusive, as determining what is in the best interests of a child." Although the Michigan court's ruling that it was in Jessica's best interests to stay with the DeBoers was never legally challenged, much of the coverage created the impression that there were two different, equally compelling arguments about what best met Jessica's needs. The *New York Times* said simply that the case wasn't "clear-cut." *National Review* called the case a "perplexing, agonizing controversy." And *People* stated that "both sides can make passionate and persuasive arguments to support their cases."

In an attempt to present balanced coverage of the mis-guided DeBoers vs. Schmidts framework, articles dredged up competing best-interests arguments that were not at all comparable in quality or credibility. Reporters were easily able to round up child-development experts not involved in the case who would attest to the certain emotional pain and negative developmental consequences of separating Jessica from her parents. However, they "balanced" these views with decidedly unscientific quotes from spokespeople for anti-adoption groups. *People,* for example, paraphrased the director of the Council for Equal Rights in Adoption as say-ing that "if you want to talk long-term problems, nothing can match the lifelong pain that adopted children often feel." Coverage did not refer to studies which found, for ex-ample, that "children placed in adoptive homes do far bet-ter in terms of standard measures of adjustment and self-esteem than . . . children raised by birth mothers who once considered adoption but decided against it." Nor did it challenge the accepted notion that, in general, biological parents make the best parents.

Coverage also distorted the issue of Jessica's best inter-ests by weighing expert testimony that she would be trau-matized against expert testimony that she would probably adapt. The second opinion obscured, but did not counter or contradict the first. All the credible experts agreed that Jes-sica would be devastated and that the move would be bad for her; they only disagreed about the degree of emotional damage she would sustain. However, the two-sided presen-tation had the effect of dismissing the fact that Jessica would be harmed. The following two examples are from the *New York Times* and *Newsweek,* respectively:

Experts in child psychology are not sure how Jessica will be affected.

"I think she will be devastated," said Dr. Steven Nickman, a assistant professor of clinical psychiatry at Harvard Medical School. "The child loses the family that she knows."

But Bettye Caldwell, an expert on child development at the University of Arkansas at Little Rock, said children are "wonderfully adaptable creatures" and Jessica will adjust if given time and support.

Does that mean [Jessica DeBoer] is certain to suffer, if not today perhaps a decade from now? Many professionals think so. "You really don't know what will happen with a crack in a foundation until it's asked to weather some external force," says Sally Rutzky. *But* there are no certainties. As David Zinn, a child psychiatrist at Northwestern University puts it, "This girl has good genes. She's a survivor."

Coverage of the case drew several other parallels which further eroded the reality that transferring two-and-a-half-year-old Jessica to the Schmidts was an egregious and harmful injustice, not simply one of two acceptable options. Most articles equated the fitness of both sets of parents. They compared the fact that Jan DeBoer had been arrested once as a young man to the fact that Dan Schmidt had demonstrated parental incompetence through neglect of the two children he already had. The mother of Dan Schmidt's second child told reporters, "He wants that child [Jessica] back and wants to make a family . . . but he doesn't care a rat's butt about Amanda." A *Newsweek* article reduced the issue of parental fitness to income and education: "[C]onventional wisdom believed the DeBoers would be better parents. In fact, the Schmidts earned slightly more money. . . . And Cara [Schmidt], who finished two years of college, has more education than Robby [DeBoer]."

This leveling of the two couples' parental fitness is particularly striking in view of the wildly different circumstances that led each to want to parent Jessica. Jan and Robby had been striving to adopt a child for over a decade. They planned and prepared to provide an adequate and appropriate world for the baby they were finally able to adopt. Dan Schmidt and Cara Clausen had a brief affair that resulted in an unplanned pregnancy. Cara kept the pregnancy a secret both from Dan whom she was no longer dating, and everyone else in her life. She went nearly the entire gestation period without prenatal care. And when the baby was born, she gave her up for adoption because she knew that she did not have the resources, emotional or financial, to provide her with what she needed for healthy, happy development.

Coverage also suggested through its structure that both the DeBoers and the Schmidts were equally to blame for the pain Jessica ultimately had to endure. The *New York Times* quoted a psychologist: "I cannot say that one set of parents is less responsible for the problems than the other." Most coverage neglected to mention that the DeBoers decided against relinquishing Jessica because they, with good reason, doubted both Cara Clausen and Dan Schmidt's fitness as parents, and because they did not want Jessica to be placed in foster care as she would have been for an undetermined amount of time had they agreed to give her up. The DeBoers appear to have been watching out for Jessica's interests, while the Schmidts seemed to be looking out only for their own. Even those articles which were the most adamant about the equal culpability of both sides in the Jessica case presented an unflattering portrait of the Schmidts' attitudes toward Jessica. One *Newsweek* article quotes Dan explaining how the DeBoers were at fault: "After they had her for nine days, they knew they couldn't keep her. . . . This is *our* flesh and blood, mine and Cara's."

Even when presented in the best possible light, the Schmidts appeared to lack any appreciation for Jessica as a human being. They both seemed incapable of recognizing that the separation and its aftermath could have deeply upset Jessica. Cara told reporters that Jessica had cried during the separation from her parents only because "the DeBoers kept her up all night to guarantee that the waiting cameras would snap a screaming child." Dan and Cara continue to deny Jessica any contact with her past. They have renamed her, even though she was far past the point of knowing her own name when she was uprooted. And they have refused any visitations between Jessica and her parents, even going so far as to send back presents sent by the DeBoers. Regarding a large toy cottage sent by the DeBoers on Jessica's third birthday, Dan told *Newsweek*, "If we keep it, we're letting them intrude whenever they want."

Coverage of the Baby Jessica case created an environment in which the Schmidts' anti-child behavior did not garner the kind of negative attention it might have if presented in a different, more pro-child light. In their dramatic portrayals of the separations, writers often made reference to Jessica's "world" with the DeBoers. *Newsweek* wrote that at the moment of separation, "the toddler's small world exploded." The same article explained, "For a two-year-old . . . the world is organized around the sound of familiar voices, the smell of her house, the way her mother holds her." However, at the same time, most coverage inadvertently diminished the importance of Jessica's relationship to her "world" by neglecting to mention many of its most important elements.

Article after article stressed that Jessica was being forced to leave behind two people she perceived as her parents, the family dog, and the house she knew as home. But not one of the major articles about the case mentioned the other significant people and environments that she would lose. As Robby DeBoer later wrote in her book *Losing Jessica*, the family held a going-away party the night before the transfer attended by Jessica's grandparents, neighbors, family friends, and her best friend, Gina.

Coverage reinforced the idea that Jessica was a discrete human being who could be separated from familiar belongings and people and still remain intact, rather than acknowledging that children's identities exist in the relationship they have with their significant caregivers. One psychologist was quoted as saying: "A small child torn from the tapestry of relationships into which she is so completely woven loses not only that familiar world but herself." While Jessica's body was strapped into a car seat and transported four hundred miles, her identity broke into many pieces, only some of which accompanied her. Most articles neglected to mention Jessica's emotional deterioration leading up to the transfer. According to Robby DeBoer, once Jessica knew she would be taken away, she "started to regress. She no longer wanted to wear 'pull ups'; diapers were a must. She fell back into using baby talk and would sometimes withdraw, an empty look on her face."

Follow-up articles written about the Baby Jessica case went out of their way to convince readers that Jessica was doing fine. They adopted the Schmidts' perspective: Three-year-old Anna Schmidt was a clean slate, unrelated to the little girl who had lived with Robby and Jan DeBoer for thirty months and essentially unaffected by her recent dramatic life change. "She's Not Baby Jessica Anymore" announced a *Newsweek* cover story. The magazine ran posed pictures of "Anna" with her "mother" (Cara Schmidt), supplanting the cultural image of a confused, frightened Jessica in a car seat. Based only on an interview with the Schmidts, the article reported that Jessica "seems happy and content," and made the essentially unsubstantiated claim that "the unhappy epilogue that was mapped out for her hasn't materialized."

Articles like the one in *Newsweek* sought to do more than simply report that Jessica was all right. They seemed to want to vindicate the decision to "return" her to her biological parents, to portray it as the best possible solution, rather than a tolerable outcome of a misguided custody ruling. The article quoted the pilot who flew Jessica from Michigan to Iowa, "I actually saw a calmness come over her the farther west we went," and a relative of the Schmidts, "When Anna came home, it was like she had just been on vacation for a while." The articles looked for evidence to support the idea that Jessica was thriving, but not for clues that might have suggested the contrary.

The out-of-sight, out-of-mind approach to reporting about Jessica's postseparation state lacks psychological depth, but vividly illustrates two powerful public sentiments about the case. First, it shows how strong the public's desire was to believe that Jessica would not be harmed by our legal system's treatment of her. We wanted to believe Cara Schmidt when she said, "Everyone guaranteed— guaranteed—that she would have short-term trauma, that she wouldn't eat, she wouldn't sleep, she'd cry. It didn't happen." *People* magazine wrote in its follow-up article that "it may come as some solace to the millions who came to care so much about her that Jessica . . . seems to be doing fine." Most people will never know how much pain Jessica was and is in, but presumably it's worse for her than the Schmidts maintain.

Coverage of the case contrasts sharply with, for example, the second half of the movie *Losing Isaiah*, starring Jessica Lange, in which the audience is subjected to the excruciating pain and bewilderment of a toddler who, like Jessica DeBoer, is separated from his psychological parents and "returned" to the biological mother he has never met. The movie, shot at many points from the perspective of the toddler, shows how he in fact doesn't simply forget about his past life and become a tabula rasa to the delight of those who support his move. He misses his parents and his bedroom and his toys, and he is frightened by the unfamiliar people and surroundings. Fortunately, Isaiah is returned to his psychological parents within a matter of days. The making of *Losing Isaiah* suggests that our culture can recognize that children do suffer in response to adult decisions. However, we are likely to recognize that suffering only in the context of unthreatening cases, like fictional ones, where we can control the outcome without disturbing the legal status quo.

The second cultural attribute that emerges from follow-up coverage is America's profound attachment to biological bonds. Despite the fact that a young girl was sent to live with complete strangers and forbidden from ever seeing her parents again, follow-up articles portrayed Jessica as if she is now where she belongs. In a scene from the *Newsweek* article, "Anna and nine-month-old Chloe clamber onto Dan's lap and take turns planting kisses on his wide, round face—*a larger version of Anna's own.*" Something about deferring to biological bonds in custody decisions feels right to Americans, and ultimately we all want to—and probably will—feel that Baby Jessica has finally "come home." On some level, we see the DeBoers as "unreal, unnatural substitutes for the real thing."

Our attachment to biological bonds, like our wishful thinking about Jessica DeBoer's psychological welfare, flies in the face of everything we know to be true about child development. There is nothing intrinsic to the biological parent-child relationship that makes it better than a nonbiological relationship. Studies on adoption, for example, "reveal no significant disadvantages of adoption as opposed to biologic parenting, and some significant advantages." Rather, good parenting depends on the development of a healthy, intimate, consistent, long-term relationship between a child and an adult. Yet our legal system continues to define "parent" based on a genetic relationship rather than a functional one. As an article in *Journal of Family Law* points out, states like Iowa that maintain the biological bias in custody decisions "are preserving an archaic rule that hinders the ability of courts to preserve the consistent family group that is so important for every child's well-being."

The myth that the biological relationship between an adult and a child constitutes a bond, whether or not the two have ever met, allows our culture to rationalize social policies that clearly favor adults at the expense of children. It facilitates our denial about the extent to which our society gives precedence to adults' desires over children's needs. For example, our conviction that Jessica will not only survive but thrive with her biological parents justifies, for example, our society's approach to the issue of who should be allowed to parent. In many ways, the Schmidts represent every biological mother and father. Our society delivers newborn children into the hands of people who are complete strangers to their new baby, and, more importantly, complete strangers to the state. Potential biological parents are not screened. Essentially, most children are "placed" at birth with whichever adults happened to conceive them, regardless of their fitness to be parents.

Our society does not hold that any adult can be a parent. Adults who choose to adopt, and who cannot afford to bypass the public adoption system, must conform to a set of standards ostensibly designed to protect the welfare of their forthcoming children. However, parents who have the privilege and the inclination to bypass the public adoption process, either through biological procreation or private adoption, do not have to meet any minimum standards. When two people conceive a child and choose to carry their pregnancy to term, they don't have to be at a suitable time in their lives in terms of age, psychological development, or career. They don't have to possess the necessary emotional or material resources to raise a child. And they don't have to be free from disorders that might compromise their ability to parent well. As Todd explains to his mother-in-law in the movie *Parenthood*, "You need a license to buy a dog. Or drive a car. Hell, you need a license to catch a fish. But they'll let any . . . asshole be a father."

American parenting ranges from excellent to incompetent to sadistic in part because American adults range from emotionally healthy to functional to severely damaged.

American parents come from the American population and they represent and reflect the population's shortcomings and limitations, including such human conditions as abusing drugs or alcohol and resorting to violence in relationships, to name just two that have an impact on parenting. Having children does not automatically erase these conditions. On the contrary, it often exacerbates them. Yet, our culture adamantly resists the practice of evaluating prospective parents for parental fitness. The idea of requiring biological parents to meet certain minimum standards evokes visions of "Big Brother" and the long arm of the state reaching into the sanctity of the family.

Opponents of screening for fitness argue that such a practice would allow the state to infringe unduly on parental rights. Currently, our society believes that adults should have the right to try parenting regardless of their fitness, because a screening process would place an inappropriate burden on potential parents as a group. In essence, our society holds that some children must be sacrificed in order that the general adult parental privilege to have a child remains unmitigated. In other words, our culture does not consider the issue of screening parents from the perspective of children.

The institution of screening practices would diminish parental rights, and, in all likelihood, would unfairly discriminate in certain cases. There is no question that the government can wield a heavy, unjust hand indeed in family life. But parents have been known to wield some pretty heavy hands themselves. The question for our society is not whether the state is competent to guide a screening of parental fitness, but whether the government is more or less competent than adults who choose or stumble into being parents. The question is, on whose side should we err, children's or adults'?

Currently, our society errs in the favor of adults. We allow adults to maintain their "right" to raise children when and how they like, *regardless of how well this system works, or doesn't work, for children in general.* As Roger McIntire, author of *Teenagers and Parents: Ten Steps for a Better Relationship*, points out: "Regardless of how incompetent adults may be, they have the right to try parenting. The child who is an unfortunate victim of the experiment is not considered." Yet our culture's reluctance to shape the family to meet the needs of children does not lead us to characterize ourselves as adult-centered. Instead, we obscure the anti-child nature of our approach to custody by perpetuating the myth that the biological relationship creates a positive bond between parent and child. This bond, according to our culture, can mitigate circumstances that threaten to compromise an adult's potential to be an adequate parent.

Once again, our culture deludes itself with the basic myth of the harmonious parent-child attachment. It appears in our society's belief in a parental instinct for child rearing that lies dormant in adults and surfaces when they bring a baby into the world. In her book *The Mother Puzzle: A New Generation Reckons with Motherhood*, Judith D. Schwartz writes that when she observes her friends who have just become parents, she finds herself "looking for changes in their very natures, expecting them to have developed certain qualities—patience, equanimity, wisdom—practically overnight."

Our faith in an inherent parenting instinct is perpetuated by popular culture. The feature film *Nine Months*, starring Hugh Grant, recounts the story of Samuel, a child psychiatrist who, despite years of clinical practice, does not particularly like children, is not comfortable around them, and is severely limited in his ability to relate to them. He definitely does not want children of his own. When he learns that his girlfriend has accidentally become pregnant, he resolves to recommend an abortion. However, his cowardice gets the best of him. He crumbles in the face of his girlfriend's desire to go ahead with the pregnancy even though she admits, "We're not ready for a child. There's not one good reason we should keep this baby."

During the following months, Samuel copes with his anger about having to become a parent by being mean to his girlfriend, missing prenatal appointments, and hanging out with a friend who broke up with his girlfriend because she wanted to have a child. Fortunately, one viewing of his girlfriend's ultrasound on videotape instantly transforms him from an immature, spineless, self-centered worm into the perfect father. He sells his sports car, furnishes the nursery, and proposes to the baby's mother in a matter of days. In the hospital just after the baby's birth, Samuel tells the new mother that he, the man who doesn't "believe in change," has changed. "The point is, I don't care what I think or don't think anymore," he tells her. "I don't give a damn about me. I'm in love with my child." In the last scene of the movie, Samuel creeps out of bed in the middle of the night to comfort his crying child. His wife finds him absorbed in dancing with his son, a picture-perfect image of parental devotion.

Every child deserves committed caring parents like the transformed Samuel. But constructing the family to meet the needs of children requires more than a working VCR. It requires that adults relinquish their right to have children however and whenever they want. For our culture, this involves acknowledging that adults' and children's needs don't always converge in the blissful symbiosis of a slow dance, and, in turn, recognizing that we aren't currently a child-centered culture when it comes to custody issues. Unfortunately, our tendency to overlook these realities makes our job all the harder. *Nine Months*, for example, parodied the notion of screening parents. Samuel laments the fact that "the state requires you to take a written test to drive a car but any complete moron can become a parent and destroy a child's life," only to learn that the best way, and perhaps the only way, to become a committed parent is to be forced into it by an unplanned pregnancy.

Despite our desire to be a child-centered culture, we firmly resist child-custody decisions made only to meet children's needs and not at all to placate adults. In the final analysis, it seems we learn little even from cases that expose the inherent anti-child bias of our system. The Baby Jessica case led the media to hold up the Baby Pete case as an example of a model solution to similar custody battles. Rather than transferring the baby in question to his biological father, the settlement allowed him to stay with his psychological parents. However, it awarded joint custody to the psychological mother and the biological father in an effort to allow all the adults involved in the case to parent Baby Pete. Article after article quoted the psychological father as saying: "Nobody lost and the baby won." The problem with holding the Baby Pete case up as a model is that it assumes that the best outcome is one in which "[e]verybody had to give up something, but everyone in the case is a winner," rather than one that prioritizes the needs of the child involved above all else. In the best child-centered outcome, several adults might be devastated by the decision, but the child would not have had to make any unnecessary sacrifices.

Even in the face of evidence to the contrary, our culture clings to the wishful misconception that we can cater to the best interests of children without sacrificing adult privileges, or, to put it another way, that we can cater to adult privileges without sacrificing children's best interests. However, there is no getting around the fact that child-centered means *not* adult-centered, even if our myths about the biological bond make it appear so. It is unethical for us to portray ourselves as champions of the interests of children when we won't mitigate the adult rights that harm them.

THREE

The Kindness of Strangers

————

If there is any pattern to be found in the variety of families
that have succeeded and failed over the course of history, it
is that children do best in societies where child rearing is
considered too important to be left entirely to parents.

STEPHANIE COONTZ

Adults in our society are not pro–child abuse. We don't insist, for example, on a parent's right to whip a child with cat-o'-nine-tails or have him hanged if he is disobedient, as Puritan Americans did. Our culture strongly censures those who mistreat their children, expressing our disapproval in the public reaction to high-profile cases in the mainstream media and in feature films. We are appropriately horrified by the overwhelming and ever-increasing number of maltreatment reports and infanticides. We wonder about what the high rates of child abuse say about our society's morals, and the more we learn about the impact of abuse on children's development, the more we worry about the implications of so much abuse for the future of our nation.

At the same time, however, our society engages in cultural policies and perpetuates cultural myths that promote the abuses we claim to abhor. Our head says no, but our hands say yes. In our efforts to protect adults from unwanted government interference in their relationships with their children, our society perpetuates a family structure that countenances child maltreatment. It leads adults to feel entitled and inclined to assault their children. In our effort to protect ourselves from the acknowledgment that our policies harm children, we refuse to recognize the family as inherently dangerous, instead characterizing parent-child abuse as a deviation from a harmonious norm, and casting the individuals involved as aberrant. As a result, we further hamstring attempts to deter abuse. By definition, deviant behavior is not predictable, and therefore not preventable.

Our culture's reactions to the murder cases of Susan Smith and Polly Klaas illustrate the ways in which we perpetuate the myth that the family home is a haven for children. When Susan Smith confessed in 1994 to drowning her two toddlers, after maintaining that they had been kidnapped by a stranger, residents of Union, South Carolina and the public at large reacted with surprise. During the days that followed Smith's confession, reporters wove the public's reaction into their narratives, repeating our surprise like a mantra, positioning us as the witnesses of a truly incomprehensible, unbelievable, unimaginable turn of events. Articles quoted neighbors and family friends protesting their incomprehension, making statements to reporters like: "What could drive a mother to do this? I'm very heartbroken."

The public expressed surprise that it was Susan Smith who killed her children and not a black man *despite the fact that children are more likely to be killed by a parent than by any other member of their community.* Our surprise at finding out that it was Susan Smith who murdered her children contrasts starkly with our resignation in response to the abduction and murder of Polly Klaas in late 1993 by a complete stranger. Polly's murder by a bearded "bogeyman" confirmed our myth that children are more at risk from strangers than family members, and unleashed a torrent of invocations to the home as haven. Ted Gest wrote in *U.S. News & World Report*:

> The latest evidence is that crime levels actually fell last year. But that does not mean that last year wasn't the scariest in American history. Overriding the statistics is the chilling realization that the big crime stories of recent months have invaded virtually every sanctuary where Americans thought they were safe . . . even their bedrooms.

After her murder, Polly's hometown of Petaluma, like her bedroom, was portrayed as the ultimate sanctuary. Article after article pointed out what authors saw as the ironic fact that before the Klaas abduction, Petaluma had been "so peaceful that Ronald Reagan's handlers chose to film his 'Morning in America' campaign commercials there."

Even more ironic, perhaps, was the fact that the picture of Petaluma painted by the media was as misleading as Reagan's political campaign. While no major articles on the Klaas story mentioned it, family violence exists in Petaluma just as it does in every other town and city in the nation. We took the opportunity of Polly's kidnapping to enact a cultural drama of horror and outrage that implicitly reconfirmed the safety of the home despite the fact that, in general, the family is the most dangerous place for children in every American community. After Polly's murder, Petaluma became the site at which we located our mythical story of family harmony under siege from "random" violence.

The discussion of "random" violence sparked by the Klaas abduction called attention to family violence and at the same time rendered it invisible. "Random" violence is by definition unexpected, unusual, and rare, yet the random kidnapping and murder of Polly Klaas dominated the media for weeks. The media reflected our culture's conviction that the slight increase in infrequent random violence is more of a threat to the American way of life than consistently frequent family violence. "While the absolute numbers [of crimes] fluctuated in the past decade, an increase in random murders was especially ominous," one article stated. "Decades ago, most murders were committed by relatives or acquaintances of the victim."

Most murders are still committed by family and friends of the victim, but this extended family violence does not generate the level of fear in the public or the level of the attention in the media that random violence does. Despite the numbers, American culture does not recognize family violence as the threat to personal safety that it is. However, an isolated incident of "random" violence like Polly's murder can throw the entire country into a state of panic. Most articles on the Klaas incident made the obligatory reference to the fact that the vast majority of child abductions are not perpetrated by a stranger, but by someone the child knows very well—a parent. Estimates suggest that approximately 350,000 children are kidnapped by a parent each year, compared to approximately 100 by strangers. Apart from these statistics, however, everything else about the Klaas coverage directly contradicted the reality that children have the most to fear from their own parents.

For example, one cover story cited the statistics, and even editorialized that family strife "is one problem that doesn't get the attention it deserves," at the same time as its section on "Child Snatchings" did not mention parent kidnappings at all. "Missing Children: The Ultimate Nightmare," an article in *Parents Magazine*, mentioned the statistics and the fact that "crimes [against children] by non-family members are not common," and then proceeded to tell parents how to protect their children from stranger abductions. The article counseled, among other things, that children "must be taught to view unfamiliar adults with suspicion," and that "[t]hree- and four-year-olds should be taught *to check with a parent* or caretaker before going with anyone."

Like the *Parents Magazine* article, a contemporary *Newsweek* sidebar entitled "How Parents Can Talk to Their Kids" on protecting children from abductions, did not mention how parents can communicate to their children that they will most likely be abducted by one of their noncustodial parents. On the contrary, it suggested, "All children should be conscious of strangers, and be discriminating and wary of them." Many parents may be placated by the article's advice that they can teach their child "what to do if a stranger calls or knocks on the door," but this advice won't amount to much when noncustodial Daddy or Mommy stops by. And for those parents reading the article who don't have custody of their children, the advice may be very reassuring. Essentially, these articles tell parents to teach their children not to trust anyone except their parents, not to go anywhere with anyone except their parents, not to let anyone touch them except their parents, and to scream when approached by anyone except their parents. When kidnapped by a noncustodial parent, the only relevant information children will have learned is that they shouldn't reach out to "strangers" for help.

In contrast, *New York* magazine published an article in

1990 entitled "Sparing the Child: How to Intervene When You Suspect Abuse," which elaborated on the role of strangers in *protecting* children from abuse. "[E]ndangered children *can* be rescued," the article promised. "Neighbors, teachers—even strangers—who care enough to recognize the signs of abuse . . . can get the authorities to take effective action." The author graphically described the kinds of things that parents are doing to children:

> Young children are being dipped into scalding water, burned with electric [irons] or curling irons or cigarettes, beaten on every part of their bodies with every imaginable domestic implement, held by the ankles and having their heads hammered on the floor like pile drivers, having bones broken. Young boys and girls are getting raped and sodomized, penetrated in every possible way. Babies are being shaken so severely that they die of brain hemorrhages.

However, the article did not detail what to do when the man burning his child with his cigarette is your spouse or the woman shaking her baby is you.

Our approach to child abductions crystallizes our completely irrational attitudes toward violence, emphasizing that which almost never occurs, and ignoring that which forms the experiential fabric of our children's lives. As we worked ourselves up over "random" violence, the media picked up the theme of violated sanctuaries like the family and the bedroom again and again *as if they were not routinely violated.* One article explained, "To many, this wave of violence is ominous because safe havens are violated," using the Klaas case as an example.

Our nostalgia for a mythical safe haven extended into nostalgia for a mythical past. *Newsweek*'s Jerry Adler pontificated, "Children can no longer retreat to a kid-size world in

which no danger loomed bigger than the school yard bully."
While he acknowledged in the same article that family
violence has always existed, he maintained that for children
in the fifties, "Unless you were black and people spat on you
when you tried to go to school, or mentally handicapped
and shut away in a misery-drenched state home, or you had
the bad luck to go flying seatbeltless through the wind-
shield of your family's car in an accident, *life was pretty good
and expected to get better.*"

Adler's article, "Kids Growing Up Scared," is particularly symptomatic of our cultural denial regarding family
violence. Beyond eulogizing a nonexistent past in which
families protected children from violence, Adler waxes nostalgic for a time when we were less aware and therefore less
concerned about interfamily child abuse—the fifties. "By
the 1950s, public interest in abuse and neglect was practically nonexistent, and even social workers did not rate it
highly as a professional concern," according to Barbara
Nelson, the author of *Making an Issue of Child Abuse: Political
Agenda Setting for Social Problems.* "It took almost [another]
decade for physicians to conclude that some parents were
violently assaulting their children, a delay caused by professional cautiousness and a profound psychological resistance to recognizing that some parental behavior departed
so radically from the ideal." Like Adler, Ronald Reagan
longed to know less about the incidence and severity of
child abuse in America. His budget cuts decreased research
on child maltreatment from $17 million in 1980 to $2 million in 1982.

Adler waxes nostalgic for denial itself. He does say, "No
one wants to return to a world in which children suffered

alone and in silence." "But," he adds, "by definition, knowl-edge spells an end to innocence." Knowledge about child abuse interferes with our illusion of the family as a haven. It is adults' innocence, not children's, that is at stake. As if to confirm that he cares much more about what adults believe than what children experience, Adler writes that "the actual physical threat to children is less important than the per-ception of danger. . . . [T]he fear of crime is almost a sepa-rate phenomenon from the real danger it poses." When Adler writes, "Something precious has gone out of Ameri-can culture, and we don't know how to get it back," the "something precious" appears to be our ignorance. He is wrong to say that we can't retrieve it. We can. And he is showing us how.

When a tearful Susan Smith told the world that a dark stranger had come out of nowhere and ripped her babies from her bosom, she was telling us what we wanted to hear, and we loved her. But when she recanted, cruelly confronting us with the truth that she herself was the dangerous stranger, she caught us in the act of our cultural fantasizing, and broke our suspension of disbelief. Quickly our sympathetic outrage and horror turned into anger and spite. Immedi-ately we turned the tables, exposing her as manipulative and duplicitous, just as she had exposed us. If Smith was in-volved in the disappearance of her sons, "she's in the wrong line of work," one teacher told *USA Today*. "She should be an actor." Case investigators surmised that Smith "orchestrated an elaborate hoax, punctuating her lies with tears." Smith's claim that she intended to kill herself, not the boys, when she went to the lake apparently made people "laugh outright . . . calling it just one more lie, and an absurd one." Empathy that might have been engendered by her obvious emotional instability was overwhelmed by our sense of betrayal. She had tried to rob us of our cherished illusion and we hated her for it.

We treated Susan Smith as the unpredictable exception to our mythical rule that children are safe with their parents. And our outrage at the abduction and murder of Polly Klaas from her pink bedroom allowed us to reaffirm the sanctity and safety of the family. Our responses to these two cases contain embedded within them our most fundamental, and inaccurate, assumptions about parent-child relations. They imply that we fully expect children to be safe with their parents, and unsafe with nonfamily members, regardless of how unprepared biological parents are for the task of raising children. We aren't surprised in general that adults will harm and exploit children; we acknowledge that they will. However, we tell ourselves that the biological bond acts as a prophylactic that prevents adults from harming their own children.

Coverage of the Smith case made repeated references to this belief. "It is like some virus wiped out the bond that means safety," one father was quoted as saying about the murders. Another woman told a reporter that the "strongest bond there is is the mother-child bond. [Susan Smith] did something that most parents would never dream of doing." Despite the staggering statistics and abundant examples of children harmed at home at the hands of parents, we cling to the nineteenth-century notion of the family as a haven from the harsh realities of society at large. As Diane E. Eyer writes in *Mother-Infant Bonding: A Scientific*

Fiction, we tell ourselves the mother-infant bond is "a symbolic act of inoculation" that will protect infants from "the current anomie of the adult world."

The myth of the home as haven makes it difficult for our culture to see family violence as systemic. The popular image of the family as "harmonious, socially integrating, and psychologically supportive" shrouds the inherently intense nature of the parent-child relationship with its potential for both violence as well as caring. Parents and children do indeed share a bond, but the link does not necessarily "mean" safety, nurturing, or comfort. It can also "mean" the opposite: cruelty, brutality, and even murder. Children are more at risk with family members because of the parent-child bond, not in spite of it.

The social sciences have taught us that parent-child relationships "differ from others not by being more harmonious, but rather by being more ambivalent." Parent-child relationships "inevitably involve antagonism as well as love, and it is precisely this intertwining of strong positive and negative feelings that distinguishes intimacy from secondary . . . relationships." Our children evoke in us both profound love and terrifying rage; a feeling of accomplishment, as well as an overwhelming sense of failure; feelings of empowerment and hopeless insecurity. "Child rearing evokes our most generous impulses—and our basest: cruelty, indifference, possessiveness, envy, and resentment, not only of the child's right to be cared for, but also of the tedious, repetitive tasks of feeding and tending." A recent mainstream article on family violence reminded readers about the "old joke": "God made [children] cute so we wouldn't kill them."

Ultimately, the nature of the parent-child bond depends

on the character, preparation, and situation of the adult involved. Diane Eyer urges that we renounce the notion of the immediate and miraculous parent-child bond. "Doing so," she writes, "would force us to recognize that strong relationships require many ingredients; they seldom endure automatically. Constructive relationships involve love, understanding, trust, time, money, sharing, giving, stimulating, and inspiring." By promoting the notion that the biological relationship between adults and their offspring adequately guarantees an appropriate child-rearing environment, we allow ourselves to deny the importance and relevance of adult characteristics that directly impact the chances that a child will be well- or even adequately parented. In general, when it comes to child rearing, our culture ignores the competence of the adults involved, and the awesome power they wield over their offspring. As a result of our avoidance of these issues, *we set parents up to fail.*

As a culture, we do acknowledge that quality caregiving requires more than the ability to conceive a child. Our society focuses on these requirements in media stories about how to choose a nanny. Good nannies, according to articles on the subject, have thought carefully about their decision to spend time with children and have studied child development. "Obviously, the most desirable candidate," according to an article in *USA Today,* "is a professional, certified nanny who has had experience and/or who has completed a college program that requires at least 16 weeks of training, with an additional 150 to 200 hours of supervised internship working directly with children." The curriculum, according to the article "should have included the highlights of child development, behavior and guidance, infant care, food preparation, nutrition, first aid, safety, and education activities for youngsters."

Somehow, articles about choosing a nanny never remark on the glaring anomaly that we are anxious to screen and train surrogate caregivers but not parents. However, the nannies-from-hell stories about all the American children "left with strangers" that illustrate how "trust can be misplaced with tragic results" seem to allow our culture to vent our collective, repressed—but appropriate—anxieties about the current state of parenthood in America. The articles often focus on the theme of what caregivers are doing when parents aren't around, echoing our silent fear of what parents are doing when the state isn't around. An article about the Olivia Riner case, in which an au pair allegedly set the house on fire, killing a baby, discussed "the unspoken nightmare" of working parents: "[T]he wonderful new nanny . . . becomes, in the unseen moments when Mom and Dad are at work or out to dinner, a cruel, even vicious abuser."

The abuses typically cited in these articles are common fare in families. They refer to types of abuse that are most typically committed by parents. Articles mention toddlers who have drowned in pools or fallen out of windows because they were left unattended. They describe in horrific detail babies who have been shaken to death. They warn about nannies who (like many parents) regularly spank and hit their charges. And they call attention to caregivers who simply aren't caring or warm or emotionally connected. In other words, they might as well be describing abusive parents and inappropriate American family homes.

Articles critical of low or nonexistent standards in daycare centers can easily be read as critiques of the vastly uneven quality of care in the average family. In early 1990, Los

Angeles relaxed family-day-care standards, allowing "[a]ny-one without a criminal record and who has a clean bill of health and a home that meets standards of cleanliness and safety" to run a day-care center. An article about the new law remarked that it explains "why finding family day care can be so traumatic for parents." It also explains why families can be so traumatic for children:

> The standards are such that there are no guarantees that a family-care home is a quality setting for a child. One provider may keep the television on all day, smoke in the house or swat toddlers for wetting their pants. Another may have studied child development and offer daily outings to the park and art projects. One provider may burn out after one year on the job because of the low pay and long hours, while others may thrive on running their own businesses.

The myth that parents don't need training because they have a biological bond to their children masks a reluctance to define and undertake parental obligations. Almost all parental failings can be defended by the sentiments: "We did our best" and "We loved you." Yet these two statements are irrelevant to good parenting from the child's perspective. Saying that you did your best on a test when you didn't study is alternately pitiable or idiotic. Yet saying you did your best as a parent when you came to parenting totally unprepared is a time-honored way to shame critical grown children.

To acknowledge that one needs training to raise children well is to acknowledge that one can be insufficiently prepared to be a parent. It also forces the realization that we should be prepared to make changes in ourselves *before becoming parents* if we want to be good parents. Being a good parent may mean sobering up, learning to control our rage, or compromising our careers. Once we recognize the seriousness of the parenting commitment, we are duty-bound to make the necessary changes and sacrifices. This is more than many of us are willing to do, even for our children. On some level, we would rather stumble through parenting than be forced by the birth of a child to give up the privileges and luxuries of a nonparent lifestyle. It's much easier in the case of parenthood to say after the fact, "I did my best," than to be truly prepared.

Our culture's denial of the importance for parents of having the necessary temperament and resources, being knowledgeable and prepared, and having carefully thought out and dedicated themselves to the decision to have children culminates in our willingness to entrust children's well-being entirely to their parents. Our culture's entrenched doctrine of *parens patriae* dictates that the state "intervene into child rearing only when families are considered to have failed." Our culture and our laws isolate children in families, leaving them essentially at the mercy of their parents, unless and until their injuries come to the attention of the child-protection system.

Our respect for the "integrity" of the familial structure that isolates children with their biological procreators for better or for worse overrides our common sense about what is best for children. "Even when the child's individual rights appear to conflict with parental authority," Laura Oren explains in the *North Carolina Law Review*, "the Court often gives a wide latitude to the integrity of the traditional family structure." This respect for the privacy rights of parents can only exist because of our misguided faith in the myth of organic family harmony, and *in spite of* what we know to be true about parent-child relations. As Cynthia Crosson Tower writes in *Understanding Child Abuse and Neglect*, "Our comfort with allowing parents complete jurisdiction over children is based on our expectations of adequate parenting rather than our recognition of the painful statistics of the incidence of child maltreatment and parental failure."

Our assumption of family harmony not only ignores the reality of violent parent-child relations, but it also facilitates policies that promote such violence. The degree of family privacy that currently defaults to families exacerbates parents' preexisting limitations and inadequacies. Nearly unconditional parental power not only does not inhibit abusive practices—it encourages them. Much abuse evades the child-protection system "because it takes place within the confines of the family and is difficult to prove, and . . . because of the state's traditional reluctance to interfere in family affairs," and this increased likelihood of "getting away with it" contributes to the incidence of abuse. Child abuse, like rape, is to a great extent a crime of opportunity. The answer to the question, "How can the group we turn to for love and understanding be so cruel and harmful?" is, according to family-violence experts, Richard J. Gelles and Murray A. Straus, "[b]ecause they can be." In addition to providing ample opportunity to harm children without getting caught, the state's reluctance to interfere in family matters is often interpreted by parents as tacit consent for, even approval of their abusive behavior.

Our respect for parental privacy is the basis for two of the factors in the "agreement" between society and the family that *contribute* to child maltreatment. They are, according to Cynthia Crosson Tower, "society's belief in the sanctity of the family and the disproportionate emphasis afforded the rights of parents compared to the rights of children." As an illustration of these contributory factors, children who are most isolated within the jurisdiction of their parents—young children who are not yet in school—are the most likely to be abused by them.

Our respect for parental privacy also encompasses our support of corporal punishment as a legitimate form of parental behavior. As a society, we not only allow, but sometimes even encourage parents to use physical violence as a form of child control. One contemporary religious article argued, "A Christian parent is wrong to say, 'I will not spank,'" and "[T]he method we choose—whether hand, switch, paddle, or belt—is a matter of personal conviction." Yet, we know that corporal punishment often leads to child abuse. Like driving under the influence of alcohol, child rearing with violence can easily get out of hand. Most "severe, injury-causing" parental assaults on children happen in the context of physical discipline.

In families where stress results in parent-child violence, a prerequisite tolerance of physical punishment exists. To the extent that this is true, child abuse is inherent in the child-rearing privileges that the law confers on parents. Our laws contribute to a slippery slope effect, because child abuse is one end of a continuum starting with the legitimate exercise of parental authority. There is no clear-cut point along it where the quantity and quality of physical force used becomes legally impermissible.

In sum, our culture promotes and perpetuates family units that breed inadequate, inappropriate, and abusive treatment of children by the adults entrusted with their care. As Gelles and Straus argue in *Intimate Violence*:

> Our society and our families are organized to not only allow but often encourage violence between intimates. The combination of social attitudes (that sometimes encourage but often just simply allow violence) with the private nature of the modern family, and the socially structured inequality that is part of every household, makes for a tinderbox of emotions and possible violent outbursts.

Despite the connection between family privacy and child abuse, we tend not to want to talk about changing the power structure within the family, and it is political suicide for any politician to even think about banning the parental privilege to use corporal punishment. Our reluctance to take on parental privacy is well illustrated by our approach to religious cults in our communities. Despite our belief that cults and those who participate in them are qualitatively different from "normal" communities and community members, religious cults in America are a logical extension—and a current manifestation—of our contemporary approach to structuring families.

From the children's point of view, growing up in David Koresh's Davidian commune in Waco, Texas wasn't substantially different from growing up in a family. Like many families, the world of the commune included an authoritarian father who demanded constant obedience to his commands, harsh physical discipline intermingled with intense love and affection, and rules handed down from above about eating, sleeping, playing, learning, and every other aspect of life. At the discretion of the adults around them, children were physically beaten with paddles and sticks, kept isolated from adults outside the immediate cult family circle, and subjected to home schooling, chores, and various behavioral drills. And, of course, they were taught a profound fear of strangers, and that "the outside world was not good, that there were people out there who wanted to hurt them and would misunderstand them."

And Koresh's family enjoyed the same privilege of being protected from outside observation and intervention as every other American family. Child-protective services and neighbors suspected for years that the children were being abused, but they couldn't prove it and they couldn't penetrate the commune's privacy to gather evidence. So they were forced to act toward the family as if the adults were taking good care of the children and should continue to enjoy the adult privilege to run their children's lives the way they saw fit. In hesitating to intervene, authorities were simply following the dictates of our family-privacy doctrine.

The federal government finally intervened in the Koresh family because it suspected the stockpiling of weapons, not because it wanted to protect the cult's children. There are children being abused in families and cults across the nation right now, and the federal government isn't preparing tanks and tear-gas assaults for more than a handful, if that. Once the Koresh family came into the public purview, however, the public was outraged that the government had not intervened sooner. Yet had the government tried to do so, it would no doubt have been criticized by the same members of the public for interfering unduly with the parental privilege of the adults in the compound.

The shield of family privacy both enabled and protected the Davidians' abusive practices. They exercised their religious right to tell their children their theories about the pending apocalypse, they exercised their parental right to administer liberal doses of physical violence, and they exercised the cultural mandate to warn their children not to trust strangers. When protective workers followed up on rumors of abuse, all they could do was ask the Davidian adults and children if anyone was being abused. Not so surprisingly, everyone denied perpetrating, experiencing, or witnessing abuse. The workers examined a few of the children, but couldn't find any evidence of serious injury, only bruises. And so the workers closed the case.

The officials of the Texas Child Protective Services later defended their actions. As the regional director explained, "[T]here is no law against having guns in a home with children," and during their few visits, "caseworkers had seen no young girls with babies." And so the organization had to conclude that "we didn't have any evidence to justify continued involvement." In further defense, an official from the Texas Department of Protection and Regulatory Services asked rhetorically: "How could you possibly expect to elicit as much [as psychiatrists later did] with one or two brief visits?" Protective workers were simply doing their job, which included respecting the adult Davidians' family privacy. "Every law-enforcement agent involved in the Koresh case would probably do the same again, given the same allegations and limitations," according to *Newsweek*. "Without more hard evidence, even the shocking report from the psychiatrists [who examined the children removed from the compound] might not have been enough to prove child abuse in court."

Workers were sensitive to the question later asked by the lawyer for Koresh's mother: "At what point does society have a right to step in and say you have to raise your family our way?" The answer for the cult members was the same as it is for all families: not before the state has proof positive that a child is being maimed, tortured, or raped. In most states, interfering based on anything short of such proof would have interfered with the right to privacy of the adults in the compound, and so we did not interfere. Questioning the rights of those adults would have meant questioning our own, as well as examining our myth of family harmony. And these were things we were apparently not ready to do.

Perhaps a greater hypocrisy of the Koresh incident was that very little of what he was doing constituted abuse under Texas state law. Apart from his sexual relationships with young girls, he did not overstep the boundaries of his parental privileges. Yes, the children were beaten with hands, paddles, sticks, and belts. Yes, they were made to sit through endless rambling religious sermons. Yes, they were forced to practice military style drills. And yes, they endured bizarre diets, sleeping patterns, and recreational activities. But no, these experiences were not illegal. All that the children experienced combined to form what would later seem to be a clearly abusive environment, even by legal standards. However, before the standoff with the FBI, child-protective workers couldn't establish grounds for removing the children because they couldn't identify discrete acts of abuse. They were looking for grains of sand on a beach, and they came away empty-handed.

It isn't an accident that authorities couldn't easily intervene in the Davidian compound to protect the children. Our culture tends to define child abuse in ways that do not threaten parental privacy and power. For example, we define acceptable levels of physical violence not based on what harms or doesn't harm children, but on what parents intend or say they intend when they use physical force as a form of child-control. While the vast majority of pediatricians and child psychologists maintain that physical violence, including spanking, is always harmful to children, regardless of how it is administered or to what degree, the majority of states hold that parents can inflict physical punishment as long as they are motivated by a desire to discipline the child. Texas law states that "the use of force but not deadly force against a child" by a parent is acceptable "when and to the degree the actor reasonably believes the force is necessary to discipline the child." Furthermore, the definition of "reasonable" is left to the standards of adults, the "standards of the community, as represented in the prosecutor, the jury or the appellate judge."

When social workers visited the Davidian compound, they did find circular bruises on the butts of several of the little girls. Under Texas law, whether the little girls were emotionally traumatized by having bruises inflicted on them with who knows what kind of tool did not have any relevance to whether or not the adults in the compound had acted illegally. All that mattered was that the adults believed that the children needed to be punished, and that they hadn't physically maimed them. Our laws force child-protective services to be accountable not to the best interests of children, but to the parental privileges of adults. Our laws regarding corporal punishment uphold the adult privilege to use as much physical force as parents think their children deserve, and that they think they can get away with. The needs and sensitivities of children do not play a role in determining the legality of the physical violence used against them.

It's worth noting that no matter how heinous the physical violence used against their children, parents usually have a reason for administering the "punishment" and attempt to defend their behavior. A past president of the National Committee for the Prevention of Child Abuse told *Ebony* magazine that he had "lost count of the toddlers brought to his care for second- and third-degree burns suffered after parents sat them in boiling water for wetting their pants or placed their small hands on hot oven doors to discourage 'stealing.'" There is no question that Koresh had his reasons for sending children down to the "whipping room," and he defended them when he and one of his wives met with protective-services workers as part of the investigation of their allegedly abusive parenting methods.

While both the parents and the state have the potential to harm children, parents get the benefit of the doubt. When it comes to child rearing, our society tends to trust parents completely and to keep the state at arm's length. Opponents of increased state intervention conflate the interests of children with their parents, implying that what hurts parents hurts their children. Yet we have all seen that adults will fight for the right to harm their children, just as men have in the past championed the right to physically assault and rape their wives.

In general, children are more likely to benefit from state monitoring of family life than they are from state absence. Opponents of intervention gloss over this critical fact: Children benefit from state intervention even when parents don't, *and especially when parents don't.* Martha Minow, a professor at Harvard Law School who specializes in family law, admits to a "fierce resistance to [state] interference" in her family, but she recognizes the potential for such "interference" as beneficial to her daughter. "My responsibilities to my child," she wrote in an editorial, "include living under a system of laws that assure her more than me."

Linda Gordon, an historian of family violence, has written that "family violence cannot be understood outside the context of the overall politics of the family." These politics include who can be a parent, what parents are required to know, what emotional resources they are required to have, what obligations they must fulfill toward their children, and what kinds of things they are allowed to do with and to their children. Yet, again and again, our culture casts child abusers as sick deviants from a healthy norm. When it comes to child abuse, we do the opposite of questioning the politics of the family—we question the sanity of the perpetrator.

For example, when we learned that Susan Smith had killed her own children, the myth of family harmony meant that the only explanation for her behavior we could come up with was that she was "not one of us." "This just don't happen in Union," according to one longtime resident. Everyone in Union, South Carolina, it seems, wanted to make it clear to the nation that Susan Smith may have grown up in Union, but that her actions didn't reflect the character of Union residents. "While the explanations [of her deed] will someday become a dark part of the county's otherwise sleepy history," one article stated, "they will never explain the coldness and cruelty of the act to people who see their babies, any babies, as the most precious things in life." Susan Smith may have spent her whole life in Union, but she wasn't *of* Union. She was, it turned out, not "part of this world, and of their values" as residents had originally thought.

Just as our myth of family harmony and our social con-
structions of child abuse and abusers determine the nature
of our cultural responses, they also determine possible ave-
nues of reform. While the crisis of spousal violence has
not been solved, important progress has been made in part
because such violence is seen within the greater political
context of the family. In most cases, the term "domestic
violence" connotes spouse-on-spouse violence, not parent-
child violence, locating the violence within the family, not
separate from it, as the term "child abuse" does. Unlike
child-abuse legislation, domestic-violence reform seeks to
lessen the power of abusers over their victims, mandating
arrest, for example, and the confiscation of weapons. Cases
of "stranger-danger" also traditionally have led to significant reforms in protecting victims of crime. Such reforms
recognize the power of individuals to disrupt other's lives,
and, like domestic-violence reforms, seek to lessen that
power. In the aftermath of the Polly Klaas case, California
passed "three strikes" legislation that mandated life sen-
tences for three-time felony offenders.

However, cases of interfamily child abuse do not generally lead to reforms that challenge the power structure of the
family. When identified as seriously abused or neglected,
children are removed from their homes and sent to live in
temporary ones until their parents are ready to try again.
Our culture continues to resist efforts to change the basic
structure of the family, through, for example, mandatory
parent training, monitoring, and support. The case of Susan
Smith did not lead to any systemic family-violence reforms.
Apparently, we were satisfied with calling Smith a "baby-
killer," clamoring for the death penalty, and nursing the
wounds she had inflicted on our fantasy of family harmony.

Had we been willing to look for ways to reform the family system in response to Smith's murder of her toddlers, we might have realized that we set her up to fail, and that the deaths of her children probably could have been avoided. We might have agreed, for example, that it was unrealistic to assume that a young woman with only a high school degree, who began having children in her teens, who was going through a divorce, who was raising two children on her own, who was working full-time, who was economically stressed, and who had a history of emotional problems, would be able to raise two children well, or even adequately. And we might have acknowledged that this was exactly what the town of Union, South Carolina did, and what we all did, when we stood by as Susan Smith's life spun out of her control, and her children drowned at the bottom of a dark lake. However, we chose instead to simply act surprised.

FOUR

False-Denial Syndrome

[A]cceptable doublespeak: Yes, of course, child sexual abuse
is rampant and awful to contemplate. But. Such an accusation is never true when it is made in any particular circumstance by any particular child against any particular man.

LOUISE ARMSTRONG

The general American consensus is that sexual abuse of children is fairly common. We disagree about the exact numbers, but we don't doubt that many adults engage teens and
small children in sexual acts, or that many children risk becoming victims of such abuse. In line with our myth of the
home as a safe haven, our society is more aggressive in its efforts to combat abuse by strangers than by people the child
knows, even though family members and family friends
make up the overwhelming majority of offenders. However,
where we choose to invest our energies, we are dedicated and
enthusiastic. Over the course of the nineties, our courts have
gone so far as to adopt ineffective and possibly unconstitu-
tional laws directed at sex offenders because there is such societal pressure to do something, anything, about the sexual
violation of children. In a column on new legislation that
alerts citizens when a convicted sex offender has been released into their community, writer Anna Quindlen pointed
out its flaws, but empathized with its supporters. "Amid a
plethora of concerns, issues and facts," she explained, "there
is no greater than this: the passion we all share to keep our
children safe and sound."

Yet our passion has limitations that are also shared. Except in cases where the police procure the confession of a menacing stranger, our culture often doubts children's allegations of abuse. Despite our acknowledgment that sexual abuse occurs all too frequently, our culture has refined a response to allegations that makes their credibility all but impossible. Our response follows a fairly consistent pattern: It transforms victims and their allies into perpetrators, evidence into counterevidence, and perpetrators into martyrs. The more explicit and lurid the allegations against adults, the more children's testimony is characterized as unreliable, even willfully false. The more accusations that surface, the less likely it is that any particular one will be believed. The less likely adults are to escape conviction, the more innocent they seem. As allegations of abuse walk our culture's discrediting gauntlet, our passion to protect our children mutates. It becomes hostility toward children who make sex abuse allegations and toward the adults who believe them.

Our culture's response to the seven-year Virginia McMartin Pre-School trial in Manhattan Beach, California established the contemporary pattern of our denial, and currently dictates the way in which we react to most allegations. *Indictment*, the HBO version of the case broadcast in 1996, consolidates the defense's strategy and the media's spin into a potent cultural guide. The drama's narrative, presented as true ("This story happened in America in our times"), takes viewers from the first allegations in 1983 to the final jury decision in 1990. Well-paced, well-written, and well-acted, the story of Peggy McMartin Buckey and Raymond Buckey's journey through the legal system takes on tragic dimensions. In the last scene, the extended McMartin family and their defense attorney stand at the edge of a pier, staring at the horizon as if on the lookout for the next wave of sex abuse hysteria. "Had Jordan [Minnesota] and McMartin been manifestations of deliberate strategy—the staging of a spectacular production, to magnificent backlash benefit, at state expense," Louise Armstrong writes in her book, *Rocking the Cradle of Sexual Politics: What Happened When Women Said Incest*, "—one would have to applaud it as brilliant."

Early in the movie, the audience is introduced to the two competing points of view that will drive the entire drama. In response to the arrests of several members of her family and several of the teachers in her school, Virginia McMartin, the matriarch of the McMartin Pre-School, says self-righteously: "Children make up stories." Soon after, the prosecuting attorney, portrayed as zealous and only slightly less crazed than the Glenn Close character in *Fatal Attraction*, confronts the attorney for the defense with the question: "Do you actually believe children would make something like this up?" The villains in the movie are those who believe the children's "stories," and the heroes are those who know better.

Cast in this light, the social workers who interview the children become the case's abusive perpetrators. They take the children into separate rooms, show them pornographic dolls with penises, anuses, breasts, and pubic hair, corrupt their innocence with explicit sexual questions, verbally abuse them with sexual innuendoes, and harass them until they articulate the damning allegations. The children are portrayed either as innocent victims of their interviewers, volunteering false information to please them, or as little troublemakers, seizing the opportunity to make mischief by inventing fantastic stories. Explaining his strategy to go after the credibility of Kee McFarlane, the lead interviewer, the defense attorney tells his client: "[The members of the jury] are going to see that if somebody should be on trial for screwing people, maybe it shouldn't be Raymond Buckey."

The defense attorney's strategy involves using McFarlane's knowledge about child development against her. When McFarlane insists that there must have been abuse because "[t]he children told me," she is first ridiculed for her naivetè, and then chastised for not having believed them when they denied, altered, or recanted their testimony. "You closed your ears to the truth that they were so desperately trying to tell you," the attorney argues. When McFarlane insists that she could not have planted the allegations in the children's heads, the attorney quotes her explanation for their initial unwillingness to disclose: "Children between three and six can be very easily tricked. They are at this developmental stage of magical thinking. It is very easy to intimidate them." This response leads the questioning toward the issue of motive: Why would McFarlane knowingly solicit false statements (if that were possible)? The attorney sets it up so that her good intentions become the explanation for her alleged evil deeds. He confronts her with his theory that she took on the case "for a very noble reason," but the opportunity to become "the Joan of Arc of the children's movement" went to her head. In the end, he argues, "the power trip was too much to resist."

As the social workers, and by extension the children, are discredited by the defense, the defendants, particularly Peggy McMartin Buckey, emerge as the true victims in the case. From the beginning, Peggy Buckey, a middle-aged woman, is portrayed as a defenseless child in a hostile world—confused, innocent, terrified, and overwhelmed. One of the attorneys remarks that she didn't even understand the sexual charges against her; she didn't even know what the word "dildo" meant. The movie contains a scene in which Buckey, in shock after being denied bail, trips and falls while being shoved by a guard toward the holding cell. In another scene, she is literally raped by the system by being forced to undergo a cavity search. A gruff female guard commands her to undress, bend over, and endure her forceful penetrations. The experience leaves Buckey scarred for life. After being acquitted, Buckey tells her attorney: "It's not over. Not for me. When something like this hits you, you don't start your life over again so easily. . . . Not at my age." The movie's endnotes inform viewers that "Peggy had a nervous breakdown and continues to suffer from agoraphobia."

Overall, actual three-dimensional children have no role in *Indictment*'s story line. Child characters appear in the beginning as mere mouthpieces for adult accusations, the passive vessels of "fertile imaginations" in which false memories are "planted" by misguided adults. They are essentially interchangeable, without perceptible identities or even names. Each appears in a short spot as a testifying witness, part of a spectrum of accusations that develops from horrifying but potentially believable to absolutely incredible. The children are never shown frightened, suffering, or crying; they appear composed, untraumatized, and untouched by the activity around them. As "Miss Peggy" takes center stage, the children disappear. The movie never explores their perspective of the events, and they are completely absent after the first act. In sum, they do not play a crucial role in the drama; they are shallow, replaceable, and ultimately expendable props for adult conflicts.

Indictment's portrayal of the players in the McMartin case, including the children, makes sense in light of the movie's underlying belief. The movie took the unequivocal position that all the defendants in the McMartin case were completely innocent and undeniably virtuous. The role of Raymond Buckey was played by C. Thomas Howell, the young boy who befriended E.T. to the delight of millions of American moviegoers. The movie does not focus on evidence that counters its belief in the innocence of the accused: the grand jury's decision to pursue a trial, the fact that two juries deadlocked on the charges against Raymond Buckey, or the words of jurors who told reporters after the verdicts that they believed the children had been abused. These editorial decisions reflect the fact that the prosecution's failure to convict was taken as proof by the media and most of the American public that the adults who had taken the children's side in the case were "tragically mistaken" about the reliability of their allegations.

The outcome of the real-life McMartin case significantly influenced the way in which later child sex abuse allegations were viewed. It prompted the press to warn against entertaining cases "in which there is little or no physical evidence and the primary witnesses are children," or in which the children's allegations are "literally unbelievable." In the mid-1990s a spate of interest in the Salem, Massachusetts witch trials equated them with today's "outbreaks of community hysteria over purported sex abuse in preschools," warning readers about the dangerous consequences for adults of believing children's allegations. "I suspect it will be virtually impossible for anyone to see the close-ups of Devil-possessed children on the big screen," a *New York Times* reviewer wrote about the 1996 film version of Arthur

Miller's *The Crucible*, "and not reconsider the incredible inventory of uncorroborated allegations . . . in child molestation trials."

Despite the ambiguity of the verdicts, the McMartin legacy continues to fuel the widespread perception that our society has experienced—and is in constant danger of re-experiencing—an "epidemic" of false allegations. The mainstream media tends to promote the notion that sexual abuse allegations, particularly those involving multiple victims and/or multiple perpetrators, reflect cultural panic, not actual abuse. The conservative publication *National Review* took the opportunity of the McMartin verdicts to agree with the liberal *Village Voice* that "the recent rash of ritual-child-sex-abuse cases" at day-care centers was "mostly hysteria." Our culture adheres to the notion that false allegations have been sweeping across the country like a highly contagious virus, even though there is no evidence to support that view. Even Richard A. Gardner, a clinical professor of child psychiatry at Columbia University College of Physicians and Surgeons in New York, who is widely cited for his concern about the role of mass hysteria in sex abuse cases, acknowledges that "the vast majority of sex abuse allegations . . . are likely to be justified (perhaps 95 percent or more)."

The media's tendency to vouch for the innocence of those accused, and even of those convicted, of child sexual abuse is clearly unwarranted, inappropriate, and prejudicial. However, its failure to tell the other side of the story has an even more damaging effect on the public's understanding of sexual abuse and the credibility of legitimate allegations. *Indictment* does not show any scenes in which the social workers are questioned by the prosecution. Kee McFarlane never gets a chance to explain the factors that have an impact on children's testimony: the context in which most abuse occurs, the complexity of children's process of disclosure, the characteristics of children's developing cognitive and verbal capacities, the nature of the abuse, and the characteristics of child abusers.

The case of Margaret Kelly Michaels and the Wee Care Day Nursery students in Maplewood, New Jersey has been characterized by the promoters of the hysteria theory as the "spawn of McMartin." An article in *Harper's Magazine* argued that "the circumstances that resulted in her arrest, trial, and imprisonment bespeak a condition of national hysteria not unlike the hysteria that seized the Massachusetts Bay Colony . . . during the excitements of the Salem witch trials." As the Salem analogy implies, the media viewed Michaels as the innocent victim of mischievous, confused, brainwashed children. Even though articles acknowledged that "child abuse does happen in day-care facilities," they implied that Michaels was as likely to be a child abuser as she was to be a flying witch.

Whether or not the allegations against Michaels were generated by hysteria, the media's coverage of her case was true to the McMartin legacy. Michaels was convicted of sexual abuse in 1988 by a jury of her peers, 115 counts against twenty children. However, her conviction did not convince the public of her guilt. *New York* magazine called Michaels's case "one of the most grotesque miscarriages of justice in recent memory." In 1993, a New Jersey appeals court overturned Michaels's conviction because of questions about the validity of the children's testimony used to convict, questions like the ones that surfaced in the McMartin trial.

While the legal decision did not prove Michaels's innocence, it provoked a fresh wave of media coverage maintaining that she couldn't possibly be guilty.

Sexual abuse of children by adults is "by its nature . . .
private, and often without corroborating evidence." In
most cases, there isn't any physical evidence and there aren't
any witnesses. Sometimes the perpetrator confesses. But
often the only evidence a prosecutor can use to get a conviction is the testimony of the child victim. Child victims of
abuse, like adult victims of date rape, have to convince the
jury that their version of events, not the perpetrator's, is the
correct one. Because of the he-said, she-said setup, date-
rape cases are notoriously difficult to prove, especially when
the victim can't give a clear, detailed account of what happened because of the role of alcohol, trauma, or fear of the
perpetrator. Children, especially very small children, face
additional complications. Preschool-age children, for example, are in the early stages of learning how to use language
and how to understand the world around them. They disclose traumatic events differently than adults. These differences do not make them less honest, as many people
believe, but they do render them ill-equipped to participate
in a legal system designed by and for adults.

Article after article about the Michaels case argued that
the children who accused Kelly Michaels of sexually abusing them must have been indoctrinated by zealous parents,
investigators, and prosecutors. Coverage pointed to the
fact that the children had not reported the abuse while it
was taking place, and that it had taken several interviews
with investigators to get them to disclose what they had
experienced. An article in *Redbook Magazine* commented
that "the most startling thing was that none had spoken of

the abuse to parents and teachers—until after investigators had interviewed them repeatedly." This criticism assumes a number of things about very young children. It assumes that if they were being abused, they would immediately tell someone. To do that, they would have to know that they could and should go against an abusive authority figure. One study found that one-third of children abused in day-care settings did not disclose for at least six months from the onset of the abuse. In all likelihood, if children are being abused they have been told that bad things will happen if they tell anyone. Michaels allegedly told the children that she would kill their parents.

In his book *Nursery Crimes: Sexual Abuse in Day Care* on substantiated abuse in day-care cases, David Finkelhor explains that abusers frequently threaten to kill their victims, their victims' parents, and their victims' pets. In some cases, "Abusers . . . killed animals and invoked magical powers to prove to the children that they would punish them if they were disclosed." It's difficult for adults to remember that children do not perceive the world in the same way that adults do. They cannot verify the plausibility of threats, such as when an adult says, "If you tell I'll turn you into a frog." They are most likely to disclose abuse accidentally, whether or not they have been threatened because "[t]hey may not understand enough of what has occurred to make a conscious decision to tell." In the Michaels case, a four-year-old who was having his temperature taken rectally told the nurse: "That's what my teacher does to me at nap time at school. . . . Her takes my temperature."

Children's disclosure of sexual abuse is poorly understood in our culture in part because it is rarely explored in popular media. For example, it is currently completely acceptable to discount allegations of abuse that surface during custody disputes. As articles point out, fabricated allegations do occur, usually when one parent coerces a child into making false allegations against the other parent. However, we rarely report that there are also reasons why true allegations might be more likely to surface during a custody dispute than at any time before in the child's life. For example, children often report incest after the offending parent has moved out when they are less afraid of retaliation, and parent-child abuse often occurs for the first time after a marriage has broken up due to the parents' increased psychological distress.

Criticizing children for not telling until after they have gone through several interviews also presumes that when asked about possible abuse, they immediately can and will give a complete description. But, as researchers have pointed out, disclosure of abuse by children is a process not an event, a process that moves from denial to tentative disclosure to active disclosure. During the phase of tentative disclosure, the children appear "confused, inaccurate, and uncertain, often vacillating from acknowledgment to denial." Active disclosure means that children "give a detailed, coherent, first-person account of the abuse."

In a study of children who were confirmed victims of sexual abuse, almost three-fourths denied the abuse when first asked. Their denial was not always indifferent or passive. For some, denial "involved impassioned statements where the child adamantly denied any contact." The vast majority of the children then exhibited tentative disclosure. During this part of the process, they said things like, "I forgot"; "It happened to Joe"; "He tried to touch me but I hit him and ran away"; and, "I was only kidding." Finally, after repeated interviews, 96 percent of the children actively disclosed. For some, the disclosure process took one session with an interviewer; for others it took several months.

One-fifth of the children in the study completely recanted their disclosures at some time during the process, saying that they had lied, that they had made up the allegations, and even that someone else like a parent or teacher had made them say what they had said. One writer wondered in the pages of the *New Yorker* "why children are not believed when, as often happens, they specifically deny charges at the time they first arise?" Yet, it would only make sense to believe their denials if they maintained them consistently through a rigorous and long-term interviewing process. Article after article implied that the allegations were false by pointing out that they occurred only after investigators started asking questions. Yet, if investigators didn't press children they suspected of being abused, or if judges threw out all the cases where a majority of children denied the abuse when first questioned, most legitimate cases would never see the light of day.

Investigators in the Kelly Michaels case may have made mistakes in the interviewing process, but they faced an extraordinarily difficult task: getting three- and four-year-olds whom they had reason to believe had been abused to actively disclose in as short a time as possible without appearing to lead, coerce, or badger them. This task made them vulnerable to criticisms like the following: "In none of their recorded interviews with state investigators did the children freely recall the alleged incidents. The investigators cajoled and bullied them into giving the accounts they gave." We criticized investigators not only for repeated interviews, but also for asking leading, suggestive questions in those interviews, such as, "Did she put the fork in your butt?" and, "How did Kelly hurt you with the knife?"

What articles about the Michaels case didn't discuss was the development of children's language. For example, they didn't point out that early on in their development, "[c]hildren decide that each item in their environment has a unique name, and each word refers to only one thing." Therefore children have difficulty with synonyms like "utensil" for " fork," or "anus" for "butt." Investigators need to use specific language with which the child is familiar. Open-ended questions and questions that contain pronouns like, "Did someone do something to you?" often fail to evoke information. Children can also be confused by long, complicated, or simply less-than-direct questions. For example, passive questions can be difficult for them to interpret because children assume "that the noun mentioned before the verb is the noun that does the action." They might think that "Were you hurt by Kelly?" means "Did you hurt Kelly?" To further complicate interviews, small children have not yet mastered the meaning of prepositions like under, against, on top of, inside, or subjugating adverbs like because, while, and since.

At the same time, small children have a relatively limited vocabulary compared to adults, and are in the process of adding new words all the time. One McMartin juror complained, "The children were never allowed to say, in their own words, what happened to them." However, children's "own" words consist of the words of those around them, such as their parents, their teachers, and in legal cases, their interviewers. Abuse victims often make seemingly age-inappropriate statements such as, "Teacher made me suck his 'talus,'" in which they incorporate the vocabulary of their abusers. Or they may incorporate words they learned during an interview because they had needed verbal help to articulate their experiences. Just because a child uses an "adult" word or phrase does not mean that what the child is expressing is false.

Small children also have great difficulty with time. They can't yet tell time, and they can't easily conceptualize the difference between yesterday and last month, much less between six months ago and three years ago. The McMartin case lasted for seven years. The Michaels trial lasted for ten months, and it took place two years after allegations were first made. Nine of eleven jurors in the McMartin case who agreed to be interviewed after the verdicts acknowledged that they believed some of the children had been sexually abused but they hadn't been able to ascertain exactly how, when, and by whom. Prosecutors had to prove that a certain act was committed by a specific member of the staff at a certain time and place to a specific child. In other words, the legal process requires information in a format that is still inconceivable to most young children.

Unfortunately, the special nature of small children leaves them open to charges of fabricating allegations. In McMartin, people who believed that the Buckeys were victims of mass hysteria claimed that the case turned on the question of "whether the children had actually gone through the horrible things they described—or imagined them following the unintentional prompting of adult investigators and therapists." Children need more time, more support, and more input from interviewers than an adult does to articulate their allegations, which makes it easy to discredit their testimony. Child witnesses are now routinely described as having fabricated abuse experiences in response to leading questions, or having false memories "implanted" in their minds, or a combination of the two.

Whenever a publication dismisses the validity of a child's testimony, it relies on the notion that children are capable of believing in and repeatedly recounting an allegation of traumatic abuse that never occurred. The press refers to studies that supposedly prove that children can be made to believe in an event that never actually occurred, that often "children describe fantasies generated during months of intense questioning." However, the findings of these studies cannot necessarily be generalized to sexual abuse cases. According to Gail S. Goodman, author of *Testifying in Criminal Court: Emotional Effects on Child Sexual Assault Victims*, "[C]hildren often react differently to questions about genital contact than to inquiries about other kinds of events." Even preschool-age children "know that genital touch, nudity, and the like are taboo." Therefore, "embarrassment, surprise, and fear can affect children's willingness to provide information."

The media tend to ignore the research that suggests children do not, as a rule, fabricate allegations involving genital touch. A notable exception is an article published in *Vogue*. Author Carol Tavris reported on a study that contradicted what most other periodicals were reporting. Researchers Gail S. Goodman and Karen Saywitz interviewed a group of young children, half of whom had undergone a physical examination, and half of whom underwent a physical exam and a genital exam. The children were asked open-ended questions about what had happened, and then a set of leading questions, including intentionally misleading ones like,

"How many times did the doctor kiss you?" According to Goodman, "when the leading questions specifically referred to sexual touches, [the children] were highly resistant—the five-year-olds answered accurately 96 percent of the time, and the seven-year-olds 99 percent of the time." The study also found that children were much more likely to omit experiences involving sexual touch, than to fabricate such experiences. Sixty percent of the children who had undergone a genital examination did not talk about it in response to open-ended questions. Three of the children (8 percent) gave false affirmations: "[T]wo simply shaking their heads to indicate 'yes' but being unable to provide further detail and one providing false detail indicating that the doctor had used a stick to perform an anal examination."

For obvious reasons, researchers will never attempt to implant memories of sexual abuse in children in a research setting; it will always be difficult if not impossible to prove that such memories can in fact be falsely internalized and recounted by children. In addition, according to Stephen J. Ceci, author of *Jeopardy in the Courtroom: A Scientific Analysis of Children's Testimony*, "The scientific research on the suggestibility of children's recollections is contradictory and confusing, even for researchers who work in this emotionally charged and contentious area." Despite reporters' claims to the contrary, children's testimony in the McMartin trial doesn't prove that children are highly suggestible when it comes to allegations of abuse. The testimony of the children cannot be considered proof that false memories of sexual abuse can be implanted unless we know for certain the allegations are false. In other words, the children in the McMartin and Michaels cases can only be proof that investigators "impress[ed] upon [them] bizarre, sadistic sexual fantasies," as one article alleged, if, in fact, it has been proved that the abuse never actually occurred, which so far it has not.

If twenty adult women, or even five, were to accuse one person of sexual assault, even without corroborating evidence or witnesses, public opinion would likely side with them against their alleged perpetrator. From that perspective, it's somewhat surprising that many of us readily dismissed the allegations of twenty small children, even after their allegations resulted in convictions. Two factors make such a dismissal of children possible. First, the cultural belief that children are significantly different from adults in their sense of right and wrong, true and false. Second, the powerful resistance many adults have to accepting "the cruelty, sadism, neglect, and narcissism that adults inflict upon children." Most of us would rather believe that adults don't engage in perverted sexual acts with toddlers.

The appellate court that overturned Michaels's conviction included the following description in their opinion:

> The children told of games where both they and Kelly took off their clothes and, according to varying accounts, laid on each other, licked each other and Kelly, including applying and licking off peanut butter and/or jelly, had intercourse with Kelly while she apparently was having her menstrual period, ate pee and poop, and performed cunnilingus on her. Kelly allegedly committed fellatio on some of the boys. Kelly was said to have played Jingle Bells on the piano during many of those games. The acts were said to have taken place in the music or choir room, the gym, lunchroom, nap room, and bathroom. Kelly was said to have pooped and peed on or in a piano bench, on the floor, on the lunch table, and made a cake out of poop that the children had to taste.

Journalists who defend Michaels make it clear that the nature of the allegations against her goes a long way toward proving that they are false. One writer commented, "The acts she has been accused of committing. . . . surpass the merely perverse and even the bizarre, existing instead in some phantasmagoric realm." Another argued that the accusations "obviously owe more to a world of make-believe than to any world where the rules of physiology or common sense apply." The allegations were ubiquitously referred to as "bizarre," "hideous," "unbelievable," "incredible," and "unspeakable." However, most of the allegations against Michaels were not, strictly speaking, unbelievable. One boy did allege that Michaels had turned him into a mouse, a statement that seemed to prove to many that all the children's allegations must have been fabricated. Again, journalists overlooked the implications of children's developing cognitive and linguistic capacities. Michaels might have said that she *would* turn the boy into a mouse if he told, or she might have pretended for a period of time that he was a mouse. In either case, most three-year-olds would not be able to communicate, or even to understand an event that involved both literal and figurative language on the part of the abuser.

In order to confuse children, abusers sometimes make them ingest drugs or alcohol, or stage events like the killing of a baby in a way that appears real to very small children. Abusers certainly have a motive both to frighten children and to dress up their acts in various guises. The more outrageous children's allegations are, the less likely they are to be believed. The *Economist,* writing about American culture, argued that "children can be coaxed or coerced by those who may believe that satanic cults are under every bed" making them "unable to distinguish between reality and fantasy." The article didn't consider the fact that the children's confusion may have stemmed from the abuse itself. We embrace the notion that interviewers implant memories and confuse children, but we rarely discuss the fact that perpetrators do the same in conjunction with frightening, painful, traumatizing acts.

Most child sexual abuse does not occur in day-care centers. It may be true, as some pundits have suggested, that we are focusing on day-care cases to avoid acknowledging more common forms of abuse, such as abuse in families. "The libel that our society has imposed on child-care workers," according to Lawrence Wright, author of *Remembering Satan*, "is a kind of projection of guilt for the damage that we ourselves have done, as parents and as a society." However, this cultural displacement does not prove that the accused day-care workers are actually innocent. In addition, discrediting of high-profile day-care cases has facilitated the discrediting of all allegations of sexual abuse. The pattern of denial that we used to discredit the Wee Care Nursery allegations has resurfaced in coverage of more conventional and more common types of abuse.

For example, a *Newsweek* cover story on child sexual abuse filtered an interfamily abuse case through the standard rhetoric of denial. The case involved an elderly couple charged and *convicted* of sexually abusing two of their female grandchildren. Although the article never explicitly states that the Souzas are innocent, it tells their story in a way that leads the reader to that conclusion. The story as a whole posits the idea that "Americans are at a fever pitch over child sex abuse these days," and it argues that the current fight against child sexual abuse is "frantic," and has gone "too far." It mentions several high-profile day-care cases, including Wee Care Nursery, but does not discuss any cases in which most people would agree, thanks to a confession for example, that abuse had clearly occurred.

The article strongly implies that the allegations against the Souzas have been fabricated by the grandchildren from the input of zealous therapists and self-help books. It notes that the allegations of the two little girls "grew more detailed—and more vivid" the more they were interviewed, without discussing how this could be accounted for by the disclosure patterns of abused children. It cites several of the allegations in a way that makes them sound impossible. For example, according to the article, one of the girls testified that "her grandparents put 'their whole hand' into her vagina, stuck 'their head' into her as well and wiggled it around. . . . [and] pressed a button to operate a machine as big as a room with hands that hurt her." The article did not discuss children's cognitive and linguistic capacities, or the way that perpetrators strive to frighten and confuse their victims.

Perhaps the most obviously biased aspect of the article was the portrayal of the Souzas as average, wholesome Americans who couldn't possibly have sexually abused anybody. It featured two large pictures of the couple, one on the cover, one at the beginning of the article. Both suggest that these two nice people are the helpless victims of a larger cultural force beyond their control. On the cover, they are both in a staged photograph looking directly at the camera with a self-righteous air, as if to say: "The charges are obviously ridiculous." In the second photo, they are standing in a window framed by pink-and-white lace curtains, looking concerned and saddened.

The article notes that both are sixty-one and have lived in the same Massachusetts town all their lives: Shirley as a nurse and Ray as a lineman at an electrical company. Apparently, "Ray coached Little League, [and] Shirley volunteered at the American Cancer Society" and their photo books are full of pictures that "show the couple and their five children at weddings and barbecues and summer vacations." The article closes with the focus on the convicted couple who have been transformed into the real victims of the case: Ray and Shirley, "whose faces are lined with worry," waiting to be sentenced. "Again and again, they say they are innocent. 'We didn't do anything,' says Shirley in a trembling voice."

Even when allegations of abuse occur outside the media spotlight, public reaction follows larger cultural patterns of denial. A study of confirmed sexual abuse cases by teachers and staff in public schools suggests that adults often focus much more attention on their own interests and the interests of their peers than on the needs of children who allege abuse. Researchers Charol Shakeshaft and Audrey Cohan found that many of the superintendents they interviewed seemed to empathize mainly with the alleged perpetrators. Many "felt that their loyalties were divided" between the alleged victim and the alleged abuser, and "they were unsure where their duty lay." Often they couldn't believe the charges at first because the alleged abuser was an outstanding member of the staff and/or a friend. Superintendents often purposely kept the allegations in-house, giving accused teachers a variety of opportunities to escape punishment. They rarely contacted the authorities or sought evidence that might confirm the allegations. "In many cases," according to Shakeshaft and Cohan, "superintendents gave the accused teachers a complete summary of the allegations prior to questioning them about the incident," and sometimes carried out the questioning of students in a way that could frighten or intimidate them.

At the same time, colleagues of the accused most often rallied to his/her defense. "Teachers often believed that the allegations were lies or that the administration was 'going after' a good teacher," according to the study. Teachers often defended the accused "right up until the time he confessed." Some of the teachers harassed students who had made the allegation, trying to get them to recant testimony, "saying they would be responsible for ruining the career of a perfectly fine teacher." The community, like the school staff, took the side of the accused against the victim. Parents and community members often attacked the superintendent handling the investigation, accusing him of persecuting an innocent staff member. And "it was common," according to the study, "for students who accused their teachers of sexual abuse to be ostracized by other students, teachers, and members of the community."

Despite our culture's anti-child responses to sexual abuse allegations, contemporary media wisdom holds that "the pendulum of public opinion [regarding sexual abuse] is returning to midpoint." Apparently, our society acknowledges that child sexual abuse occurs, but is no longer as "frantic to root it out and stomp it to death no matter where it lurks—or doesn't." We have realized, according to this perspective, that many of the children we thought had been sexually abused had been simply brainwashed into thinking they had been abused. We had, it turns out, "planted false—and damaging—memories in children." We made, it turns out, the crucial mistake of being too "child-oriented." "A social attitude of greater incredulity and less 'respect' of the verbalization of children," according to Richard A. Gardner, "would have played a role . . . in squelching the sex abuse hysteria that we are witnessing." Armed with new legal precedents and scientific studies, the media tells us, we are finally on the road to trying child sexual abuse cases justly and effectively.

Unfortunately, the above conventional wisdom is more fairy tale than reality. Far from acknowledging our sexual abuse of children, we are deeply engaged in a sophisticated rhetoric of denial that masquerades as sensible, scientific, balanced pro-child sentiment. In an article on allegations of sex abuse in day-care centers, Lawrence Wright wondered why "there is such a cultural bias toward stories of abuse—and especially toward grotesque and absurd tales." But arguably the bias is in quite the other direction. The general consensus is that the Buckeys, Kelly Michaels, and others accused of similar acts are victims of a witch-hunt, not actual sex offenders. An article in *Newsweek* commented in 1995 that Wenatchee, Washington, the site of an alleged adult-led sex ring involving children, might be "careening toward its own version of the McMartin Pre-School case, where there are plenty of accusations but little truth to them."

Generally speaking, our culture can accept the truism that child sexual abuse is widespread, but can't internalize it. Our culture's rhetorical framework doesn't allow the reality of sexual abuse to permeate our consciousness. The way we tell stories about child sexual abuse implies that we could never do such a thing, that average Americans are living a life that does not involve such acts. We construct both the narrator and the audience of stories about child sexual abuse as people who can be adequately disgusted because they don't participate in such behavior. The fact that, statistically speaking, a portion of any body of viewers of a show on sex offenses against children are themselves perpetrators becomes unthinkable.

We continue to see perpetrators of abuse as "them" not "us." Child abusers don't have horns and tails, and they almost always proclaim their innocence with a persuasive and consistent demeanor, yet we cling to the notion that we would know an abuser if we spent any time with one. We couldn't believe that Margaret Kelly Michaels, that "pleasant-looking, open-faced woman, one of five brothers and sisters raised in a middle-class Pittsburgh neighborhood," could have inserted serrated knives into small children's anuses. We couldn't conjure up that image. The way in which information about child sexual abuse is distributed guarantees that it can never be seen as part of the status quo. It can never amount to something basic, something "we" do, but remains a conglomeration of fragments of evidence, acts allegedly committed by "others," each too insignificant in itself to change the big picture.

We also resist focusing attention on the narratives of sex offenders. We shy away from the stories of confessed offenders. It seems we don't want to know about the horrible things that have actually been done to children, especially when delivered in a context we can't dismiss. And we don't want to know that most of the people who coerce children into sex aren't easily distinguishable from the rest of us. At the same time our culture doesn't scrutinize alleged perpetrators' testimony, perhaps because it hits too close to home. Perpetrators are much more likely to lie about abuse than victims, yet we don't elaborate on the motives a perpetrator has for lying or on the countless ways perpetrators rationalize, minimize, and discount what they do to children or on the suggestibility and contamination of their testimony. If we did focus more on perpetrators, we would shift emphasis onto the reality of child sexual abuse and the credibility of abuse victims, and clearly this is a shift we don't yet want to make.

Even though we acknowledge that sexual abuse of children is widespread, we have great difficulty as a culture acknowledging what such a statement actually means for children. It means that many children experience hurtful, harmful things at the hands of adults charged with their care. Yet when we come up against descriptions of what an adult has allegedly done to a child, we balk. As a culture, we tend to minimize the frequency and harmfulness of sexual abuse in a variety of ways. For example, we frequently equate the trauma experienced by child who has been sexually abused with the trauma of an adult who has (allegedly) been falsely accused of abusing a child. For example, *Time* columnist Margaret Carlson wrote: "About the worst thing that can happen to a child is to be sexually molested. About the worst thing that can happen to an adult is to be wrongly accused of committing such a heinous crime."

We also equate the trauma of being sexually abused with the trauma of having internalized allegedly false abuse experiences. Several judges have written in their opinions that believing in a false experience is as damaging as experiencing actual abuse, and that the resulting memories are "as real to the child as any other," and the children's "behavior is just the same as if they were abused." *National Review* went even further, calling the way that the children in the Michaels case were interviewed "officially sanctioned child abuse," and claiming that those who "believe they have been subjected to unspeakable acts . . . suffer the same psychological trauma they would if these acts had really occurred." It's hard to imagine the media peddling the argument that a grown man's fantasy of being anally raped would have the same impact on him as an actual rape. It makes no sense that children's reactions to fantasy would be equivalent to their reactions to actual rape, even if both were intense. And there is absolutely no way such a hypothesis could be proved.

But the equation has clear advantages. The idea that abusive experiences and false memories of abuse (if there is such a thing) have the same impact on a child significantly minimizes the horror of actual abuse. It provides a way for adults to feel better about dismissing allegations, especially when they can't be proven definitively false. They can portray their reluctance to believe as an effort to protect children from the "abuse" of an investigation. The idea also provides a convenient method for disregarding the trauma manifested by children who allege abuse. We can claim that children in the McMartin case continue to suffer from post-traumatic stress disorder because they made the mistake of believing hysterical social workers, or that the children in the Michaels case who are now teenagers still believe they were abused because they can't tell reality from fantasy.

Our culture's patterned response to child abuse allegations may give us temporary relief from awareness, but it has serious, long-term consequences for society. Not only are we perpetuating a culture in which many children who have been sexually abused can't be believed or supported, and in which sex offenders can too easily escape sanction. But we are also promoting the development of sex offenders and, therefore, the promulgation of sex offenses against children. Children who have been abused and have not received effective intervention and treatment are more likely to grow up to abuse children themselves, or to enable the abuse of children by, for example, raising children with an abuser. Our society's rejection of children's stories and our inability to make children's well-being paramount in sex abuse cases means that the next generation will be living in an even more dangerous world. Our efforts to protect ourselves from the reality of child abuse put our society's children at ever greater risk.

FIVE

Immaculate Dysfunction

It is hard to think of a topic in recent years that has attracted more misinformation, more convoluted reasoning
or more sheer meanness than teenage pregnancy. In some
circles, the bearing of children by mothers who are themselves scarcely out of childhood seems to serve as a symbol
of all the miseries that bedevil us as a society—a drain on
the public treasury, a rot eating away the tissue of the
moral order, even the root cause of poverty in our time.

KAI ERIKSON

Our culture may question the existence of certain kinds of
harm inflicted on children, but where there is undeniable
proof of harm, most adults express concern. This societal
concern motivates the social policy process. It leads to the
identification of the adult behaviors responsible and the
proposal of potential solutions. The incontrovertible negative consequences of adolescent sexuality and reproduction,
such as sexually transmitted diseases, including AIDS and
teen pregnancy, constantly spark this process. Adults recognize that they play a role in the sexual behavior of young
people, and that they must, to some extent, alter their own
conduct if they want young people to behave differently.
The cultural image of the childbearing stork contains
within it the reminder that children do not choose their
living environments, and, therefore, cannot be the exclusive
masters of their own fate.

However, when adults mischaracterize their role in the

noxious circumstances of children's lives, they make things worse. Their efforts both compound the problem and undermine public support for young people in difficulty. In the case of teen sexuality and reproduction, adults consistently cast themselves in the role of communicating unhealthy values, a role that obscures the two most significant factors in unhealthy adolescent sexuality—childhood sexual abuse (perpetrated by adults) and childhood poverty (orchestrated by adults). When adult efforts to transmit healthier values fail to ameliorate teens' health and life circumstances (which they are doomed to do since they don't address root causes), teens are criticized for not responding appropriately. In a perverse transformation, misguided social policies created by adults become vehicles for blaming young people for their own problems.

A key element in this transformation is our cultural concept of childhood that owes much of its shape to the influence of a book entitled *The Disappearance of Childhood*, by Neil Postman. First published in 1982, and reprinted in 1994, the book has been widely cited in the media for over fifteen years, especially in the context of articles heralding childhood's end. The book argues that television erodes the state of childhood by exposing children to the "secrets" of the adult world. This argument has given many cultural pundits the notion that young people are more influenced by media messages about adult "secrets" than by the adult "secret" behavior they experience, and therefore young people have more to fear from the television than from abusive adults and unjust adult policies. As a result, articles that lament the perceived erosion of childhood innocence do not focus on rape, sexual exploitation, or poverty. Instead, they identify media, "the saturation of American popular culture with sexual messages, themes, images, exhortations," as the true culprit.

In an article about "vanished childhood," Bruno Bettelheim, the late renowned child psychologist, summarized Postman's ideas about television, and then extrapolated that the early age at which children reach puberty and "the provocative images" they see in the media are "two forces [that] together help explain why girls and boys are engaging in sex—and consequently are also having children." Articles about childhood's end often make this unwarranted leap from knowledge to action. A *New York Times* article entitled "Little Big People" connected exposure to television shows like *Married . . . With Children* to the phenomenon of a group of fourth-grade girls who were (according to their parents) "so sexually precocious that they were hotly pursuing certain boys and refusing to speak to others." It quoted a concerned mother who suggested that television not only inspires imitation in ten-year-old girls, but implants sexual sophistication: "The girls wore halter tops and tiny bicycle shorts," the woman complained. "It's hard to know whether they just wanted to look like Julia Roberts in *Pretty Woman* or whether they knew what they were up to."

Our culture's concept of childhood minimizes the adult function in adolescent welfare, thereby exaggerating young people's control over their own lives. The idea that information determines children's behavior, and even their identities, allows our culture to perceive sexually active and pregnant teens as in control of their experiences. We portray teens not as victims of uncontrollable people and social forces (other than their hormones), but as decision makers (albeit poor ones). We sustain this portrayal despite extensive social science research that underscores the active role of adult coercion in young people's sexual behavior. In his book *The Scapegoat Generation: America's War on Adolescents*, author Mike A. Males presents a harrowing overview of rape in children's lives. He cites a survey that concluded that "27 percent of the women and 16 percent of the men [in the sample] had been sexually abused in childhood. The average age at the time of victimization was nine for victims, thirty for abusers." Males points out that "most 'sexually active' girls under age fifteen were initiated into sex by rape by older males"; "For most of these girls, a rape had been their only 'sex.'"

Adults also play a major role in "teen" pregnancy, according to Males. Sexual abuse in childhood is "the single biggest predictor of teenage pregnancy over the past forty years." In one survey, "Two-thirds of the pregnant and parenting teens . . . had been sexually abused or raped." A 1995 study found, "Sexually abused girls were 'sexually active' at much younger ages . . . and tended to have partners five to six years older, factors which increased the chances of early pregnancy four-fold." Men eighteen and older father 80 percent of babies born to girls eighteen and younger; half of these fathers are over twenty. Birth records shows that for girls fifteen and under who give birth, "40 percent of the fathers are senior high males and 50 percent are post-high-school adult men averaging five to six years older than the mothers." In other words, pregnancy is more often than not a consequence, and often a manifestation, of the adult sexual exploitation of children.

Our society uses media messages to understand how children might feel about sex. However, we assiduously avoid

letting the media tell us anything about our adult selves.
Our culture's response to Calvin Klein's 1995 ad campaign
featuring "intimate snapshots of very young men and
women in a provocative state of undress" skirted the obvious: adults are sexually attracted to minors. Instead, articles
interviewed teens to gauge their reactions. Even when we
could acknowledge that "[t]hese ads enter the heart of adult
darkness, where toying with the sexuality of teens is think-
able," we couldn't follow through to point out that to
millions of adults sexual toying with teens is not just think-
able, it's doable, and done.

For the most part, our neglect of the adult role in children's sexual experiences is not malicious. We don't con-
sciously hide evidence of adult sexual impropriety involving
children. We simply can't incorporate what we know to be
true into what we believe to be the case. For example, as our
culture's scapegoating of pregnant teens rose to a fevered
pitch in 1995-96, every major magazine and newspaper dutifully published at least one article on the adult male role in
"teen" pregnancy. *U.S. News & World Report* clearly stated,
"The problem with teen sex is not simply that teens are having sex. Adults, in disturbing numbers, are having sex with
teens." Joe Klein wrote in *Newsweek* that pregnant teens
"aren't just amoral, premature tarts—they are prey." However, the next time a related media event occurred—sexual
harassment in high schools—we once again neglected to
bring up adult-teen sex.

In less than a decade, our culture has effected a positive
paradigm shift regarding young people and sexual violence.
We have begun to acknowledge that the world of childhood
is not free from "adult" problems. We now realize to some

extent that "the transgressions of the playground both reflect and help constitute the oppressive sexual politics of our
larger culture." In 1990, *U. S. News & World Report* columnist
John Leo confidently dismissed the notion of sexual harassment among teenagers. In reference to a new sexual harassment code at a high school in Massachusetts, he wrote that
"these rules are ideal for a time capsule. Let's just stuff them
there and skip the whole idea of imposing them on the un-
suspecting young." Less than six years later, he had changed
his tune. He continued to deride what he referred to as
the "harsh attitude toward tot-harassers" in schools, but he
grudgingly acknowledged: "It's true that crude sexual incidents occur . . . some reaching down to lower grades."

The Clarence Thomas hearings and subsequent research
prompted Leo's improved attitude, and the broader cultural
shift. In 1993, the American Association of University
Women Educational Foundation (AAUW) released the findings of a survey on sexual harassment in the schools. The
study found that harassment among teens was prevalent,
harmful, and ignored by school personnel. Major magazines and newspapers dutifully reported that "85 percent of
girls in grades 8 through 11, and 76 percent of boys in the
same grades, said they had been the subject of unwelcome
sexual behavior at least once in their school lives." In other
words, "The hallways of America's high schools and junior
high schools . . . are daunting, sexually charged terrain
where most girls and many boys can routinely expect to be
grabbed, poked, pinched or put down in explicitly sexual
ways." Harassment was found to be not only extremely
common, but also extremely harmful; it had "consequences
that go beyond the realm of simple coming-of-age rituals,"
according to one article. And students of both sexes agreed

that school personnel responded inadequately, if at all, to complaints and incidents of harassing behavior.

By the time a North Carolina elementary school had suspended six-year-old Johnathan Prevette on charges of sexual harassment, the media had been reprogrammed. Articles did complain that the school had been too extreme, manifesting what one author called "political correctness gone amok." But they also added that sexual harassment in the schools was a serious problem that needed attention. "While some schools are overreacting," the *New York Times* pointed out, "many others still fail to respond adequately to complaints of persistent harassment that blight students' school life." Unfortunately, however, our culture still had at least one more dramatic shift to make before we could say that we truly had acknowledged the extent and severity of sexual violence in the lives of young people. When confronted with data about sexual harassment in the schools, we collectively overlooked a crucial aspect of the problem: the role of adults as perpetrators.

The AAUW report received a great deal of media attention. However, that attention was oddly selective. Only a handful of articles reported the AAUW findings involving staff-to-student harassment. According to the survey, one in five girls and one in twelve boys reported having been harassed by a school employee "such as a teacher, coach, bus driver, teacher's aide, security guard, principal, or counselor." The few articles that did mention this data dedicated one easily dismissed sentence at most. Every other component of the coverage focused on teen-to-teen harassment. We essentially ignored the fact that a significant minority of school personnel subject students to sexual violence, including exhibitionism, verbal abuse, sexual abuse, and rape, and that the educational system and surrounding communities have not adequately addressed the problem.

In general, coverage completely resisted discussing harassment by adults. If it mentioned adult harassment at all, it implied that such harassment wasn't terribly significant. Had reporters writing about the Prevette case been so inclined, they could have informed readers that sexual harassment by school personnel is a major problem in secondary schools, more widespread even than the AAUW survey suggested. A study presented in *Youth & Society* in 1993 found that half of the subjects interviewed "cited incidents where they felt another student had been treated inappropriately." Nearly one-third of this inappropriate behavior "consisted of affairs or dating between high school students and teachers." Another survey of college students found that over 17 percent of males and 82 percent of females had experienced sexual harassment by faculty or staff while in high school; 13 percent said they had had a sexual relationship with a teacher while in high school.

While articles were perfectly ready to generalize about the harmful "status quo" of harassing teens in schools, they did not call attention to a pattern of harassment on the part of school staff. There were no angry editorials written about the "adults-will-be-harassers" mentality on school campuses, as there had been about the "boys-will-be-boys" attitude. The articles didn't explore why faculty and staff harassed students, what impact such harassment had on students, or what steps schools should take to discipline adult offenders. It was as if the statistics about sexual violence perpetrated by adults against the young people in their care had simply fallen on deaf ears. Coverage of the AAUW report demonstrates how our society can acknowledge a problem statistically without acknowledging it culturally.

Our attitudes toward teens who are sexually involved with older adults provides another illustration of acknowledgment without acceptance. Coverage of the Joey Buttafuoco-Amy Fisher liaison illustrates the myth that sexually active teens, even teens that we acknowledge are being exploited to some extent by adults, are in control of their situations and should be held entirely accountable for them. According to police, Buttafuoco, a man in his midthirties, admitted when he was first brought in for questioning to having had a sexual relationship with the teenage Amy Fisher. Shortly afterward, he retracted his admission. Up until the day he pled guilty to charges of statutory rape, Buttafuoco steadfastly maintained that Amy was simply an obsessive teenager, whom he barely knew, who had a crush on him. Most of America believed all along that he had been having sex with the young, attractive girl. However, he was not subjected to the harsh scrutiny that his teenage partner had to endure. Buttafuoco remained a somewhat lecherous, somewhat pathetic figure who had exercised poor judgment. Amy became the "Long Island Lolita" who suffered from a "fatal attraction."

Our culture somehow transformed Amy Fisher, an abused, troubled young girl, into an object of derision, rather than of sympathy. We accomplished this by downplaying and misrepresenting her difficult childhood, and by casting her as a sexually promiscuous deviant who controlled her environment rather than as a child in need, deserving of our protection and care. Like the prosecuting attorney, we came to believe that it would be as accurate to characterize Amy as "a 17-year-old girl who lives at home with her parents and goes to high school," as it would be to describe John Gotti as "a businessman from New York."

When police apprehended Amy Fisher, a seventeen-year-old high school senior, she told them that she had been having an affair with Joey Buttafuoco for over a year, and that he had promised to take care of her forever if she got rid of his wife, Mary Jo. "Now I see a blob with stretch marks. Now, oh, my God, I can't believe that was me!" she said recently in a prison interview. "But back then he was so charming. There's a word. It is brainwashing." According to Amy, the explanation for her relationship with Buttafuoco, was simple and sad: "I was a young girl. Who had family problems. And met the wrong man."

Amy's vulnerability had been cultivated by an emotionally and sexually abusive childhood and exacerbated by a morally and sexually corrupt community. An alleged victim of incest at the hands of her father, unprotected by her mother, she acted out in school; she got into fights and car accidents, and she ran away, once for as long as two weeks. Beginning when she was a sixteen-year-old high school junior, Buttafuoco had sex with her four to five times a week, in motels, parking lots, and his boat. "I was lonely and so scared of my father," Amy told a reporter, "and here's this older man and he takes care of me and he tells me I'm beautiful. I felt honored." Within a few months, Buttafuoco allegedly hooked her up with an escort service run out of a house just six blocks from his family's auto body repair shop. Older men, many of them regular clients, many presumably residents of the area, paid her hundreds of dollars to have sex with them after school.

Amy Fisher's allegations of incest were never publicly corroborated. And both her father and his attorney protested his innocence. However, the media was not content with simply presenting both sides. Amy's revelations were either ignored or dismissed out of hand. Articles portrayed Mr. and Mrs. Fisher as sweet and doting; their only fault was perhaps that they were too generous. One magazine characterized the Fishers as "an adoring and indulgent family." "She was their only child; they gave her all they could," according to another. "She had her own room with matching furniture, her own phone, an endless supply of stuffed animals." Coverage stressed how Amy's parents had bought her a car when she turned sixteen, and a second car when she crashed the first.

In general, coverage expressed bewilderment at Amy's behavior, embracing the "fascinating and irresistible paradox: how a young, attractive woman from an affluent family could go so utterly wrong." In general, we did not remind ourselves that "adolescents who are out of control and sexually acting out very frequently have prior histories of being severely traumatized." At the same time, coverage bent over backward to exonerate Amy's community of any wrongdoing. *Time* magazine described Merrick, Long Island as "a montage of Middle American normality. . . . This is where the American Dream still works, where crime is something glimpsed on a news cast, where the next generation prompts hope and not despair." It insisted that "Fisher's sordid story still would seem to have little to reveal about the norms of her community."

The article didn't mention that this is the same community that, for over a decade, had both tolerated and frequented the local ABBA Escort Service that employed the teenage Amy Fisher. The woman who ran the prostitution ring had been arrested and fined in 1990, and then had been allowed to go immediately back into business. This is the same community made up of restaurant patrons, motel clerks, and acquaintances of the Buttafuocos who stood by as a thirty-six-year-old married man with two children pursued a very public sexual affair with a teenager. He made no secret of his activities, allegedly boasting to his colleagues in the auto body repair shop that he had given Amy her first orgasm.

After whitewashing Amy Fisher's childhood and her social environment, coverage got on with the business of portraying her as a sex-obsessed vixen. Articles and television shows regarded the videotape of Amy turning a trick with a twenty-nine-year-old man as a confirmation of her sexual control, rather than as a sad commentary on her dysfunction. The Nassau County district attorney described Amy as "so shrewd and so manipulative and so brazen" because she had allegedly tried to turn tricks without giving the woman who ran the prostitution ring her share. The most widely quoted dialogue of the video was Amy's response to an offer from the john to work a bachelor party: "I'm wild. I don't care. I love sex."

The Crush, a movie released in 1993, accomplishes a similar distortion of a troubled young girl's behavior. Darian Forrester (played by real-life teen Alicia Silverstone) is the sexy, pouty fourteen-year-old daughter of two sweet, affluent working parents whose only fault is that they are overindulgent. Enter Nick Eliot, a handsome twenty-eight-year-old magazine writer who becomes the object of Darian's obsessive desire. To its credit, the movie shows how Nick "blurs the line," as his girlfriend points out, by initially responding to Darian's persistent advances. He drives her to Shelter Point and allows her to give him a long, deep kiss, and several times he finds himself aroused by her barely pubescent sexuality. But then, who wouldn't become flustered and sweaty at the sight of a bikini-clad Alicia Silverstone? the movie seems to be asking. Every straight man in the audience can certainly identify with the poor, tortured Nick Eliot. He shows remarkable restraint, all things considered.

Darian, on the other hand, is portrayed as beyond comprehension. Her provocative mix of youth and sexual sophistication gets us all hot and bothered, but it doesn't make her a sympathetic character. We empathize with Nick as a scorned Darian begins to destroy every aspect of his life with her cunning intelligence and vengeful ingenuity. We are even afraid for him, afraid of a fourteen-year-old girl! But this is no ordinary teenager, we learn. She never took to the carousel that her father restored for her. "I ride real horses now," she reminds him. Except for a couple of violent tantrums, she is completely unchildlike—cool, calculating, and collected. She is unperturbed by a glimpse of Nick's naked body, comfortable with any tawdry sexual subject, able to pull off a false rape allegation worthy of an Oscar. This spoiled woman-child's only weakness is her inability to tolerate not getting exactly what she wants.

When we portray teenage girls as fatally attracted to older men, we seem to be suggesting that they are driven, controlled by their overwhelming sexual desire. Yet we also characterize these same girls as supremely in control—of themselves, the objects of their desire, and their environments. After all, Amy Fisher traded sex for money and for services from men, such as procuring weapons and spying on Mary Jo. And the last scene of *The Crush* shows Darian Forrester on the brink of being freed from a mental institution because she has fooled her doctor, who is also her latest crush, into believing she is really a nice girl. Ultimately, we resolve the contradiction of our portrayal by making both the trait of being out of control and the trait of being in control mean the same thing—that the girl has the capacity to consent.

As the cases of both Amy Fisher and *The Crush*'s Darian Forrester illustrate, we equate children's sexual knowledge with their psychological maturity. Because of their sexual sophistication, we couldn't perceive either Amy or Darian as children, and therefore we couldn't imagine them as vulnerable. At one point Nick Eliot asks Darian, "Are you sure you are only fourteen?" He already knows the answer, but his rhetorical question implies that the only difference between her and a grown-up is a seemingly arbitrary number. Nick resists Darian's advances to protect himself from getting into trouble, not to protect her. Joey Buttafuoco apparently couldn't think of any convincing reason not to have sex with sixteen-year-old Amy. While we suspected that Joey Buttafuoco was lying about not having had sex with Amy, we never presumed that he had coerced her.

Woody Allen rationalized his relationship with Soon-Yi Previn, the young daughter of his partner, Mia Farrow, by describing her as "a grown sophisticated person," who was "probably more mature than I am." He seemed to echo a widely held cultural belief that young people, even abused and neglected young people, have the psychological resources to control their sexual experiences with older adults outside their immediate family circle. This belief pervades the story line of his movie *Husbands and Wives*. The main character, Gabe, played by Woody Allen, understands the inherent imbalance in relationships between older men and young women. He explains that many professors seduce their pupils "because it's a cinch. [Their students] look up to them. They're older men. Their students are flattered by the attention." However, the film portrays Rainer (Juliette Lewis), the female student with whom Gabe becomes involved, as the stronger, more experienced, more sexually aggressive of the two.

In a moment of anger, Gabe snaps at Rainer: "I don't need a lecture on maturity or writing from a twenty-year-old twit." But, in general, both he and the movie portray the young woman as worldly-wise and surprisingly assertive. She tells Gabe about how she took up with several older men and then quickly discarded them. We meet one ex-lover who is also her ex-analyst, waiting for her outside her family's apartment, devastated by the breakup. In response to her tales, Gabe remarks: "My God, you've got material for your first novel and the sequel and an opera by Puccini here. Incredible." Rainer also has the courage and intelligence to give Gabe a scathing critique of the attitudes toward women in his semi-autobiographical novel. "The way your main character views women. It's so retrograde. It's so shallow," she tells him.

Gabe claims to have found Rainer's criticisms of his work and the argument that followed to be alluring. "It attracted me to her in some way, that she was not just a passive little worshipful pupil." However, Gabe decides not to pursue a sexual relationship with her, even after she gets him to give her a long, deep kiss at her birthday party. He seems to imply that he is not taking up with her because it is inappropriate, but what he tells her gives the impression that her emotional strength is what changed his mind. She didn't turn out to be the starry-eyed "twit" he had presumed her to be, a girl who would fawn over his compliments and his work. And he knows she would eventually leave him. "I just feel I know how this is going to come out," he tells her. Rainer, disappointed, accepts his decision. "Okay," she agrees. "I know how it would end [if we started seeing each other]."

There are, no doubt, twenty-year-old women who are strong enough to control their sexual relationships with older men as Rainer appears to be. But many young women are strong-armed into sexual relationships with older men, and the pregnancies that often result, by difficult circumstances including psychological vulnerability and socioeconomic hardship. The psychological makeup of pregnant teens strongly implicates not so much the girls themselves as their social environments—environments created and maintained by adults. "The correlation between childhood poverty and later teenage childbearing is so strong," according to Mike A. Males, "that during the 1960–1993 period, the teen birth rate could be calculated with 90 percent accuracy from the previous decade's child poverty rate." Males points out that "U.S. teens who enjoy low youth poverty rates similar to those in Europe . . . display low teenage pregnancy. . . rates similar to those of Europe." From a social science perspective, a teenager's pregnant body represents the intersection of adult-perpetrated exploitation with adult-fostered vulnerability.

Mainstream coverage of sexually active teens generally fails to point out the extent to which their behavior is adaptive. Many young women "try to fulfill their emotional needs through sex." Many young women "may be exercising their best option in bleak circumstances when they latch onto older men who promise them a 'way out' of homes characterized by poverty, violence, and rape." Often poor socioeconomic circumstances make having a baby at a young age a good, and perhaps the best, "choice" available. Teenage girls growing up in poverty who postpone child-bearing until adulthood "need to possess not just average but above-average psychological resources and strengths" and will often not be any better off economically than their peers who bear children as teens. However, there is a good chance that they will be worse off emotionally. Pregnant teens show dramatic improvement in their behavioral health and emotional well-being. "The adolescent mother, in contrast with the sexually active adolescent who is not a mother, feels better about herself and engages in fewer overt undesirable behaviors," according to a 1990 study.

Unfortunately, our society continues to devise policy as if all girls had the psychological and social resources necessary to resist destructive sexual relationships and early parenthood. In a speech given in response to receiving a teen pregnancy report, President Clinton acknowledged that "we have to . . . take seriously the role in this problem of older men." He then proceeded to argue that in terms of prevention, the country needed to focus on changing teens. "First and foremost, community programs must stress abstinence and personal responsibility. A program cannot be successful unless it gives our children the moral leadership they need." According to *U.S. News & World Report*, the federal government has spent over $30 million since 1981 to develop "abstinence only" education programs, and President Clinton made abstinence a "cornerstone" of his $400 million campaign against teen pregnancy, officially launched in 1996. In the nineties, the mainstream media also began promoting absti-nence as an essential component in sex-education programs. Magazines ran stories with such positive headlines as "Prac-ticing the Safest Sex of All," "Fifteen Cheers for Abstinence," and "Making the Case for Abstinence."

In many ways, this decade's pro-abstinence position re-flects a better understanding of teens' sexual experiences. It is a response in part to studies that suggest that many teens want to learn how to resist unwanted sexual advances. One survey found that 84 percent of teens "wanted to know how to say no to someone pressuring them for sex." Some of the better abstinence-based programs seek to teach teens how to say no to sex before they are ready and when they don't want to engage in it. But the lessons don't necessarily help them to say no to adults, especially to family members and other authority figures, and don't generally give them the resources to escape their difficult environments. As Mike A. Males points out:

> those who postulate that abstinence or sex education is a panacea to "teen pregnancy" are contending that young girls, most with histories of poverty and sexual abuse, can be taught or persuaded to enforce abstinence or contra-ception upon significantly older male partners—some of whom don't take "no" for an answer.

Sex education courses in the schools vary greatly in con-tent and quality. However, if mainstream coverage is any in-dication, most programs continue to portray peers and the media as the greatest threats to inappropriate sexual experi-ences, and they do not discuss the role of adults in the sex-ual exploitation of teens. Mainstream articles tend to laud programs that teach role-playing in "classic" situations: for example, "Boy takes girl on an expensive date and then insists on sex." A *Newsweek* article expressed support for a program "aimed at those thirteen- and fourteen-year-olds who were nervous about sex, but likely to plunge ahead because of peer pressure." Articles also criticize the "supersexed world of pop culture" arguing, as one did, that "when you're a teenager. . . . [w]hat counts is what flits by on the tube and pulses through the headphones of your Discman." Even those rare articles that acknowledge the role of adult males in "teen" sex and pregnancy never wonder about the logic of averting sexual abuse by teaching an eleven-year-old girl to just say no to her thirty-five-year-old father, stepfather, uncle, coach, or baby-sitter. Certainly, children should be taught that they can and should say no to unwanted sexual advances. But to be effective, programs must, in addition, teach them what to do when such advances come from adults they trust, and to provide them with the resources they need to assert themselves.

Teaching teens how to resist peers and the media is valuable, but it falls far short of what they need. If we acknowledged that teens face the greatest threat to their sexual health from adults and adult-perpetuated circumstances, we would also have to acknowledge that it is unfair and unrealistic to put the burden on young people to stem the tide of adult-child sexual exploitation. Currently, most pregnancy-prevention programs still do more to perpetuate adult myths about teens and sex than they do to meet teenagers' need for healthy, safe sexuality. In addition, they often teach children that they can say no when they lack the psychological and/or practical resources to do so and when they might be better off saying yes, especially in the short run, a lesson that is as absurd as it is cruel.

The ideology of teen pregnancy-prevention programs reveals a great deal about adult perceptions of children's lives. Statistics about child sexual abuse and childhood poverty seem to have had little impact on the popular misconception that the biggest trauma most teens have to face is an unsatisfactory social life. Coverage of the "Baby Think It Over" doll, for example, paints an intensely distorted portrait. The doll, designed "to provide adolescents an up-in-the-middle-of-the-night reality check on what parenting is all about," can be programmed "to cry at random intervals, to mimic an infant's sleeping patterns and demands for food." One article touted it as a much-needed alternative to lectures that "aren't effective when weighed against peer pressures and passion of the moment." The doll apparently has the ability to deliver "a dose of near-reality" and a "realistic taste of parenthood" that causes teens to "think twice about the consequences of their sexual behavior."

Coverage praised the doll's ability to "disrupt [teens'] social life. The constant care and attention it requires changes a teenager's lifestyle profoundly." Inevitably, the articles on the doll's use in various schools quoted teen girls whose sleep and activities with peers had been curtailed. "It woke me up three times in the middle of the night," one girl was quoted as saying. "I had to take it everywhere, even to the coffee shop. It was embarrassing and really put a damper on my social life." Another girl was described as having been "embarrassed at times about carrying a baby around in public to hangouts with friends, to the school's basketball games, even to her other classes. Getting up throughout the night proved to be more exhausting than she could have imagined." In other words, the coverage suggested that teens' lives are so essentially safe, comfortable, and sheltered from the exigencies of the "real" world that a sleepless night or interrupted pizza party will really shake them up.

Lance Morrow argued in an essay in *Time* that the "mentality of abstinence" goes a long way toward providing a context of "shelter," "safety," and "security" for adolescents making the passage from childhood to adulthood. But arguably the opposite is true. Pro-abstinence rhetoric denies adolescents shelter. It relieves adults of the responsibility for creating and maintaining a safe, secure environment in which children can grow. Children do not control their environments, nor can they be expected to protect themselves from the adults around them regardless of their maturity, particularly when they have already been made vulnerable by adult abuse and neglect. Yet pro-abstinence coverage conveys the implicit message that teens can control their lives, and aren't particularly vulnerable or victimized.

And pro-abstinence rhetoric effectively denies children the opportunity to safely explore their sexuality with themselves and their peers in healthy, developmentally appropriate ways. Abstinence programs downplay the need for information about sexuality, birth control, and safe sex, and rarely discriminate between unhealthy and healthy teenage sexual experiences. Concerned about teen pregnancy and disease, yet unwilling to acknowledge our role, we are coercing children into saying no to all sex, including healthy sexual exploration. Overall, our response to "teen" pregnancy illustrates how far we are willing to go at children's expense to avoid taking accountability for what we do to them.

Over the course of the 1990s, the unmarried, pregnant teen (and, by extension, the young, single mother she becomes) has been cast as the paramount enemy of American prosperity. We have traced the root cause of our social ills, and we have found it literally inside the amoral character of our teenagers. Our media and our policies continue to portray teens who have babies as carried away by a desire for inappropriate pleasure. In this way, we avoid a more dire reading of their state. What if participating in unprotected sex means that they are being coerced or they don't feel they are worth safe sex? What if choosing to have a baby means that they don't feel they have access to a better future, and they are probably right? Perhaps we have embraced abstinence-based programs in part because we don't want to acknowledge just how poor a job we are doing as a society of taking care of our young people. If all we have to do is teach children to tune out the television and say no to their peers, then, we imagine, the situations they are in can't be terribly serious. However, if children are exploited because adults who should be protecting them are preying on them, and/or because they lack the emotional and practical resources to avoid or to want to avoid such exploitation, then their situation is indeed grim.

Our culture vilifies the growing number of teen mothers without realizing that we are indicting ourselves. It may be true that "every threat to the fabric of this country—from poverty to crime to homelessness—is connected to out-of-wedlock teen pregnancy," as one article argued, or that "America's future is being placed at risk by the cycle of children who are having children." But it does not follow that teen sex or "teen" pregnancies are a cause. In fact, they are a result. From a policy perspective, welfare reform efforts that deny benefits to teen mothers strain understanding. Not only do studies show that higher welfare payments are "consistently correlated with lower, not higher, rates of unwed childbearing among teenage mothers." There is also no way to decrease "teen" pregnancy without addressing adult behaviors and economic policies. The idea that we can decrease the incidence of childhood sexual abuse and childhood poverty by talking tough to children defies logic.

However, it is consistent with our culture's ambivalent and contradictory attitudes toward childhood. Even though we believe that childhood should be a sheltered state in which children can play, explore, and develop in safety, we fail to provide such a shelter for most children. Our policies mandate that children experience the circumstances of their parents, however dire, even though children are much more harmed by socioeconomic hardship than adults. In our democratic, theoretically classless, society, it is difficult to acknowledge that children's futures are more often than not determined by accident of birth. Childhood doesn't relocate children to a special safe world. It confines them to the adult world of their parents without the benefit of adult rights and privileges.

Children cannot create a safe environment for themselves by saying no to sex and pregnancy any more than they can improve their diets by refusing to eat. The point that we insist on overlooking is that the onset of puberty isn't the beginning of most children's difficulties. It is just one more challenge in their already dangerous and difficult lives. To acknowledge that children don't control their destinies, our society must face the extent to which we fail to care for the next generation. The irony of preaching responsibility to teens when we have never taken adequate responsibility for *them* is somehow lost on us. How can we lecture children about the importance of taking responsibility for their offspring when our society is doing less and less about the intergenerational transmission of child abuse and poverty in which so many teens are powerless casualties? Adult tirades against teen irresponsibility are displaced messages. We should be directing them at ourselves.

SIX

Bad Seeds

The adult temptation is to swing wildly from notions of childhood innocence to guilt, ignoring all the while the simple fact that children must live in a world that adults create. The urgent question . . . should not be about the innocence or guilt of our children, but about adults. The age of our innocence—and guilt. What we need to learn from our kids.

RICHARD RODRIGUEZ

The mainstream media does not always deny the role of trauma in shaping children and influencing their behavior. Coverage of violent crimes committed by teens, for example, often points out that teens act out violently in response to physical and sexual abuse, chronic material hardship, inadequate opportunities to develop their potential, and a lack of nurturing and guidance. Coverage incorporates the assumption that young people act out violently because they have been subjected to bad social conditions, not because they are fundamentally bad individuals. In keeping with this basic belief, coverage tends to make the point that punishment is an inappropriate and unworkable response to teen crime; the solution lies in rehabilitation and in prevention. As the nation has become increasingly focused on reforming the juvenile-justice system, the press has done a commendable job of reporting on relevant social science findings, dispelling myths and contextualizing fads.

Yet the public and policymakers don't seem to have been listening. A *Glamour* poll found that 97 percent of respondents felt that the current system was "too lenient with juvenile offenders." Only 3 percent felt that teens who break the law "need more help, not more punishment." A news analysis in *Utne Reader* summarized that "the very concept of rehabilitation has fallen out of favor." And in the last few years, states have restructured the juvenile-justice system to a degree unprecedented in this century, eliminating protections for juvenile offenders and transferring ever greater numbers of them into the adult-corrections system.

The media blames misguided juvenile-justice policies on members of the public and on the politicians who cater to their fears. But the American public is as much a dominant set of assumptions and beliefs as it is a group of people. The media necessarily influence and are influenced by a shared set of cultural notions. When members of the media criticize public attitudes, they are, by definition, criticizing themselves. In fact, origins and traces of "the public's" outlook on adolescent criminality can be found in the media. Public prejudices saturate more overt, and sound, pieces of information, corrupting them the way subliminal messages subvert stated intentions. As a result, mainstream coverage undermines—and ultimately sabotages—its humanistic, pro-prevention message. And no one, apparently, is the wiser.

A 1996 *New York Times* editorial entitled "Wrong Approach to Teen-Age Crime" illustrates the mainstream media's well-intentioned, but ultimately ineffective stance. On the surface, the editorial argues for prevention over punishment. It denounces contemporary efforts to prosecute teens as adults, to house adult and juvenile prisoners in the same facilities, and to lower the age at which the death penalty can be imposed, calling them "not the answer to juvenile crime." Instead, the editorial promotes a recent study by the Rand Corporation that argues for investment in programs "that prevent youngsters from committing crimes in the first place."

The editorial implies that punitive policies stem from misguided public attitudes, suggesting that politicians are pursuing the "wrong approach" because "get-tough-on-kids proposals" are "politically appealing." It seems unaware that its own structure encourages the same punitive responses it wants to check. It frames the teen-crime debate in the same way most mainstream coverage does—from the perspective of adult, not child, welfare. The editorial constantly emphasizes adult self-interest. For example, it opposes punishment because prevention is "more cost-effective" and because punitive measures will not "reduce juvenile crime." In other words, the media argues that we should pursue prevention-oriented policies, not because they constitute a more humane and just way to treat our children, but because they will save us money and decrease our likelihood of becoming victims of crime.

The audience of the mainstream press, i.e., the public, is encouraged to empathize with adult concerns rather than with children's needs. This strategy creates a context in which the experiences of young people in trouble are inconsequential, and empathy for them is irrelevant. Coverage rarely promotes the idea that an act of violent crime is a form of teen dysfunction and a sign that a young person is in pain and need of help, even though this idea is consistent with the ideology of a pro-prevention message: Violence originates in human suffering, and much human suffering can be prevented. The *Times* editorial cited above ends with the reassurance that prevention measures will be more effective than punitive ones in decreasing crime in the long term, and may "rescue more than a few youngsters in the bargain." The goal of providing young people safe and happy childhoods is only an afterthought, peripheral to the main argument of the editorial. It is also characterized as a perk of the essential exchange: cost-effective spending for "public" safety, i.e., the safety of adults and of the younger humans they particularly value.

In effect, mainstream coverage about children's delinquency marginalizes the children's issues such as poverty and abuse that cause such delinquency. Articles assiduously calculate future rates of crimes children will commit based on current trends, but rarely calculate future rates of circumstances children will endure such as childhood poverty and violent treatment at the hands of adults. Articles predict a future epidemic of murder based on an upcoming increase in the number of adolescents without discussing research proving that when poverty rates are held constant, adolescents have "unusually low rates of violence" compared to adults. Coverage detracts readers' attention from the systemic aspects of our society that can be changed. As a result, the media is saturated with a cynical attitude toward teen crime that has a corrosive effect on prevention ideology.

In a *U.S. News & World Report* article, the author acknowledged that juvenile crime reflects childhood hardship. However, he begins the article by arguing, "Even if Congress enacts a costly federal war on crime, America should brace itself for a new surge of youthful violence." In other words, the article, entitled "The New Crime Wave," does not seem to believe that our society can adequately nurture its young people *no matter how hard it tries*. Articles like this one play to adult fears about their own welfare, not to adult concerns about the welfare of children. As an article entitled "Street Crime: An Agenda for Change" put it: "The mandate for action is clear: Help them now, or *fear them later*." Mainstream coverage indirectly promotes the idea that teen crime is inevitable, rather than preventable, an idea that could well account for what one article described as "a general failure of will, a kind of paralysis in the face of the growing dimensions of the problem."

Our culture's attitude of resignation toward teen crime also manifests itself in the way we portray young people who act out violently. The American Psychological Association's Commission on Violence recently confirmed that violence is learned. Therefore it can be unlearned, and never learned. Yet our stated belief in the determinant role of nurture in children's violent behavior conflicts with a pervasive image in culture of children as innately violent and savage, inadequately "tamed" by adult society. Writing in the *New York Times*, Brent Staples, author of *Parallel Time: Growing Up in Black and White*, compared children in Chicago public housing projects to the fictional children in William Golding's *Lord of the Flies*. "Without adults to keep them in check," he wrote, "the boys turn to blood lust and murder." In this context, it's not surprising that articles consistently characterize children who act out violently as a "breed," like the new "breed" of "superpredators" who "have absolutely no respect for human life" and who "kill and maim on impulse, without any intelligible motive." An article in *Time* argued that "atrocious crimes" committed recently "have awakened the country to the beast that has broken loose in some of America's young people."

Coverage further perpetuates the notion of "bad seeds" by making repeated references to teen criminal behavior as a form of disease, an "epidemic" that is spreading like a contagious virus, as opposed to an adaptive behavior painfully learned by one child at a time. An article entitled "A Generation of Stone Killers" quoted an expert who argues that the "malign ethos" of these children "has metastasized to the suburbs" like a cancer. Coverage tends to promote the idea that the impending increase in the number of teenagers will translate into an increase in crime without investigating why there is a correlation between teens and violence. "As today's five-year-old children become tomorrow's teenagers," according to a conservative commentator, "America faces the most violent juvenile crime surge in history," because "[m]ore violent crime is committed by older teenagers than by any other age group." This logic dictates that crimes committed by teens function as a "demographic reality" rather than as an indicator of social conditions, ignoring the fact that when "race, class, gender, era, family background, and locality" are taken into account, according to Mike Males, author of *The Scapegoat Generation: America's War on Adolescents*, "young age doesn't predict much of anything."

The characterization of children as nonhumans (e.g., wild beasts, evil seeds, viruses, miscreants, etc.) and their violent behavior as instinctive and irrational erodes the adult empathy necessary to motivate preventative efforts. It creates a context in which Senator Orrin G. Hatch's comment, "We've got to quit coddling these violent kids like nothing is going on," is considered appealing rather than barbaric, responsible rather than hypocritical. It facilitates adult support for juvenile boot camps, even though such camps do not transform angry young people into well-adjusted citizens. As one article pointed out: "News footage of panting, shaven-headed young men in khaki jumpsuits, doing push-ups at the foot of a snarling drill instructor, satisfie[s] the deep public appetite for seeing some civility pounded into thugs who terrorize their neighborhoods." As long as children are viewed as animals that need to be tamed and diseases that need to be quarantined, adult hostility will thrive and adult compassion for children's difficult, adult-orchestrated circumstances will be hard to come by.

The idea that children who commit crimes aren't human also contributes to misguided public attitudes about children's motivations. Coverage often suggests that young people's motives for committing crimes have more to do with their innate lack of morals than their background. Assigning simplistic and trivial motives to young people erases all the difficult circumstances that went into forming these teens. A child who has grown up in a home saturated with alcoholism and domestic violence, in the dysfunctional foster-care system, or surviving on the streets is transformed by news coverage into an alien being who took a life over a pair of shoes.

Sometimes articles do an impressive job of summarizing social science knowledge about violent children, pointing out, for example, that they are "animated by a chillingly rational response to an environment that is saturated with violence and stress." However, they implicitly discount children's environments when they characterize their motives. "These are the reasons children are dying in America's mean streets at the hands of other children," according to the article cited above: "sneakers and lambskin coats, whispers and trivial insults over menacing looks, scuffles over pocket change, and, of course, drug turf." Reporters unwittingly become revisionist historians, writing the role of childhood poverty and abuse out of the teen-crime narrative.

For example, a short *Newsweek* article on the death of a five-year-old at the hands of a ten- and an eleven-year-old routinely referred to the older boys as "killers." Subtitled "Should We Cage a New Breed of Vicious Kids?" it did not discuss the boys' backgrounds, and the closest it came to an explanation of their behavior was to refer to them as "two of the toughest bullies their South Side Chicago neighborhood had to offer," who dropped the smaller boy out of a fourteenth-floor apartment because he had "refused to steal candy for them." This article quoted an Illinois Department of Child and Family Services spokesperson: "There are some people who view these two boys as victims of society. . . . It's our view that the only victim in this case is dead." The article closed with an emphasis on how dangerous these boys and others like them will be when they grow up, quoting an attorney: "We've become a nation being terrorized by our children."

Once children who act out violently have been dehumanized in the eyes of the public, the decidedly unscientific notion that certain young people are "beyond reform" can flourish. As one reporter who had embraced this concept wrote, "[T]here is something resembling an emerging ideological consensus on one thing: some kids are beyond help." Even though there is no scientific consensus on the notion of irreparable youth, the media has adopted it with enthusiasm, and conflated it with urban lore about "superpredators." The media's stance on incorrigible teens feeds and rationalizes the transfer of minors into the adult-justice system. If certain children are beyond rehabilitation, why not lock them up with adult offenders and throw away the key? As a family-court judge wrote in *Ladies' Home Journal*: "When it comes to kids who rape, maim and kill, their age quickly becomes unimportant." In other words, we regard children who act out violently as *not* children, in addition to being less human than adults. Our culture, according to Barry Krisberg, president of the National Council on Crime and Delinquency, "is trying to lower the age of adulthood rather than see what is happening as a failure of society."

What gets lost in mainstream coverage is the extent to which young people, both those who act out violently and those who don't, suffer at the hands of adults. Because children are dependent on adults, physically small, and emotionally vulnerable, they suffer more violence and more sexual assaults than adults, and they are more traumatized by those assaults than adults would be. For every one violent or sexual offense committed by a minor, there are three perpetrated by adults against children. Many children witness and endure violence in their families, and children in urban neighborhoods witness and experience violence in their schools and communities as well. In addition, children don't have the rights and privileges accorded to adults. In most cases, they can't change families, schools, or neighborhoods, or isolate themselves from violence for even a part of each day. Alex Kotlowitz, author of *There Are No Children Here: The Story of Two Boys Growing Up in the Other America*, has written, "Violence has become an integral part of growing up in our cities." The situation is so bad that many of the children growing up, he points out, "suffer from the same kind of post-traumatic stress disorder we have seen in soldiers returning from combat." Incredibly, we

continue to see children who commit crimes as the problem, not as a manifestation of the problem, and not, of
course, as the victims of the problem.

The coverage of the murder of Jose and Kitty Menendez by
their two sons, Lyle, twenty-one, and Erik, eighteen, provides a detailed illustration of how cultural attitudes can
eclipse social science knowledge when the issue is violent
crime. In 1992, *Time* magazine announced that public attitudes toward children who kill their parents were undergoing a transformation. Instead of being regarded as "the
ultimate pariahs," "evil," or "bad seeds," these children were
now "drawing more understanding." Certainly, the public
reaction toward Gina Grant's rejection from Harvard
University in 1995 seemed to support that view. Although
Harvard stood by its decision to rescind her admission after
finding out that she had killed her mother when she was
fourteen, many Harvard students and faculty spoke out
in her favor. And the media, for the most part, presented
her case in a favorable light and questioned the wisdom of
Harvard's decision.

Supporters acknowledged that Gina Grant had blud-
geoned her inebriated mother to death in self-defense. In
fear for her life, the fourteen-year-old girl had twice knocked
a knife out of her enraged mother's hand, before grabbing a
heavy candlestick and repeatedly swinging it at her head. In
other words, she had been driven to break the law by circumstances that were beyond her control. Even though she had
become a perpetrator of violence, she remained a victim,
deserving of sympathy not condemnation. By reporting on
her exemplary academic and extracurricular high school
record, media coverage underscored the widely held belief

that her crime did not make her a bad person. Articles also quoted the praise of her many friends and supporters. Her former lawyer called her "an exceptionally bright, affable, well-adjusted and charitable student." And her mother's brother was quoted as saying that she "is and always was a kind and loving and good girl."

Yet, while Gina Grant pled no contest to voluntary manslaughter, spent six months in a juvenile facility, and is now enrolled as an undergraduate student at Tufts University, most other convicted parricide perpetrators, including the infamous Menendez brothers, are serving life terms without parole in prisons all over the country. The sympathetic public reaction to Grant does support the view that our culture has more compassion and understanding than it used to for young people who commit crimes. But this compassion has clearly not permeated our overall response to young people who are driven to commit crimes by difficult childhood circumstances. In fact, most children who kill their parents receive first-degree murder convictions.

The popular response to Gina Grant constitutes a pronounced exception to our culture's general attitude toward young people who break the law. Despite our support of individual cases like Gina's, and our rhetoric of understanding and compassion, we still believe that teens should be held entirely responsible—and severely punished—for their actions, regardless of the nature of their childhoods. Gina Grant's case and that of Lyle and Erik Menendez provoked different legal and social reactions, but shared many characteristics. The inconsistency in our responses reveals more about our culture's beliefs and attitudes than it does about the merits of the individual cases. Ultimately our response to Gina Grant's case does not contradict our widely held notion that it is appropriate to punish children for desperate crimes born of childhood circumstances they did not choose and could not control.

According to Kathleen M. Heide, author of *Why Kids Kill Parents: Child Abuse and Adolescent Homicide*, young people who kill their parents have been severely abused and neglected. Children who kill their parents experience treatment that resembles torture in its unrelenting brutality. Mark Martone, who is serving time for shooting his father, remembers having to spend the night in the cellar when he was five years old, handcuffed to the rafters, dangling, as punishment for admitting that he was afraid of the dark. Sometimes when his father was angry, he would stick a gun in his son's mouth and tell him he was "going to blow [his] brains out." Both Gina Grant and the Menendez brothers have consistently maintained that they endured long-term, severe psychological and physical abuse at the hands of disturbed, sadistic parents.

Gina Grant's father died of cancer when she was eleven. After his death, her mother's alcoholism worsened and she became a vicious drunk who, according to an article in the *New Yorker*, regularly launched into "wild, abusive tirades" directed at Gina. In the years following, she blamed Gina for her father's death, "berated her incessantly, and refused to allow her to keep a photograph of her father in the house." Unexplained bruises and bone fractures suggest that Gina was routinely physically assaulted by her mother, who sometimes initiated physical fights with her. Once, according to court records, "her mother had hit her hard enough to raise bruises for such lapses as failing to wax the kitchen floor."

Even those who do not believe the Menendez brothers

were sexually abused by their father acknowledge that their home life was miserable under his tyranny. Prosecutor Pamela Bozanich conceded that the Menendez parents "obviously had terrific flaws," and described the family as "Father Knows Best Meets Godzilla." The prosecution team decided not to counter the testimony of over thirty witnesses who testified about the parents' abuse of their sons. Even an article in *New York* magazine, that was overwhelmingly critical of the brothers, called their parents "loathsome."

Driven to make his sons exact replicas of himself and "perfect," Jose Menendez allegedly used physical force and psychological manipulation to control his boys, exploiting their childhood vulnerability, stunting their emotional development, and crushing their spirits. Menendez was so oppressive that he could make his first son "urinate in his pants with fear simply by staring at him." Like a cruel trainer, Jose physically tortured his children in an effort to control their behavior. One of the tennis coaches Jose employed while the family lived in Princeton, New Jersey "testified that of the difficult tennis parents he has known, Jose was 'one of the worst,' forcing his children to play in the cold, the rain, on Christmas and even when they were sick." "When Erik's swimming disappointed his father," according to court testimony, "Jose held him underwater until he almost drowned." Another time, when Erik "cried after an injection, Jose decided to toughen him up by torturing him with needles, ropes and 'wooden implements.'"

Far from being the caring but helpless wife who cowers at her husband's feet alongside her children, by all accounts Kitty Menendez's cruelty to her children rivaled her husband's. Mentally imbalanced and alcoholic, Kitty terrorized her children with her eccentric, cruel, and vicious behavior, according to court testimony. In fits of anger, she left her sons behind in shopping malls or made them watch while she attacked their stuffed animals. She flew into rages, verbally abusing and throwing things at her sons. She once "cut herself and smeared her blood on Lyle." She sometimes locked Lyle and Erik in their rooms "until they were forced to defecate in plastic containers." And sometimes she dragged them around by their hair, pushing them under beds or into closets in the large Menendez house. In a routine that played itself out over and over again for Lyle like a recurring nightmare, she called him a "bastard," and told him that she wished he had never been born.

As horrific as they are, descriptions of isolated events can never fully convey the dark environment in which Jose and Kitty Menendez raised their two sons. The boys wet their beds far into their teens. Their parents often brought the soiled sheets to the breakfast table, ridiculing and humiliating the boys, sometimes even rubbing their faces in the urine-soaked linens. The parents kept a ferret who roamed freely around the house, defecating in places where the boys would later be sent when they "misbehaved." Kitty and Jose tolerated the other's abusive treatment of the children, and often collaborated in it. Once when Lyle asked his mother about the whereabouts of his new pet rabbit, she told him to ask his father about it. Jose told him to check in the trash, and there Lyle found the rabbit, dead and bloody, its head smashed in.

The culture of violence established and perpetuated by Jose and Kitty Menendez, including the omnipresent threat of excruciating pain and death, was allegedly interwoven with sexual acts. Lyle testified that his father instigated a sexual relationship with him when he was six. With the methodical and unwavering persistence characteristic of incest perpetrators, Jose's abuse allegedly began with rubdowns and massages after sports practices, slowly incorporated genital fondling, oral sex, forced anal sex, anal sex with foreign objects, and sexual sadism, and culminated in what came to be an almost daily violent sexual routine. Jose sexually abused Lyle for over two years, and he continued with Erik until a few days before his death.

According to Lyle, Jose would "put me on my knees. He'd guide me in all my movements, and I'd have oral sex with him." When Lyle resisted, Jose jabbed him with pins. Often Jose made his son lean against the sink in the bathroom, while he sodomized him with toothbrushes, needles, and knives. Also typical of sexual abusers, Jose shrouded his assaults in an explanatory, normalizing narrative. He showed his sons violent pornographic videos. He told them that his sexual interactions were a way of showing his love. And he lectured them about how Greek soldiers had sex with each other before going into battle as a way of bonding and preparing themselves for the challenges ahead.

Lyle's testimony about the sexual abuse he and his brother had endured at the hands of his powerful, overbearing father moved many in the courtroom, including reporters, to tears. "Sometimes putting his knuckles to his mouth in an effort to compose himself, sometimes squeezing and wiping his eyes, sometimes burying his head in his sleeve," Lyle described in excruciating detail the experiences of his childhood. As one journalist wrote, the brothers' "emotions were impossible to dismiss." However, while Gina Grant's testimony about her abusive mother helped to lessen her sentence, Lyle and Erik Menendez's testimony, like the testimony of many children who have killed their parents, ultimately provoked disbelief and hostility. Despite the fact that the brothers' testimony was convincing, validated by psychiatrists, and unperturbed by lengthy and difficult cross-examinations, their allegations, particularly those concerning sexual abuse, were eventually treated as suspect by the media. Rather than gaining sympathy, the brothers were accused of having fabricated their painful experiences. An article in *Commentary* magazine labeled the accounts of abuse as "all apparent lies," arguing that even Erik's attorney "could not have believed . . . the gruesome stories . . . of how, from an early age, [Erik] was forced to satisfy his father's sexual desires."

Most coverage, however, dismissed the accounts of abuse in a less obvious, perhaps even less conscious, manner by imposing a dramatic context on the case. By constantly evoking the Hollywood backdrop of the parricide, writers surrounded the case in an aura of the fantastic, the fictive, the incredible, and the surreal. Jose was repeatedly described as a wealthy entertainment executive, Kitty as a former beauty queen and socialite, and Lyle and Erik as handsome, tennis-playing young men. An article in the *New York Times* began: "Just minutes from the studios where the most bizarre crime plots are hatched for movies and television, a searing real-life story of blood, money and alleged patricide is unfolding." An article in *Esquire* described the particulars of the case "as hoary as an episode in a television series." Other articles in mainstream publications talked about life imitating art and art imitating life in a way that made everything about the case seem, at best, tenuously connected to reality.

Another sensational aspect of the Menendez coverage

was the characterization of the court testimony as performance art. A *Time* article stated that "channel grazers happening past Court TV . . . might well have mistaken the proceedings for a staged show, complete with great clothes and great cheekbones." While articles stated with confidence that the verdicts would be determined by "the strength and believability of the testimony," together they presented a very confusing definition of "believability." The prosecuting attorney's cryptic, but widely quoted, description of Lyle's testimony as a "performance by Laurence Olivier which rapidly degenerated into Sylvester Stallone" encapsulates the paradox of the credibility issue: Whether their testimony was perceived as realistic or not, it could not be credible viewed in the context of a dramatic performance.

Those who found the brothers convincing accused them of good acting, and those who found them unconvincing accused them of bad acting. No matter how the brothers' testimony came across, they were perceived as performing rather than presenting reality. For example, one article that rejected the brothers' version of events cited both the impression that their "performance" was poor, as well as the certainty that it was superb, to bolster its argument against their credibility. The trial, the author wrote,

> has the look of a bad TV movie. The brothers' testimony, despite its tearfulness seems hollow. We all know that defendants are scripted to some degree, but in this case one gets the sense that we're seeing not simply a script, but an artfully crafted melodrama.

Somehow, despite the fact that our "understanding" culture knows that children who kill their parents have been horrendously abused, we felt good, even self-righteous, about dismissing Lyle and Erik Menendez's testimony. In most ways, the Menendez case resembled the paradigm of the typical parricide case. Ironically, it was the similarities that provoked the most hostile public reaction. The fact that Jose and Kitty were unarmed when they were shot, the fact that they were shot more than fifteen times, the fact that the brothers initially lied about their role in the killings, the fact that they seemed to show no remorse, the fact that they spent money in the months following, and the fact that they said they loved their parents—all were used to suggest that they were manipulative, dishonest, evil people who had killed for money. Yet all those facts were more likely signs that they killed their parents out of a desperate fear for their well-being. But once we as a culture had agreed that the brothers were not victims of abuse, it was easy to doubt all other aspects of their case, no matter how well they matched those of a classic parricide.

According to Kathleen M. Heide, young people who kill their parents "kill only when they feel there is no one to help them," and "honestly think they have no other way out." The night that Gina Grant killed her mother, she feared for her life. She felt she had exhausted all other possibilities of surviving her mother's abuse. She believed that if she didn't kill her mother, her mother would kill her. Her mother's behavior was getting worse every day. She was drinking more, as well as abusing sedatives. She "had been flying into violent rages, breaking into Gina's room in the middle of the night and threatening to kill her." Gina had become so afraid of what her mother might do that she removed the gun that her mother kept under her mattress. The night of the killing, as her drunken, raging mother kept coming at her with a knife, Gina picked up a heavy candlestick and started swinging.

The Menendez brothers also testified that they felt they had no choice but to kill their parents when they did. Erik told his therapist in a session following the killing: "[My father] was someone that I loved and I almost had no choice to do what I did. And I hate myself for doing it." The night that Lyle and Erik Menendez killed their parents, they believed that Jose and Kitty were in the process of plotting to kill them. Like a battered woman, "a child can be so terrorized by years of sexual, physical and emotional abuse that he or she genuinely reads menace—accurate or not—into a look, a gesture, an ambiguous word that an outsider might not consider a dire threat." Three days before Lyle confronted Jose about the fact that he was still sexually abusing Erik, he had interpreted his father's response as a death threat. During the trial, "[i]mitating his father's menacing tone," Lyle described his father's reaction: "You listen to me. . . . What I do with my son is none of your business. I warn you, don't throw your life away." Lyle still insisted that he would disclose the sexual abuse of Erik if his father didn't stop. To this his father allegedly replied, "We all make choices in life, son. Erik made his. You've made yours."

A few days later, Kitty told Erik that if Lyle "had just kept his mouth shut, things might have worked out in this family." At that point, "the brothers were convinced the decision to kill them had been made," and they became overwhelmed by a "mind-numbing, adrenaline-pumping fear" for their lives. According to court testimony, the morning of the killing

after another alleged attempt by Jose to enter Erik's room, the brothers concluded that Erik had to get out of the house. Lyle, making conversation, asked his father for the phone number of a tennis camp he planned to attend. Jose replied, "What does it matter anymore?" Lyle said he took

that "to be my dad's sarcastic way of saying, 'You're dead!'"
The boys told Kitty they were going out to meet some
friends; she ordered them to stay in the house. Jose told
Erik to go upstairs and wait for him. Lyle screamed, "No,
you're not going to touch Erik!" Jose summoned Kitty to
the TV room and closed the doors. Said Lyle: "I thought
this was the end. I thought they were going inside the TV
room to plan to kill us." He ran upstairs to get Erik. Both
brothers got their guns, and blam! And blam! again and 13
more times.

Critics of the brothers were quick to write off the possibility that they could have been so afraid. The media wondered repeatedly why Lyle and Erik didn't just "walk away,"
especially if they were abused. As a friend of Kitty's asked *Time*
magazine rhetorically: "If Lyle and Erik were true victims,
why didn't they just move out?" Even though victims of domestic violence become hypersensitive to signs of impending
attacks, one article stated that "there was no evidence that
[Jose] intended, or had reason, to kill" Lyle and Erik. A column in *Time* complained that in the brothers' case, "the law
has been so stretched that an 'unreasonable' belief that one
is in danger of serious harm—one no sane person would har-
bor—can be sufficient grounds for self-defense."

Another article argued that the brothers "cannot reasonably be said to have faced imminent death at the hands of
their father. They were strong, agile, young men . . . free to
come and go as they pleased, and they did not suffer from a
shortage of cash." An editorial in the *New York Times* also
called attention to the fact that the brothers were not at a
physical disadvantage as proof that they had no reason to
be afraid. The author described Lyle and Erik as "two young

men in their physical prime who kill with shotguns . . . then plead fear of harm from a middle-aged father and mother." The nonsensical suggestion that the brothers couldn't have been afraid because "no sane person" would be, or because they were "in their physical prime" reveals our society's collective desire to dismiss the reality of the psychological torment they endured. The belief that they were "two grown men who could have left home if life was so intolerable," as one article described them, betrays our desire to forget they were ever children—vulnerable, weak, helpless boys, brutally and unrelentingly tortured for over two decades by the adults entrusted with their care.

Lyle and Erik were also heavily criticized for having shot their parents while they were watching television. Yet typical parricide perpetrators almost always attack their parents when they are in a vulnerable position. "That may be the only time youngsters can overpower their abusers," according to an article on parricide, "but it makes the killing appear to be cold-blooded murder." In addition, they usually "overkill" their parents, shooting, hitting, or stabbing far more times than are necessary to kill them, in part because they are terrified that their parents might survive and come after them, and in part because they become overwhelmed with long-repressed rage.

Young people who kill their parents often clumsily try to cover up the evidence of their culpability. They are in shock during and after the killing. Sometimes they disassociate and forget that they were responsible; sometimes they refuse to accept that their parents are actually dead. Gina Grant initially tried to make the killing look like a suicide. Her boyfriend helped her to place a knife in her mother's neck and wrap her hand around it. Still insisting that she had not killed her, Grant later implicated her boyfriend. It wasn't until she spent time with a psychiatrist that she was able, with the help of drugs that reduced her inhibitions, to tell what had really happened. Lyle and Erik picked up the bullet casings and dispensed with the murder weapon before calling the authorities. They maintained their innocence, and suggested that Mafia hit men had been responsible. It took Lyle and Erik much longer than Gina to come to terms with what had happened and to acknowledge their role.

Another characteristic of parricide perpetrators that works against them in court is what appears to be a lack of remorse. The abuse they have suffered, the enormity of what they have done, and the dramatic change in their lives lead them to detach from their emotions and from what has occurred. Police reported that "only hours after killing her mother [Gina Grant] had joked to a female officer accompanying her into the ladies' room, 'Don't worry, I don't have body parts in my pocket.'" Within days, however, Gina was "suffering chronic nightmares and needed to be sedated in order to sleep."

Many articles about the Menendez brothers remarked on their smug, relaxed appearance immediately after the killings and in court. One argued that the brothers "seem loose, untroubled, unafraid, an indication they haven't been advised of proper courtroom etiquette." An article in *Time* editorialized: "Far from appearing crushed with grief, after the slayings the boys set off on a $700,000 shopping spree." Another article pointed out that the brothers "did not put on a very convincing show of grief." Yet appearing genuinely remorseful could have been taken as a sign that they weren't damaged enough to have killed their parents out of fear. Lyle and Erik suffered from characteristic emotional detachment. In an interview given a few months after the killings, Erik explained, "Once we realized what had happened . . . it started sinking into our heads: These aren't just two people. These are our parents." Lyle added, "There was initial hysterics and then, after that night was over, I just sort of entered into my dad's sort of mode. . . . Sort of like an ESP sort of thing."

Many articles found it ridiculous and offensive that Lyle and Erik continued to maintain that they had loved their parents after having killed them. One article quoted the priest who officiated at the funeral, "I would be shocked if they could speak about their parents the way they did and be able to do that much violence to them." Yet love and hate are quite often inextricably linked in abusive family relationships. A young man who shot his father after years of abuse told *Time* magazine: "It may sound sick, but I did love him. . . . I still love him. I mean, he was my father."

Parricide perpetrators often strike juries and others who follow their cases as "unlikable." They have grown up in a sadistic, brutal, terrifying environment, and they are often adept at lying, manipulating, and detaching: all skills they have learned to survive. Often, the more seriously they have been abused, the more "unlikable" they seem. Sadly, therefore, the more severely a child has been abused, the less likely he is to be understood or pitied. While no one who sat through the Menendez trial would have traded childhoods, public sympathy was in short supply. A *Newsweek* article argued, "Given the straightforward facts of what [they] did . . . it's hard to imagine feeling sorry for them." An article in

Time magazine complained that Lyle Menendez's court-room demeanor "has not exactly shown the brothers to be lovable enough to deserve outright acquittal."

In general, our culture understands but frequently rejects the notion that people are shaped by their environment and by their experiences. Just because Lyle and Erik were both eighteen or over at the time of the murders doesn't mean they ceased to be the same two brothers with the same childhoods. They will never be able to "walk away" from their formative experiences. We cannot judge them by imagining what we would have done in their shoes because we don't have imaginations vivid or brave enough to evoke what they endured. No matter what we feel the brothers should or could have done, we must accept that they knew their parents better than anyone else ever could, and that, like most of us, they didn't want to die. The prosecution felt that it was making a convincing point when it characterized the brothers as "spoiled rich children." However, it is precisely because they were still "children" in relation to their abusive parents, that they had to do what they did. As Erik's lawyer explained: "These children are not their chronological age or biological age regarding their parents but are still imprisoned children."

Our culture consistently treated the brothers as if they had the strength and options of full-grown adults who had had nurturing childhoods. Over and over, critics of the brothers singled out what was evidence of their having been severely abused, as if it proved they had every opportunity to control their situation. For example, the brothers' testimony was considered particularly suspicious because they never told anyone outside the immediate family about the abuse. One article doubted the accounts of sexual abuse because "[n]o one in the extended Menendez family has testified to being aware that sexual abuse occurred. The brothers themselves never told anyone during all those years of the supposed abuse." Yet we know that incest perpetrators are notoriously secretive about their activities, and that, in general, the more seriously a child is abused, the less likely he is to tell anyone, especially if he has bravely tried at least once to notify someone and the attempt has been unsuccessful.

"I spent my whole childhood trying to get help, and none ever came," says Roy Rowe, nineteen, who last year was sentenced to four-to-twelve years for killing his stepfather. According to an article about his case:

> Neighbors . . . sometimes called the police when the screams grew too loud from the beatings—with a paddle, a belt and a two-by-four—that Roy's stepfather gave him, his younger sister and brother, and his mother. Teachers reported their suspicions of abuse; relatives tried to intervene. But each time, police officers and social workers left the children in the home. On his seventeenth birthday, Roy shot and killed his stepfather on their front porch as he came home from work.

After keeping the family secret for years, Gina Grant finally confided to her best friend's mother that she was afraid her mother was going to kill her. This woman called the police and told an officer that Gina's mother "was a violent alcoholic, and that the daughter was afraid for her life." The officer said she couldn't file an anonymous complaint; the woman who called didn't want to file the complaint in her name since then Gina might not be able to visit anymore, and the complaint disintegrated. Nine days later, Gina killed her mother.

When Lyle confided to his mother that "Dad was touching me," she told him that he was "exaggerating" and that Jose had to punish Lyle when he did things wrong. When Lyle was in his teens, he confronted his father about his sexual abuse of Erik. Jose told him that what he did with his son was his business, and, characteristically for incest perpetrators, that he would kill him if he told anyone. Lyle testified that he and Erik had thought about going to the police, but had reasoned that it would not help them. "We discussed: Would the police side with us, believe us?" Lyle testified. He and Erik concluded that the police wouldn't believe them or side with them against their father, but that "filing charges would definitely have put us in a position to be killed."

Lyle and Erik have been criticized for not telling either their therapist or the authorities about the abuse until a year after the killings. Yet, in addition to being afraid, "It's very common for people who have been molested to not come forward with that information. . . . There are powerful feelings of shame, self-blame, humiliation." However, one critical article attacked Erik's lawyer for saying that Erik hadn't talked about the abuse because he felt ashamed: "A lawyer brazen enough to suggest that anyone would willingly confess to having shotgunned his parents to death but be embarrassed to discuss sex with his therapist is just the sort of lawyer Erik Menendez needed." This article distorted and dismissed what is known about the psychological makeup of sex-abuse victims and once again demonstrated our culture's resistance to the Menendez brothers' childhood experiences.

The idea that Lyle and Erik had killed their parents in response to an abusive situation was immediately labeled a "designer defense" employed to trick the jury into acquitting the brothers. Despite its basis in human psychology and behavior, one critic called defenses like it "exotic." Another complained that supporters had "constructed voguish victimization defenses, portraying the accused as the products of some sweeping social or parental failure." The defense was criticized for the testimony it presented about the abuse perpetrated on the boys by their parents. Many articles suggested that the defense was bringing up the abuse "to convince the jury that Jose and Kitty were so awful they deserved to die." The defense countered that "we brought up the fact that these people sodomized and tortured and punished and smacked and derided and tormented [the boys] all their lives to show that these are the kind of people that you might be afraid of." Yet many people felt the accounts of abuse were irrelevant. The judge presiding over the case said at one point, "We're not talking about a child-custody case here," before refusing to allow any more witnesses to testify about abuse.

The prosecution did not deny that the brothers had been mistreated by their parents; they simply didn't believe the abuse was relevant to the case. They didn't want to be "derailed by the defense's claims that Lyle and Erik were sexually and emotionally abused by their parents." Instead, they argued that the brothers had killed "out of hatred, [and] out of greed for a $14 million inheritance." While articles were quick to critique the battered-child defense, few scrutinized the claim that the brothers killed out of greed even though, unlike the abuse defense, the concept of killing for greed is not based on a psychological or behavioral paradigm of behavior—it is a cliché. As one article noted, "[T]he motive of simple greed . . . doesn't, in and of itself, seem sufficient." Another commented, "[G]reed alone. . . . seems a particularly unsatisfactory explanation for . . . a crime that violates such fundamental laws of human behavior."

While many articles cited the screenplay written by Erik as evidence of the greed motive, even its narrative was more complex. While it was repeatedly summed up in the press as a screenplay about "an 18-year-old who murders his parents for their money," the protagonist seems motivated by something far darker. As he greets his parents just before killing them, "[h]is voice is of attempted compassion but the hatred completely overwhelms it." Prosecutors began to emphasize the "hatred" aspect of the motive after witnesses had painted a vivid and disturbing portrait of Jose and Kitty. But they did not revise their strategy to incorporate this new motivation. Where did Lyle and Erik get their intense hatred of their parents and, if the prosecutors were right, their immoral willingness to take life for money?

One critic of the Menendez defense acknowledged that "the moral vacuum in which the brothers were raised makes a textbook case for the argument that morals and filial piety are socially constructed." Yet he follows this up by saying, "Having endured a privileged but somewhat amoral childhood does not constitute a legal defense." In other words, many critics felt that even if the brothers had been shaped by an abusive childhood, their past should not factor into the legal response to their crime. In many ways, the crux of the Menendez case, and of the larger debate on teen crime, has to do with responsibility: Who is responsible when a young person breaks the law? In societal terms, the fundamental question of the Menendez case seems to have been: If young people, who have experienced abuse that they did not choose and could not escape, kill in fear for their lives after having tried to the degree they felt they safely could to find another solution, how responsible are they for their violent actions? Our culture's answer at this point in history appears to be: completely responsible.

While it's true, as Erik's attorney pointed out, that our culture has "learned a lot . . . about the psychology of abusive relationships, about the cruelty, oppression and inescapability of child abuse and molestation, [and] about the terror that marks virtually every moment for the victims of chronic domestic violence," we have not, as a result, become much more "understanding" of individuals like the Menendez brothers. On the contrary, Lyle and Erik Menendez have become the reviled poster boys of "victimism." *Time* magazine wrote that "victim chic has found its finest expression in Lyle and Erik," and an editorial in the *New York Times* characterized the killing of their parents as "emblematic of the troubling American preference for taking on the role of the victim."

We resented the characterization of the brothers as "victims," regardless of their childhood experiences. Rather than regard the defense's strategy as a product of our increased understanding of human behavior, we wrote it off as an attempt to evade responsibility. The Menendez brothers were swept up in what many regarded as a growing trend, "this growing compulsion of Americans," as one article described it, "to find someone or something else to blame for whatever is wrong . . . about their lives." As Erik's attorney explained:

The forces that drive [women and children] to act are fear and terror, the motivations of the weak, the oppressed, the tortured and the broken. And they are scorned and ridiculed and hated for it.

For many, the Menendez case illustrated that our understanding of the origins of dysfunction had gone too far. An article in *Vogue* complained, "When you convince a jury that events and conditions kill people, it is much easier to sympathize with the actual killers." A *Time* magazine article commented, "The brothers went from parents that understood too much to a jury that did." An article in *Glamour* acknowledged, "It's one of the achievements of the late twentieth century that the widespread trauma of abuse is finally being recognized and its effects on behavior understood. Yet," the author adds, "there's a dark side." The author sees the "dark side" as a use of this understanding to "duck responsibility." An article in *Time* entitled "Oprah! Oprah in the Court!" noted approvingly that Oprah Winfrey was "willing to concede some culpability" for the trend in which "juries are increasingly willing to make allowance for mitigating circumstances," and are, "more sympathetic to novel defense strategies."

Apparently, we don't feel that awareness of psychology, or sentiments like sympathy and understanding belong in the courtroom, at least not where people who have been abused as children are concerned. Many people were pleased with the murder-one verdicts in the second Menendez trial. As an article in the *New Yorker* described it, "Last week, the legal odyssey of America's most notorious orphans took a long-awaited turn." According to an interview with Los Angeles District Attorney Gil Garcetti, instead of empathizing, we should turn a deaf ear. Garcetti, according to the article, "admits that in the Menendez brothers' cases, he and his team underestimated 'the emotional pull' the abuse defense had on the jurors," and in the future "Garcetti hopes to head off such tendencies among jurors by changing the system."

If Garcetti likes a system that bars understanding for young people who have been abused, he has reason to be pleased with our current one. Gina Grant would probably still be in prison if it weren't for one sympathetic judge who made lifetime enemies with the state's juvenile-parole board as a result of helping her escape the juvenile-justice system. The county sheriff described her as a "sociopath with no conscience" and felt she should be tried as an adult so that she could receive the maximum sentence. The commissioner of the state's Department of Youth Services wrote that teenagers like Gina "are responsible for the choices they make about their own actions," and they shouldn't "see themselves as hapless victims whose antisocial actions should be excused because of their backgrounds."

Critics of the judge who rescued Gina from a hostile system would no doubt accuse him of being a "victimism" sympathizer who helped Gina evade responsibility for killing her mother. However, in many ways, he was the only one in Gina's environment who took any responsibility. The judge's actions acknowledged that both her community and the juvenile-justice system had failed her, and that she deserved, at the very least, the support needed to pursue a life free of life-threatening, soul-crushing abuse. While we self-righteously declare, "When we resist victim excuses, we're resisting an abdication of personal responsibility," what we are actually doing is abdicating collective responsibility for children.

Of all the hundreds of articles on the Menendez case,

only one wondered why no one had intervened in the family when the boys were young, and then only in the form of a concluding quote:

> Charlene Elmore, nurse at the Princeton Day School who spent a great deal of time with Lyle, says she has been asking herself, "Why didn't we pick up on something that had gone astray?" She begins to cry. "The thing that hurts me most is to think that a kid that I watched grow up could go to the gas chamber. . . . How did we miss something?"

Where were all those witnesses who testified about Jose and Kitty's monstrous behavior? What about the local child-protective services and the local police? How did we all miss something, and why didn't we step up after the killings to take responsibility for our failure? Adults are right to maintain the belief expressed in *U.S. News & World Report* that "you can't run a society, or cope with its problems, if people are not held accountable for what they do." But to be fair they must extend that belief to include members of society who tolerate children's suffering, whether at the hands of abusive parents or abusive policies.

Our resistance to society's role in the Menendez killings is so profound that we don't even know we should be contrite. The author of a sarcastic article in *Vogue* magazine on the Menendez case seemed to boast about her resistance to responsibility. In response to bumper stickers that read, I BELIEVE LYLE AND ERIK, the author wrote, "So what? When I was in ninth grade, my biology partner blew his parents away, Menendez-style. . . . Everybody knew the parents were drunks and that they were physically abusive to their adopted son, but nobody thought for a minute that he shouldn't be prosecuted." The author goes on to complain that since that episode, "there has arisen this insane notion that we deserve a perfect life with nice parents . . . and that anything short of that is grounds for committing murder."

Children who act out violently don't have "a perfect life with nice parents," except in the movies. In *The Good Son*, a 1993 thriller starring Macaulay Culkin, Henry is a boy who is violent and sadistic for no apparent reason. He lives with his two dedicated, caring affluent parents and sweet little sister in a beautiful house in a safe neighborhood. Yet he delights in causing others pain. He is responsible for the drowning of his baby brother and several attempted murders, including hurling his sister onto the thin ice of a frozen pond and pushing his mother off a cliff. He shows no ability to empathize with the suffering of others and no inclination to feel remorse. And he refuses to take accountability for what he does, often blaming his cousin, the perennially innocent and good Mark. Mark believes that Henry is simply evil. " 'Evil' is a word people use when they have given up trying to understand someone," his therapists tells him in a feeble rebuttal. "There is a reason for everything, if we could just find it." The film portrays the therapist as a kind, but hopelessly naive and misguided woman, who is no match for a child like Henry. Like the therapist, the other adults around Henry are so intent on being understanding that they become pathetic and ineffective. Mark ultimately has to take matters into his own hands.

Like *The Good Son*, coverage of recent attempts to hold parents liable for their children's crimes suggests that some children "go bad" for no reason. In a critique of parental responsibility legislation, columnist Ellen Goodman wrote, "We know about good parents whose kids went wrong all by themselves." The notion of innate evil performs a similar function as the attitude that children are essentially savage and/or can be incorrigible: Both relieve adults of any responsibility for the childhood circumstances of children in trouble, and both facilitate punitive rather than preventive approaches to juvenile crime. Evil, by definition, cannot be predicted or prevented. There is no question that children who act out need to be held accountable for what they do. But it doesn't follow that adults should be absolved of responsibility. Holding children alone responsible for the consequences of their misfortune is not only unfair, it is unwise. Our culture's material and psychological salvation lies in prevention, and children can neither prevent, nor control, the circumstances of their own childhoods.

SEVEN

Cash Values

_____

> One thing is sure: our failure to invest either public re-
> sources or private time in the raising of children has left
> many families fragile and overburdened, unable to do a
> decent job in raising the next generation. True, some chil-
> dren continue to be raised in supportive communities by
> thoughtful, attentive parents, but the larger fact is that
> the whole drift of our society, our government policies,
> and our private adult choices is toward blighting our
> youngsters and stunting their potential. An anti-child
> spirit is loose in the land.
>
> SYLVIA ANN HEWLETT

Even though adult society resists taking accountability for
children's sexual and criminal behavior, it does acknowledge
that young people can't be entirely to blame for the circumstances that lead to their dysfunction. Politicians don't
argue that preschool-age children are responsible for the
poverty of their families and their communities, or for the
violence they endure at the hands of their caregivers and in
the streets of their neighborhoods. Our culture generally
views young children as innocent victims of adult individuals and policies, and we want to help them even when we
don't want to help their parents. We believe, to some extent,
that our society should guarantee all children the necessities
of life, and that we are all responsible when their basic
needs aren't met. Consistent with our state's fundamental
contract with parents, we advocate intervention only after

175

adults have demonstrated that they can't or won't care for their children. As a result, parents shoulder the bulk of the responsibility for meeting their children's needs and the bulk of the blame when their children suffer deprivations.

Holding parents responsible for the well-being of their children is an important state function. Adults who choose to have children should focus most of their energies on providing a wonderful life for them, and they should not be allowed to deprive them of basics such as food, shelter, clothing, medical care, and education. However, our society insists on holding parents accountable even when they lack the necessary resources to honor their commitment to child rearing. We expect parents to meet their children's needs even as we perpetuate social and economic systems that make their duty impossible to perform. In line with our culture's general inability to recognize the role of social forces (other than media culture) in children's lives, we refuse to acknowledge that even the best parents can't function in a dysfunctional environment, and that dysfunctional environments aren't likely to produce good parents. Blaming parents has both camouflaged and facilitated our government's declining commitment to children, making it more and more difficult to hold it responsible for its failures and atrocities. Our society's manner of holding parents accountable is making a bad situation worse.

Cultural discourse about "family values" illustrates the dominant role of blaming parents in social-policy debates. Within less than two weeks of Vice President Dan Quayle's now infamous 1992 speech entitled "Restoring Basic Values," *Newsweek* declared that his words had "jolted the country, igniting a long-simmering debate about cultural values and the American family." Quayle's rhetoric about America's "poverty of values" and his attack on the television character Murphy Brown inspired cultural commentators everywhere. The ensuing "family values" debate built on Quayle's initial gesture of blaming every conceivable social ill on the "breakdown of family structure" over the past forty years, by which he meant the increase in the rate of divorce and in the number of children born to unmarried women. According to an article in *National Journal*, "'Family values' is the latest incarnation of the social issue in American politics."

Given its broad resonance with American popular culture, the family-values debate has come to encompass a wide variety of often conflicting theories on the causes, consequences, and themes of the nature of American society. (For example, Quayle blamed the "lawless social anarchy" that took place in Los Angeles in 1992 on a shortage of family values.) However, most politicians and pundits who participate in the debate agree on two basic premises: that most social problems have their origins in the breakdown of the American family, and that this breakdown has its origins in widespread moral decay. "That there is something called 'the family'—Papa Bear, Mama Bear, Brother Bear and Sister Bear—that it is the best setting for raising children, and that it is in trouble because of a decline in 'values,'" observed *Nation* columnist Katha Pollitt, "are bromides accepted by commentators of all political stripes."

Government policies affecting families have changed dramatically over the past twenty years, but during the 1994 elections, adult morals were center stage in the family-policy debate. "From coast to coast, moral decline is rocketing to the top of the agenda for campaign 1994," wrote a *Los Angeles Times* political writer. "[C]andidates are lining up to lament the trend in American family life—and linking problems from crime to the decay of the cities to a perceived breakdown in the transmission of values." Political commentators generally accepted the Republican implication that "intact" equaled "morally upstanding," and they touted broad bipartisan consensus on the importance of "intact" families as a sign of social progress. Democrats who embraced these family-values assumptions were congratulated for putting politics aside for the benefit of American society. However, the preponderance of cultural disputes since Quayle's family-values speech have not led to constructive family-policy debates. They have instead centered them on how much worse unmarried adults are for children than married ones, erasing the role of socioeconomic circumstances in family dysfunction.

The most crucial question about family functioning in the United States remains virtually unasked: Does even the two-parent family have a good chance at raising physically, emotionally, and socially healthy children in contemporary American society? The answer, according to poverty figures, is "no." Due to dramatic increases in child poverty over the past two decades, one in four American children now lives below the federally established poverty line. The *National Center for Children in Poverty* reports that over six million children under the age of six are officially poor in the United States. Another four and a half million live just above the poverty line (approximately $14,500 for a family of four). Most poor children live with parents who work. Over one-third live in families where parental employment is the only source of income. Over two million poor children under six live in married-couple families.

Despite the magnitude of childhood poverty, our culture continues to debate socioeconomic circumstances as if they were mainly related to parental morals and behavior. We avoid straight talk about government-poverty policy, instead discussing poor families in the context of child abuse and neglect. Viewing child poverty through the lens of the child-protection system underestimates its role in children's lives and perpetuates parent blaming, further distracting our focus and our energies from our dysfunctional economic system. Our culture's reaction to the death of Elisa Izquierdo at the hands of her mother illustrates how the misguided rhetoric of the child-protection debate (and therefore of the child-poverty debate) obscures root causes of child suffering, perpetually alienating the possibility of constructive reform.

Elisa Izquierdo, a six-year-old living in New York, died a horrible death. Although the most gruesome details have probably been buried with her broken body, what we do know rivals anything our culture has ever committed to film, fiction, or canvas. Apparently convinced that Elisa had been put under a spell that had to be beaten out of her, Awilda Lopez tortured her daughter regularly. She slapped, punched, burned, and twisted Elisa's limbs. Mrs. Lopez raped and sodomized her with toothbrushes, hairbrushes, and other household implements. She confessed to having finally killed Elisa by throwing her against a wall, after having, among other things, made her eat her own feces and mopped the floor with her head.

In the three excruciating years leading up to Elisa's death, many people had some idea of her intense suffering. And many of them communicated their knowledge to New York's Child Welfare Agency (CWA), the government agency charged with protecting children from abuse and neglect at the hands of their caregivers. Neighbors, who couldn't avoid hearing Elisa's moaning and pleading that emanated from Awilda Lopez's apartment, made several calls to the police. The principal and social worker of Elisa's elementary school, who saw that Elisa had bruises all over her small body including her head, and had an uneven walk suggestive of injury, reported their observations to a deputy director of CWA's Manhattan division. And the director of a parenting program, who had worked with Awilda Lopez and had firsthand knowledge of her abusive behavior, repeatedly contacted Elisa's CWA caseworker about the escalating crisis between Awilda Lopez and her daughter as recently as six months before Elisa's death.

Due to CWA's knowledge of Elisa's situation, the logical response to Elisa's death, according to press accounts, was to point fingers at New York's child-protection system. *Time*'s cover story editorialized that "the aspect of the tragedy's aftermath that has dumbfounded the city" was "that Elisa's case was known to the system, and yet the system so shamefully failed her." *Time*'s story helped to turn Elisa Izquierdo into a poster child for child maltreatment. It accompanied a picture of Elisa on its cover with the text: "Let down by the system, murdered by her mom, a little girl symbolizes America's failure to protect its children." A *New York Times* editorial echoed this construction in its statement that Elisa's death "has focused national attention on . . . the nation's most vulnerable children—victims of abuse and neglect." And an article in *National Review* argued that Elisa's death "opens a window on a fatally confused bureaucratic system." However, neither *Time*, the *New York Times* editorial, the *National Review* article, nor most coverage of

Elisa's case pointed out that in many ways Elisa is not, in fact, an appropriate symbol for the child-protection reform movement.

America's debate about protecting children from maltreatment suffers from a lack of perspective. It conflates all types of abuse and neglect into one massive category—"child maltreatment," or, more popularly, "child abuse." Elisa should not have been made a symbol for the systemic problems in our child-protection system because she suffered from abuse, not neglect. Although the distinction between the two types of maltreatment is not clear-cut, the definition of each is not exact, and the two often happen to the same child at the hands of the same caregivers, the terms are different in significant ways. In general, according to *Child Welfare: Policies and Practice*, child abuse is "an act of commission" that involves physical abuse, sexual abuse, psychological abuse, or a combination. In theory, a well-funded child-protection system can effectively handle moderately abusive families by either teaching parents how to modify their violent behavior, or placing their child with a safe, nurturing family.

Child neglect, on the other hand, is "an act of omission" involving a failure "to provide one or more of the ingredients generally deemed essential for developing a person's physical, intellectual and emotional capacities." Not surprisingly, the vast majority of child-neglect cases involve socioeconomically disadvantaged families. These cases cannot be effectively treated by a child-protection system, even a well-funded one. The system cannot, with few exceptions, treat a family's poverty, nor can it treat the poverty endemic to a family's community. Also, child-protection services, which are by definition crisis-oriented and short-term, cannot adequately treat the poverty-related psychological problems often manifested by poor neglectful parents.

Incidents of child neglect make up the largest and fastest-growing category of reported maltreatment. Fully 65 percent of all reported cases stem from neglect, and more children die from neglect than from abuse. The number of neglect cases is likely to continue its gruesome upward climb thanks to the Republican-led "reform" of our country's social services system. An increase in the number of children living in poverty will mean an increase in neglect if for no other reason than poverty itself is a form of neglect. As an article in the journal *Criminal Justice and Behavior* argued, "[I]n a society with immense resources, poverty per se constitutes neglect. . . . Of all the risk factors to the health and development of children, poverty is undoubtedly the most damaging." Poverty, and by implication the state, is the most harmful and the least-reported perpetrator of child maltreatment. And the state is not one of the families that the child-protection system was designed to treat.

Unfortunately, driven by marginally representative, but irresistibly compelling, anecdotes, our child-protection debate continues to confuse rather than to clarify. In the early 1990s, the media began to tell inspiring, hope-filled stories about a new trend in child-protection referred to as "family preservation." Rather than removing children from dangerous or inadequate families, family-preservation efforts sought to keep troubled parents and children together with the help of intensive, short-term services. The *New York Times* called it a "major—and promising—shift in emphasis that could save lives and money." *Newsweek* commented that "in a line of work with too few happy endings, it is a particularly gratifying option." Family preservation gained momentum from the Adoption Assistance and Child Welfare Act of 1980, which required agencies to make "reasonable efforts" to prevent the removal of children from families identified as abusive or neglectful. The new approach also benefited from the fact that, as a concept, particularly as pitched in the mass media, it proved irresistible on both sides of the aisle. It promised to be both more humane than traditional child-welfare efforts, and cheaper. It could, apparently, keep children out of the dysfunctional foster-care system, help parents to be more effective and competent, and save the state money—all at the same time. As one reporter noted in 1990, "[C]ritics of the concept are hard to find."

The media sold the family-preservation concept with the help of heartwarming anecdotes. For example, one article introduced readers to a twenty-six-year-old single woman with five small children. After receiving family-preservation services, she realized that she had been depressed for many years. "It was just me in this dark closet," she told the reporter, until her family-preservation caseworker "came in and opened it up, and the sun came in." Her caseworker was able to be there at crisis-prone times, like the children's bedtime. She taught "techniques like taking a 'time out,' which allowed the mother to control her temper and remain firmly authoritative." She also provided transportation to other services such as counseling, and helped the young mother to budget her time and money.

In one scene described by the reporter, the mother "[d]rawing on her recent lessons about composure and patience . . . tried to reason with her children, using a newly discovered inner reserve":

> I used to tell them, 'Leave me alone'. . . . But I'm learning
> that it's better to talk to them and punish them than to hit
> them. . . . I'm more in control and acting better [toward my
> children]. . . . They hug and kiss each other all the time.

The article reported that the program was helping the mother to raise her children rather than lose them to the foster-care system, and was giving her the opportunity and resources to explore employment options. "Her boys are starting to settle down and follow instructions . . . and her daughter, who is 7, is showing more interest in school work and reading."

Despite its much-heralded introduction, family preservation soon began to find its critics. Inevitably, it didn't turn out to be as humane and cost-effective as it had been touted. Within a few years, the press began to turn on it with the same intensity it had once used to proclaim its wonders. Articles came out citing dead children, unchanged (and unrepentant) parents, and false savings. Yet through all the coverage generated by the trend, both pro and con, the fundamental causes of child-protection failures were somehow never exposed. As a culture, we engaged in a five-year debate about child protection, without moving any closer to realistic solutions. Meanwhile, the ranks of maltreated children grew, the number of foster-care children swelled, the entire child-welfare system continued its inexorable decline, and we worked on legislation that would significantly decrease funding for child-protective services and most social services designed to support children and families.

Family-preservation services have always been discussed

in the larger context of the economics of child protection. When the media first began to introduce the concept of family preservation, it always included details about how preservation services would save the state money by keeping children out of the foster-care system. At the same time, family preservation was sold as the antidote to child-protection policies that discriminated against poor parents. As an editorial in the *Nation* argued, "most advocates for poor and minority families support family-preservation programs because they believe that child-welfare agencies unfairly remove kids from broken homes without first trying to help the parents." Family preservation promised to slow the removal of children whose parents' only crime was poverty. According to early articles touting the concept, family preservation promised an irresistibly quick fix to what had traditionally been portrayed as an intractable social problem.

Apparently, family-preservation caseworkers could "quickly identify problems and rectify them," and within a matter of a few weeks could "help create environments in which families are able to begin functioning." One article reported, "In many cases, one small change can help turn a family around, and social workers can draw on special funds to assist them. They might pay for a septic tank or buy car tires so a parent can get to work." Another argued that "often the stress on a child's own family could be worked out at home, with no need for foster placement, if only more money were available for emergency counseling to get families through crises like drug dependence or losing a job." Even though the foster-care system takes on children because of their parents' drug abuse, homelessness, economic

hardship, illness, and imprisonment, many of these problems supposedly "can be solved simply by helping unemployed parents get back on their feet."

In the context of this quick-fix scenario, the popular
press was willing to acknowledge that poverty wasn't good
for children. "Poverty is the main cause of neglect," according to an article in the *Los Angeles Times*. "Most often . . .
families in [family-preservation] programs have trouble providing enough food, housing and clothing for their children, all of which are considered problems of neglect."
Poverty didn't seem so bad if its negative consequences for
children could be cured with a few swift strokes of government intervention. Who could resist the rhetorical appeal
made by Peter Digre, director of Los Angeles County's
child-protection agency: "Rather than putting five kids in
foster care, why not spend $500 for a refrigerator if that's
what they need?"

The media embraced the concept of poverty as superfi-
cial, and therefore easily removable. Articles citing the many
services offered to families involved in preservation programs never failed to mention housecleaning. A typical article explained, "Caseworkers will tailor their contributions
to the family's needs. For instance, the worker might help
parents scrub the floors, plan a budget, obtain housing, get
into drug treatment or learn how to discipline children
without beating them." Another reported that caseworkers
"provide families with food stamps, clothing, household
goods, cleaning supplies and transportation." A clean
house often ranked in significance with treating a drug
problem and having a well-stocked refrigerator.

The association between poverty and filth resonated

with reporters, perhaps because it was the only obvious way
to describe what poverty looked like. When police stumbled
upon the "Chicago 19," nineteen neglected children in a
Chicago house, every news report focused on the "squalor"
of the situation. *Time* opened its description of the children
with the lines: "Lying two deep on a pair of dirty mattresses.
Or sprawled on the apartment's cold floor amid food
scraps, cigarette butts and human excrement." *Newsweek*
felt that "nothing was more emblematic than the kitchen."
It reported:

> The stove was inoperable, its oven door yawning wide. The
> sink held fetid dishes that one cop said "were not from
> that day, not from that week, maybe not from this year."
> And although the six mothers living there collected a total
> of $4,500 a month in welfare and food stamps, there was
> barely any food in the house.

Citing dirty dishes as emblematic of the children's situation
may have spoken volumes to people used to living in clean
houses, but it didn't address one of the essential questions
raised by the discovery of the Chicago 19: How much of the
child neglect evident in the apartment was in the mothers'
control and how much was related to the mothers' poverty?

To its credit, the *Newsweek* article pointed out that the
Chicago 19 were found in "what most people would consider
a troubled home. But to veterans of the city's juvenile courts,
it's just another 'dirty house' case." The attorneys for the
mothers charged with neglect would probably argue that
their clients weren't guilty; their children "weren't malnour-
ished, weren't physically or sexually abused and weren't left
without adult supervision." But the article did, like most
coverage of the case, imply that the problem in the situation

rested squarely with the mothers, not their poverty level, not their impoverished surroundings—not, in other words, their socioeconomic status. When the family-preservation backlash struck, the media perpetuated this implication. When it turned out that the short-term, intense services had not prevented foster-care placements as predicted, the media did discuss both incorrigible parents and intractable poverty. But it left the public with no viable understanding of the issues involved, making it very easy for all of us to hold individual parents responsible not only for the suffering of their children, but for their own poverty as well.

The media's discussion of family preservation's false promise of cost-effectiveness reported on two kinds of studies. The first "had found no evidence that children in family-preservation programs were less likely to be placed in foster care than those who receive standard treatment." And the second found that family preservation didn't actually reduce foster-care placements because agencies were delivering services to families who weren't at risk of losing their children in the first place. However, coverage focused on the findings of the second type of study, not the first. The *New York Times* argued that the "Achilles' heel" of family preservation lay in the fact that "a program developed to prevent families from breaking up serves families that were not going to break up anyway." The media generally avoided an informative discussion about why family-preservation services didn't work with so many families who were at risk for placement. They did, however, air the views of various pundits, who used the opportunity to vent their own particular policy-related biases about poverty.

Some liberal-leaning child-protection experts located the failure of family preservation not in parents, but in their environments. Richard Wexler, author of *Wounded Innocents: The Real Victims of the War Against Child Abuse*, has been widely quoted in the family-preservation debate. He argues that many children are removed from their families "because the family's poverty has been confused with 'neglect.'" He cites statistics about the number of children placed because their parents lacked adequate housing and/or adequate health care. These views suggest that family preservation can work as long as it is adequately funded to provide the concrete services poor families need.

An article in the *Washington Post* argued, "[F]amilies can be overwhelmed by unemployment, ill health, paternal abandonment and poverty." The article pointed out that such circumstances don't make the people who endure them bad. "It makes them families who need support. That can include helping a single mother fix up her house so she won't lose her children because a landlord has let his property fall apart." Critics of family preservation, according to this school of thought, are waging "an insensitive assault on poor families. . . . who have fallen short of society's high standards in their struggle to feed, clothe and house their families on pitifully inadequate resources."

Most conservative pundits located the failure of family preservation in the parents who received such services. They embraced Dan Quayle's notion of a "poverty of values." They argued that the family-preservation philosophy misguidedly "translates deficits of values into deficits of resources" and wrongly assumes that "the maltreating parent does not necessarily lack the values to raise a child responsibly . . . but simply the resources to do so." According to this view, family preservationists overlook the inherent negative characteristics of the parents, and avoid a discussion of personal responsibility. "Left out of the analysis is why the family is *not* providing for the child—might not drugs or sheer irresponsibility play a more important role than poverty?" This view suggests that family-preservation services can't work because they cater to bad people who can't be changed through kindness or generosity. Maltreating parents, therefore, shouldn't be regarded as victims of circumstances, but as actors who choose to live in squalor and harm their children. In this view, poor parents can control their own poverty, or at least any negative impact it could have on their children. Therefore, if they are deemed guilty of neglect, they should lose their children to the child-protection system.

Both these views on child maltreatment and poverty make valid points, and both have serious limitations. The mainstream liberal view underestimates the child-protection system's ability to cope with profound poverty. Articles acknowledge that the number of reports of child maltreatment has risen in response to "homelessness and the . . . deteriorating economy," and then argue that family-preservation services can "keep families together . . . by battling destructive forces that often lead to dissolution." Family-preservation services cannot "battle" poverty. As Ann Hartman, editor-in-chief of the journal *Social Work* has eloquently argued: "We must not expect that children will be protected and nurtured through the heroic efforts of families and social workers in an uncaring, hostile, and depriving environment." Family-preservation services can in some cases provide the material and psychological support necessary to connect families to existing social services. They can "mobilize needed services and resources, but [they] cannot substitute for such resources."

Selling the idea that we should provide all eligible families with family-preservation services obscures the reality that a family's poverty cannot be cleaned up in a few weeks. Articles shy away from the ugly truth that a society which tolerates widespread poverty as ours does, must also tolerate discrimination against poor parents on the part of the child-protection system. Poverty is so detrimental to children that many suffer from "neglect" even when their parents are doing the best they can.

While it is certainly true that "child placement has been used not only as a solution to child abuse and neglect but often as a substitute for financial and social assistance to needy families," it does not follow that children should never be removed simply because their parents are poor. As long as our society is not willing to address the multifaceted environment of poverty, we will have to remove children from their communities. Poverty, according to David Hamburg, author of *Today's Children: Creating a Future for a Generation in Crisis*, presents a variety of physical and psychological hazards to children:

> Poor children are at higher risk of succumbing to death, disease, disability, or injury than are economically advantaged children. They are more likely to have parents with formidable vulnerabilities that expose them to multiple hazards. . . . [T]hey may grow up malnourished and have untreated childhood illnesses or uncorrected early problems of hearing and vision, accidents, and injury. They may experience higher degrees of stress and violence in their social environment on a continuing, long-term basis. . . . In school, they will be observed to be underdeveloped in their social skills, emotionally troubled, and linguistically and cognitively well behind their peers born into more fortunate circumstances. So, poverty is a profound

and pervasive exacerbating factor in illness, disability, emotional distress, and educational failure.

Promoting family-preservation services may make us feel more humane and just; however, it does very little to improve children's socioeconomic circumstances. Increased funding for such services when other social services are being defunded should make us wary, not grateful. Ideally, family preservation "challenges the community to recognize the limitations of services that are currently being offered to respond to the basic needs of people in trouble." Practically, it seems to have further obscured the damaging elements in children's environments that are beyond parental control.

The mainstream conservative view willfully overestimates the individual parent's ability to cope with profound poverty. It may be true that "[f]amily preservation . . . plays an important ideological role in the culture's flight from honesty about the problems of the underclass" in that it shifts focus from an individual's character to an individual's circumstances. However, in many cases of poor parents who maltreat their children, character and circumstance are interrelated. These parents suffer not so much from a "poverty of values" as they do from the values of poverty. Sometimes they are doing their best in an impossible situation, and sometimes they are doing a mediocre-to-poor job in an impossible situation. Either way, their efforts to protect their children from dire poverty are relatively futile.

Conservatives are correct to call attention to the ineffectiveness of family-preservation services in the face of certain parental pathologies. However, these pathologies have nothing to do with moral decay. For example, a disproportionate number of poor mothers suffer from depression directly related to their poverty. In brief, as an article in the journal *Families in Society* explains, "Parents who are poor are constantly confronted with their powerlessness in relation to the world. They internalize feelings of incompetence and inadequacy, which lead to overwhelming anxiety and depression." Depression often leads to inappropriate parenting: "episodes of harsh, punitive, and intrusive interactions alternate with gross inattention and obliviousness." In addition, depressed mothers often abuse alcohol and other drugs as a form of self-medication to ease the pain caused by their psychological condition. Substance abuse then compounds existing child maltreatment. However, contrary to what many conservatives suggest, these parents are not untreatable. Their parental defects result not from poor values, but poor mental health, a shortage of appropriate drug treatment and psychological services, and any hope of a better future. While severely depressed, impoverished, maltreating parents cannot benefit significantly from short-term family-preservation services, they and their children could become functional in a functional and supportive society.

Even the conservative columnist George F. Will acknowledged that the state can short-circuit "the family pathologies that drive the intergenerational transmission of poverty" by teaching young, poor, emotionally disturbed mothers to be good parents. In a column entitled "Mothers Who Don't Know How," Will reported, "Very early intervention, involving close and protracted supervision of young unmarried mothers, can 'jumpstart' their mothering skills." He concluded, however, that giving these women what they need to raise happy, healthy children can't be "a public health policy." Why? Because *there are too many single mothers who need this long, painstaking, labor-intensive and therefore expensive attention.* In 1994, Will backtracked, saying, "Cultural regeneration cannot be legislated; least of all can it be skill-fully implemented by the federal government."

Our too-little, too-late approach to poor families means that many of the underprivileged children who come to the attention of the child-protection system become perma-nently caught up in it. On the one hand, existing child-protection programs are insufficient in length and intensity to improve the socioeconomic circumstances of poor abu-sive and neglectful families. On the other, judges are un-likely to terminate parental rights in these cases because the parents have not committed a particularly heinous act, nor have they completely abandoned their children. As a result, underprivileged children are trapped: "Their parents can-not adequately care for them; existing services do not im-prove parental functioning; they cannot be returned home; and they cannot be placed for adoption." Children end up staying in a succession of foster-care settings while their parents are given years to become adequate parents with in-adequate resources. Many children end up too old or too damaged to be adopted or to be returned to their biological families. Many spend their childhoods in group homes, still wards of the state when they turn eighteen.

In sum, our society is using foster care to treat "what is, in essence, a poverty problem." We use child-protection pol-icy to camouflage our unwillingness to maintain a social in-frastructure that provides adults the supports, resources, and services they need to care for their children. In essence, we sacrifice children to the child-protection system to cope with our dysfunctional economy. We deny what is actually happening by blaming parents, arguing that we had to re-move the children because their parents were bad, or that we tried to help but their bad parents wouldn't cooperate.

We have great difficulty acknowledging that parents who are doing their best lose their children to the system every day. Homelessness is a leading cause of placement. We have even greater difficulty recognizing that "bad" parents are products of the same impoverished circumstances that now threaten their children. The intergenerational transmission of poverty means, by definition, that the different generations are caught up in social forces for the most part beyond their control. Whether or not they do dishes has everything to do with the life prospects they have endured and inherited.

Unfortunately, the passage of time further cripples our sickly rhetoric about children and poverty. Poor children who grow up neglected, whether in their families or in our foster-care system, are less likely to benefit from short-term services, and more likely to neglect their own children. This seemingly intractable and intergenerational transmission of neglect bolsters the conservative argument that people are poor and neglectful because of their character, not because of their circumstances. Unfortunately, then, as poverty deepens and broadens its realm, we will find it easier to blame the poor and their children for their plight, and easier to avoid a discussion about poverty as a destructive force in its own right.

As American cities have decayed over the past twenty years, our culture's dominant coping strategy has been to blame the inhabitants of that decay once they become parents. Increasingly, the victims are still children when we begin to chastise them for causing poverty. In fact, teenage mothers were the focus of a recent surge of support for creating a system of state-run orphanages to cope with the consequences of welfare reform. According to George F. Will, "[T]he serious idea being considered by serious people is that infants whose mothers are say, 16, unmarried, uneducated, unemployed, addicted and abusive might be better off in institutions." In other words, girls who have grown up in poverty and who exhibit the disadvantages and coping mechanisms associated with childhood poverty, such as drug use and early motherhood, should be punished so that their children can have a different life.

It doesn't seem to have occurred to supporters of current welfare reform that the sixteen-year-old pregnant girl is almost as much a victim as her baby-to-be. They are both poor children, both victims of circumstances far beyond their control. An editorial in *National Review* suggested that "if the parent is a teenage drug addict whose boyfriend beats her children, then she is not raising them to anything but woe, and an institution becomes a desirable alternative." Apparently, the fate of the young girl becomes irrelevant. Logically, our empathy for a baby born into a difficult life should extend to its young mother, also recently born into the same difficult circumstances. But it doesn't. We want to rescue the baby because we know how unhealthy and damaging those life circumstances are, but we have very little empathy for the young girl or boy who has already been damaged by those same circumstances.

Our culture's recent debate about orphanages suffered from most of the distortions of our culture's larger child-protection debate. As one columnist pointed out, even liberals equated "poor" with "bad"; they "mentally substitute[d] 'unfit parent' for 'welfare mother.'" The media repeatedly confused being an AFDC recipient with being an abusive and neglectful parent, without acknowledging that most recipients are not abusive, or that, for many, their poverty and their neglect are intricately related. One article explained that the "impulse behind the orphanage revival is the concern . . . for the catastrophic decline of proper child-rearing practices among the poor." Like the term "orphan" itself, coverage implied that the defining characteristic of the children in question was that they didn't have functional parents, not that they failed to be born into a functional economic environment, even though the orphanage plan involved removing children from their teen parents *before any parenting had even taken place.* Children whose fathers wouldn't or couldn't support them, and whose mothers couldn't find a job that would pay enough for living expenses including adequate child care, would be effectively separated from their families on those grounds alone. In general, children whose parents have an adequate source of income are not removed from their families unless and until an egregious act of abuse or neglect has occurred.

However, coverage did inadvertently support the view that good parents were only one component of a healthy environment. In describing what ideal orphanages would be like, the emphasis was on resources directly related to economic status, such as quality child care, safe neighborhoods, good schools, and adequate medical care, all things a poor parent, particularly a poor working parent, cannot provide, no matter how dedicated. According to an article in *Insight on the News*, the founders of a chain of residential care facilities "envisioned a typical American family with four to six kids living in a typical middle-class, Norman Rockwell-type neighborhood." The program buys a house, hires "house parents," and raises children. The founders acknowledge that the program costs money (about $85,000 a year per household), but the irony of investing in "house parents" rather than parents seems to be lost on them. While they build Rockwellian communities for poor children, they steadfastly maintain that the problem for children in the inner cities is not their impoverished communities, but their immoral parents. Apparently, these children "don't have parents who provide the things that allow them to survive in society. . . . from teaching morals and ethics to how to interact with other people."

Poor parents should not be idealized any more than any group of parents should be. Some parents are too violent, too crazy, or too broken to care for their children regardless of the supports they have. But the concept of immorality obscures the fact that people don't parent in a vacuum. Their ability to be good parents depends on their backgrounds and their resources. Adults don't leave their pasts behind any more than children who get pregnant or commit violent crimes stop being children. Most parents could be adequate for their children if our society made treating and ultimately eradicating poverty and its damaging effects our public health policy. In functional communities, parents wouldn't have to worry about running out of money for food, utilities, housing, and medical care. Instead, parents would be trained and supported to focus on parenting, and access to a wide variety of activities and opportunities would enhance their strengths and compensate for their weaknesses. Removing children from poor parents at birth is as misguided as leaving children isolated with their middle- and upper-class parents until they get hurt.

Neither approach recognizes the crucial role of social infrastructure in raising children well, and neither approach will ameliorate that infrastructure.

In the media flurry following Elisa Izquierdo's death, two liberal commentators tried to turn the cultural conversation to the taboo subject of poverty. *Nation* columnist Katha Pollitt pointed out, correctly, that it is a "fantasy" to imagine that "government can simultaneously deprive poor families of the wherewithal to survive while stopping child abuse," and that "fighting social inequality" is the only "realistic program," for fighting child maltreatment. And Jonathan Kozol, author of *Amazing Grace: The Lives of Children and the Conscience of a Nation*, argued that "in the death zones of America's postmodern ghetto, stripped of jobs and human services and sanitation, plagued by AIDS, tuberculosis, pediatric asthma and endemic clinical depression . . . deaths like [Elisa's] are part of a predictable scenario."

However, Pollitt and Kozol did not succeed in instigating a "realistic" discussion. They may have inadvertently contributed to its continued avoidance. As long as we only discuss child poverty in the context of child protection, we will have a hard time motivating ourselves to do anything about it. The association of poverty with child protection immediately brings the discussion to the level of the individual and the anecdote. The image of Awilda Lopez mopping the floor with Elisa's head will continue to dominate and derail rational overtures about child maltreatment until we find a new, credible social forum for our much-needed discussion about children and economic justice.

Currently, both the liberal and conservative perspectives on family preservation facilitate our society's ability to ignore the larger, more significant issue of poverty. The liberal view treats family function as if it were a housecleaning away even for poor families, and suggests that it is better to leave children in poverty than to remove them from their parents. The conservative view argues that poverty is not a significant factor in child maltreatment. So, we sustain a policy paradox. As we decrease social services for families, we increase child-protection services. Sometimes we remove children from their families, putting the blame for abuse and neglect entirely on the parents. Sometimes we offer the families meager and inadequate services, acknowledging that economic hardship might have played a role in the child maltreatment that occurred. But we always strenuously avoid looking at the big picture.

Our refusal to discuss the impact of poverty on children except in the context of child protection inevitably keeps us focused on the failure of individuals, and distracted from the failure of our socioeconomic policies. And within the context of child protection, we keep our attention trained on horrific instances of physical and sexual abuse, and rarely on the sustained, systematic deformation of neglect. Contemporary poverty rhetoric cannot lead us toward progressive reform because, in the final analysis, no trend in child protection, whether toward family preservation or efficient termination of parental rights, can work in a dysfunctional economic environment. Until we confront poverty itself, the child-protection system will continue to face a choice between two evils: leaving children in dangerous environments with insufficient services to significantly ameliorate their situation, or jostling them around for years in an overwhelmed foster-care system. Our displaced focus continues to unfairly undermine our culture's faith in our government's ability to support families and to protect children, making matters ever worse.

EIGHT

The Business of Caring

___

[C]hildren are changing fast from kids to consumers.
Savvy marketers are both capitalizing on the trend and
speeding it along.

PATRICIA SELLERS

Our culture does not have much sympathy for the plight of
impoverished parents, and does not empathize with their inability to adequately care for their children. However, we are
not insensitive to the difficulties facing parents who work
full-time, earn enough to exist above the poverty line, live in
the suburbs, and still have a hard time raising their children.
We recognize that for them, trying their hardest may not be
enough through no fault of their own. These families who
"play by the rules," as President Clinton described them, are
working harder and longer than their parents did, earning
less, getting fewer and less comprehensive medical benefits,
and raising their children with less time, energy, supervision,
and community resources. In their case, we are beginning to
appreciate that quality child rearing requires more than two
married, dedicated adults. For more and more families, work
and child rearing just don't mix.

Yet, our society has been surprisingly reticent to challenge business to work for families. Corporate America
strongly resisted family-leave legislation that would allow
employees to take time off to care for a family member, and
the result was an unpaid, relatively short leave available to

fewer than half the nation's workers. In general, we allow business to regard the family responsibilities of employees as their own problem, even though more parents are in the workforce than ever before. As government slowly abandons families, our society's children are becoming everybody's problem and nobody's responsibility. The only members of our society that are benefiting, at least financially, from our current approach to child rearing are corporate executives. They have found myriad ways to turn children's losses into corporate gains. And our culture's response so far has been to accommodate, not to censure.

In effect, our culture tacitly supports a dramatically inequitable contract between business and children. We tolerate, and sometimes even praise, corporate America's exploitation of the vulnerabilities of today's children. At the same time, we condone, and sometimes even encourage, its efforts to "fight back" against those same vulnerabilities as soon as they cease to yield a profit. As our civic infrastructure deteriorates and families face increasing economic and temporal stresses, we perpetuate the myth that the financial interests of business and the developmental interests of children are converging. When it's clear that they aren't, we blame individual parents and their children. Our culture perpetuates a rhetorical environment in which this corporate behavior continues unabated with little to no public outcry. In terms of working families, we stand by, relatively unperturbed, as our business sector takes advantage of the growing number of unattended and under-attended children while heartily resisting family-friendly policies necessary to meet their employees' child-care needs.

Contemporary articles about retailers who target their sales pitches at children illustrate our rhetorical contract.

These articles tend to celebrate retailers' marketing efforts. They lead, inevitably, with a focus on the theme of children's pleasure. "The scene," one article about an "activity room" at Ikea, a furniture chain, began: "screaming children cavorting in a knee-deep sea of green, red, yellow and blue plastic balls." "Here," it continued, "the little ones watch videos, draw pictures or immerse themselves in the popular ballroom." Another article on pay-per-use indoor playgrounds opened: "Kids! Come have a ball! Or 60,000 of them!" An article about "Kids Only" theaters in shopping malls introduced readers to a three-year-old who "armed with a cup of popcorn," gets to "catch up with his favorite characters on the big screen" while his mom shops.

These articles acknowledge that retailers cater to children's desires in order to increase sales, not out of a selfless desire to serve the public good. As one article put it, "Today's merchandisers are relying on a host of child-friendly retailing methods to attract the tots and lure in mom and dad." Targeting kids makes sense, according to this article, because "kids not only spend lots of money, they have a big say in how everyone else does." Since "adults can't spend anything while they're chasing the little ones around the aisles," the same article explains, "retailers are relying on a grab bag of tricks to keep tykes busy while parents empty their wallets." In addition, retailers and reporters understand that "where mom and dad shop couldn't be more important these days" because of the weak economy. "Child-friendly" retailing can be "the key to economic revival" in troubled economic times.

However, the same articles downplay corporate self-interest, and instead emphasize the idea that retailers are providing much-needed services to today's families. The "days of shopping with a 40-pound ball and chain may be over" according to an article in *Newsweek*. It predicts that drop-off child-care services "may be the wave of the future" because "kids love them, and parents who can't find baby-sitters are relieved not to have to drag reluctant shoppers around with them." Another reported that the "goal" of the on-site services of a child-care chain, KinderCare, is "to give families more time with their offspring (and to keep them as clients)." It opened with a lead much like a sales pitch: "A neatly pressed blazer, a take-home chocolate mousse cake, a well-coifed toddler, free 'Bambi' rentals, all available in one place—it sounds like a Yupscale convenience fantasy." It argued that KinderCare stays open late on Fridays to "allow parents to spend a little quality time with each other."

The articles consistently stress the way in which retailers are servicing needs created by the decline of our society's civic infrastructure and the influx of mothers into the workforce. "As public playgrounds grow increasingly seedy," an article on pay-per-use playgrounds points out, "the for-profit centers offer clean, safe, supervised activity." Once again, the inferred goal of the "service" is to meet families' needs. "In an attempt to soup up" the sedentary lifestyle of today's children, the article argues, "the new facilities cater to the concerns of two-earner families, staying open in the evenings, long after traditional public playgrounds have grown dark and unusable." The moral of the article is that pay-per-use playgrounds, despite their for-profit nature, are not only convenient, they are good for families. "The most fun of all," according to the article, "is getting to do what parents used to do in the days before two-career families and two-hour commutes: play with their kids."

In essence, articles on "child-friendly" retail services posit and perpetuate the notion that the need for families to flourish and the mandate of businesses to maximize profits can and do dovetail. We don't need to worry, according to this cultural illusion, about cash-strapped counties and inadequate child-care options for working parents because corporate America is ready to step in and pick up the slack—with style! Apparently, capitalism works for the working family and everybody wins. It is only in light of this belief that our culture's response to "stealth baby-sitting" makes sense.

"Stealth baby-sitting" is an expression used, and possibly coined, by *Newsweek* in an article on "the increasingly shady practice of parents—often professional and suburban—to park junior in local multimedia and toy stores while they run off on errands." "Stealth baby-sitting" results from a conflict between retailers' profits and parents' needs. On the one hand, "Targeting affluent families, specialty toy stores have turned into virtual playgrounds." On the other, parents often want or need to take advantage of these "playgrounds" without choosing to spend money in the retail outlet that provides them. Rather than questioning the myth of dovetailing interests, coverage of "stealth baby-sitting" points fingers: it defends retailers' efforts to exploit children for profit, while it accuses parents and children of "abusing the privilege" of child-oriented services.

An article in the *Wall Street Journal* commended Ikea's efforts to "fight back" against parents who used its free baby-sitting services while shopping in nearby stores. The article reported favorably on Ikea's new policy that "restricts children's visits to 30 minutes. After that they repeatedly page parents and then call police." Far from sympathizing with the plight of parents who strive to be the good consumers they are exhorted to be but lack adequate child-care options, or with the children who would rather play than be dragged around another store, articles like this one side confidently with retailers.

The *Wall Street Journal* called the impact of "stealth babysitting" on retailers "more than just a nuisance" and *Newsweek* described it as "pervasive problem." Both explored the "marketing dilemma" faced by retailers: how to attract and entertain children whose parents will spend money, while keeping out those whose parents won't. While they acknowledge that these "child-friendly" services attract both the children of potential consumers and those of nonconsumers, they also identify with the fact that "[e]liminating that kid-friendly environment could hurt sales." Retailers do have the option of expelling children whose parents aren't spending money, but "always at the risk of alienating customers."

Meanwhile, coverage has only disdain for participating families. Nonconsuming parents who take advantage of child-friendly retail services are characterized as incompetent, unprincipled, and flaky—as guilty as retailers are innocent. The *Wall Street Journal* asks rhetorically, "What kind of parent would do such a thing?" and answers with a quote from a retailer: "I feel like asking these parents, 'What are you idiotic?'" In an anecdote, *Newsweek* described a father who "blows into a downtown toy store with two kids in tow," and, "After mumbling something about coming right back, he disappears, leaving his youngsters." It described unattended children in even less flattering terms: "temporarily abandoned kids hog the game displays for hours at a time (if they don't break them) from potential customers."

Contrary to popular wisdom, two parents are not sufficient to raise children. In an economy in which the majority of families depend on two or more incomes, it takes at least three caregivers to raise a child. Parents are solely responsible for the round-the-clock care of their young children, and, as a result, most pairs of working parents must procure the services of a relative, baby-sitter, nanny, or professional caregiver. In addition, they must procure these services in a society that, in general, is "neglectful of families and their needs," and specifically, undervalues the work of caring for children.

One doesn't have to look far, therefore, to find examples of dedicated pairs of married adults who can't themselves meet their children's material and psychological needs. In January 1996, *Time* devoted five pages to an article on American families. The article crystallized the state of the American family in its portrait of the Maldonados. Aurelio Maldonado (a bill collector), his wife Rita (a legal secretary), their son Adrian (six years old), and daughter Clarissa (five months) "make up the classic family of four," we learn from the article. "[T]heir income of $44,000—a bit more than half earned by Rita—is smack in the middle nationally." Despite their family values, their family structure does not permit them to be the kind of parents they would like to be:

> The couple would like to keep Adrian in the Roman Catholic school system but cannot because first-grade tuition would be $2,500 a year. After attending a Catholic

kindergarten, Adrian is a first-grader in a public school that his father says is "not the kind of environment anyone would want for their kids." Rita's parents now baby-sit for Clarissa while her mother works, but the grandparents plan to move to Texas in a year or two, and the Maldonados will somehow have to scrape up the money for day care. Says Lio: "Rita would love to stay home with our daughter, but we have to combine both salaries to make ends meet."

Despite the conventional wisdom that what society needs is more intact families, most mainstream magazines and newspapers have published articles in the 1990s that document the struggle of two-parent families to function adequately for their children. Real wages have decreased over the past two decades, and most women with children who work full-time do so out of economic necessity even when married. A *National Journal* article editorialized, "Whether or not the 1950s represented heaven, the twin hells for those trying to rear children in the 1990s are less money and less family time, whether the home has one parent or two." Even *Business Week* acknowledged, "With a growing population of dual-career couples . . . balancing the demands of home and work has become the great game of the American middle class."

It is fairly common knowledge that dual-wage-earner families are now the norm. We also acknowledge that "somehow neither work nor the family has changed enough to make this a tenable situation." Even though over 60 percent of American women with school-age children are in the workforce, "the nation still clings to the old every-woman-for-herself method of securing child care." We have just begun to recognize the devastating consequences of this refusal to accommodate the children of working parents.

David Elkind, author of *The Ties That Stress: The New Family Imbalance*, calls the lack of affordable, accessible high-quality child care the "tragedy of the post-modern family." However, we are still far from redressing the problem.

While infant day care may be controversial, studies generally confirm, "Most children can thrive in high-quality, out-of-home care." We have proven to ourselves over and over again the commonsense truism that "children cared for by sensitive, responsive providers in high-quality settings [show] greater cognitive development," and, conversely, mediocre to poor care impedes healthy development.

> Finding the best environment for your child is important, especially during the first few years of life. Research has shown that the brain experiences its greatest growth before age three, and that a child's intellectual outlook is affected by his environment. It may sound overly dramatic to say that a child's future is decided by where she spends the first three years of life, but in those years, a baby learns to trust, to pursue curiosity, and to interact with people. A child who does not connect with a warm and loving adult during these early years may fall behind.

Despite our knowledge about children's vulnerabilities and needs, articles on child care point out that "the need for safe, affordable child care has reached crisis level." As one article put it, "for most working parents, child care today doesn't work." Millions of American children spend forty-plus hours per week in care that ranges from depressing to dangerous, custodial to cruel. Given how much time young children spend in child-care settings and how vital their early years are for healthy emotional, cognitive, and physical development, it is easy to conclude, as an article in

Fortune did, that "the short supply of high-quality day care is the greatest obstacle to better prospects for America's children."

Roughly one-third of young children of employed mothers spend long days in child-care centers. Of these five million children, according to a 1995 study, fewer than 600,000 receive care that meets their needs for "health, safety, warm relationships, and learning." Of the remaining almost four and a half million, 3,800,000—almost 75 percent—are getting only custodial care that does not meet their needs to grow and develop into healthy beings, and another 600,000 are receiving care that is so inadequate, harmful, unsafe and unsanitary that it interferes with their basic development. Overall, "Most [center] child care is mediocre in quality, sufficiently poor to interfere with children's emotional and intellectual development."

Another five million children of employed mothers spend their days in "family day care" provided in the houses of relative and nonrelative caregivers. Of these children, only 9 percent are receiving good quality care, according to a 1994 study. In general, "family day care is 'barely adequate' in providing the sensitive, responsive environment considered critical to the healthy development of children." Over a third of the settings are "considered of such poor quality that they [are] potentially harmful to a child's healthy growth," and over half are only "adequate or 'custodial,' meaning they would not harm, but neither would they enhance, a child's development."

For school-age children, the outlook is similarly bleak: "[T]he number of young children who routinely spend part of the day unsupervised has been mushrooming." According to *Time* magazine, "42 percent of all American kids between the ages of five and nine are home alone often or at least occasionally. (For older children, the figure rises to 77 percent)." Estimates vary, but some studies suggest that "up to 10 million children are alone most afternoons—or for longer stretches—virtually every weekday." Rather than participating in developmentally appropriate, intellectually stimulating, safe activities, most of these children are under virtual house arrest. They experience boredom, loneliness, and feelings of abandonment. They are more likely to get depressed, to get into trouble in school and with sex, drugs, and crime. And many are constantly terrified, frightened by every noise, every knock on the front door, and every phone call.

"As a nation, we have not paid enough attention to the daily environment of 5 million of our preschool children," according to a spokeswoman for the National Association for the Education of Young Children in Washington. However, not all of us have taken an out-of-sight, out-of-mind attitude. Business has been paying an inordinate amount of attention to unattended and underattended young Americans. While its voluminous research and targeting efforts have not benefited these children, who continue to languish and suffer in ever greater numbers, they have paid off for corporate America—big time. And when it comes to covering American business, the mainstream press has taken its cue from corporate America itself. Its praise for the "services" corporate America is providing, its faith in the myth that the needs of business and those of children can and do dovetail, and its tendency to criticize parents and children who aren't benefiting from the "corporate organization of childhood" are all cribbed from the corporate party line. In the pages of advertising trades and business sections, corporations market their sophisticated and seductive version of their contract with America's children, and, so far, it appears that our culture is completely sold.

There isn't any question that corporations do what they do with, to, and for children for the sole purpose of making as much money as possible. Due to several dramatic socioeconomic and demographic shifts over the past two decades, "[c]hildren either directly make or influence more purchases than ever before." According to a widely quoted estimate, children and preteens spend approximately nine billion dollars a year, and influence the spending of another $130 billion. Teens spend over $80 billion annually, a third of which is discretionary. Both the preteen and teen markets are expected to continue to grow over the next ten years. They are, in fact, the fastest-growing sectors of the economy. These sales figures "have captured advertisers' attention, including those for whom the teenage market is not their core segment." Children are touted in the trades as "some of the hottest targets in marketing," and "[o]ne of the fastest-growing target audiences." Corporations have sought to tap into and increase this mushrooming youth market, creating an "explosion in youth-oriented marketing strategies" and a dramatic increase in advertising aimed at young people. The youth market has become "a niche that everyone is attacking." In 1990, we invested over $500 million dollars to "reach" the preteen market alone.

In order to be successful, advertisers need a great deal of specific, current information about their target group. "Visuals count . . . even those visuals that seemingly have nothing to do with the product sale," one ad executive explains. "Locations, sets, props, wardrobe, colors, numbers, sexes and ages of people all reflect a lifestyle that is either in step with the target prospect or out to lunch." Companies conduct focus groups, snail mail surveys, and online polls to gather data. When conducted with children, these methods are "designed to get to know how they, and only they, act and react, to understand their ever-changing tastes and desires."

Over the past ten years, advertisers have learned a great deal about children. The most important lesson has been that the "child consumer isn't just a pint-size version of an adult." In fact, for a variety of developmental reasons, children are much better consumers than adults—they are almost ideal. According to James Garbarino, author of *Raising Children in a Socially Toxic Environment*, "Childhood is . . . a period of socialization, of adult investment in the creation of socially relevant skills, beliefs, and motives." In other words, for the same reasons that high-quality child care is so important to young children, childhood is a great time to instill brand recognition and to nurture brand loyalty. "Smart marketers recognize that it's easier to start a habit than stop one," the publisher of *Seventeen* magazine told *Mediaweek*. "If they can get young consumers to feel good about their product, then they're ahead of the game in the future." As a result, writes *Direct Marketing*, "the manufacturer, wholesaler and retailer are combining forces to make sure they have tomorrow's adult customer, which is today's child."

Add to the receptive soil of a young child's brain the fertilizing fact that "preschoolers spend more time watching TV than doing anything else except sleeping." The average child has seen approximately 350,000 to 400,000 television commercials by the time he or she turns eighteen. In addition, "[C]hildren younger than 5 can't tell the difference between commercials and programs, and until the age of 7 or 8 children don't understand a commercial's selling intent." The result of this mixture is an advertiser's wet dream: a truly attentive, trusting, receptive, impressionable target. Once billions of consumer dollars are involved, it shouldn't be surprising to learn that advertisers are "falling over one another to reach the nation's 32 million kiddoes between the ages of 4 and 12" as well as the burgeoning teen-consumer contingent. "The kids' market is attractive," according to *Fortune*, "because the money is there, and because corralling a young consumer and keeping him loyal sets a course for predictable sales growth."

Through research, corporations have also learned that today's children are particularly vulnerable to advertising messages because of the changing nature of the family. To begin with, children are getting less and less constructive adult guidance because they spend so much of their time in mediocre child care and/or home alone. "With the traditional household becoming less of a fixture," according to *Advertising Age*, "more children are having their emotional needs go unmet." The same article quoted an advertising executive's comment that children today "still need that ideal family and the security and bonding," but "[w]hat's happened is that kids are feeling insecurity." Fortunately for advertisers, "the less time parents and children spend together, and the fewer thoughts and activities they share, the more powerful secondary influences are likely to be." Marketing research firms often interview mothers and children separately in order to approximate actual living situations.

At the same time and for the same reasons, children are making more of the household purchasing decisions. "Working and single parents are so time-pressed," according to *Business Week*, "that they cede more influence on purchases to kids." Children are being forced to become more self-reliant. As one ad executive told *Advertising Age*, "two-income families leave kids more independent at a younger age." Targeting advertising directly to children is, as one article described it, "a pragmatic strategy based on a simple truth: Now that mom is away from home nearly as often as dad is, there isn't much point in fashioning media messages that follow the traditional route from advertiser to parent to child." In addition, researchers have identified another contemporary factor in children's increasing influence: what they call "the G factor," also knows as "runaway guilt." As one researcher told the *New York Times*, "There are more and more working mothers, and one of the things we know that generates is guilt." This guilt often leads parents to give children more discretionary income and more say in purchasing decisions.

To top it all off, television is becoming a more and more integral part of children's lives. There are obvious correlations between unattended and underattended children and television viewing. In most child-care settings, children are only getting what's called "custodial care," which "means kids are safe but not mentally stimulated: they're plopped in front of the TV and basically ignored by adults." Latchkey children who come home directly after school to an empty house turn to the television as a substitute for human companionship and extracurricular activities. In the era of the two-working-parent family, watching TV has become equivalent to having a part-time job for many children. According to a survey conducted in 1989, "2- to 5-year-olds now watch television about 25 hours a week; 6- to 11-year-olds watch about 22 hours, and 12- to 17-year-olds watch about 23 hours." The average child, according to *Time*, "will have watched 5,000 hours of TV by the time he enters first grade and 19,000 hours by the end of high school—more time than he will spend in class." The correlation between our inadequate child-care system and children watching television has certainly not been lost on marketers. In 1991, the president of the Fox Children's Network commented in an article, "We have inherited the responsibilities of being a baby-sitter for millions of kids."

Despite their mercenary intent, marketers often portray their million-dollar efforts to exploit today's children and families as a form of public service. "Kids have no childhood today," the president of Nickelodeon/Nick at Nite children's cable channel told the *Christian Science Monitor*. "Also, they have no community. Look at all the families where both parents work. The youngsters need us to pick up trends; to understand." An article in *Forbes* described a new Hallmark greeting card series called "To Kids with Love" in similarly altruistic terms. "For parents who leave for work before the kids get up and return after the young ones are tucked in bed," according to the article, "a greeting card can complement parental attention or affection—and can be purchased in a hurry for as little as 95 cents."

The way the food industry has moved into the children's market provides an illustrative case study of the typical strategies and rhetoric that surround most commercial exploitation of children. Like most industries, food conglomerates find they have a lot to gain from targeting children in the 1990s. With "that current American phenomenon, the disappearance of the family dinner in time-starved dual-income or single-parent families" according to the trades, "it was a natural for the food folks to try and cash in." One expert predicts the market will expand to $250 million "as parents try to cram more into a day." In addition, with the concurrent rise of the microwave, food companies are "frantic to develop new, microwavable meals and snacks," two-thirds of which they are marketing directly to children. "In their bids to grab their share of the . . . market, Tyson and ConAgra have rolled out nationally with complete frozen dinners, called Looney Tunes Meals and Banquet Kid Cuisine, respectively." And then of course there are the fast-food chains. McDonald's continues to dominate the "kid business," but Burger King has joined the fray as a major player. "[W]ith fast-food sales sluggish," according to an article in *Forbes*, "Burger King has begun aggressively going after kids with new TV ads."

And like other industries, food companies have found that children today are excellent targets for advertising messages. Food companies make liberal use of bright packages with kid-style characters and product offers of free puzzles, games, toys and other items. For example, Kraft has created a new animated series for children around "Cheesasaurus Rex," the character featured on boxes of Kraft "Macaroni 'n Cheese." In addition, children don't always know what food is supposed to taste like, which means they are particularly good targets for microwave food products that often lack tastes and textures appealing to more experienced eaters. And perhaps most important, eating habits—like brand associations—when "established in early years persist into adulthood."

Add to this heightened receptivity the fact that children are playing an ever greater role in family food shopping. The food industry is "particularly intrigued by the youth market," according to *Business Week*, because "junior is juggling supermarket shopping with school." In the "two-working-parent family prevalent today," children are now shouldering more household responsibilities, including food shopping and cooking their own meals. The good news for the industry is that "these responsibilities have brought kids closer to buying decisions," or, to put it in market-speak, children are "really becoming partners in the brand decision process."

The food industry has done a particularly successful job of portraying itself as a good friend to today's stressed-out families. Both public-relations rhetoric and commercials tout the idea that the food industry is there to help parents cope with their overwhelmingly busy lives. "Mom's got to run and dad's got to fly, but little Graham and Gillian still have to eat," an article in *Marketing and Media Decisions* explains. "Recognizing this, some major food marketers are offering parents a helping hand." An ad for Kid Cuisine from ConAgra promotes a message of convenience. It shows a child "calmly discussing how convenient, fun, nutritious and good tasting the meals are while his mother races around the kitchen in the background." An ad for Hormel microwavable dinners for kids "features small children triumphantly heating their own snacks."

In the lineup of food companies posing as friendly neighbors to stressed-out parents and their neglected children, none has done a more pervasive, sophisticated or insidious job than McDonald's. In the early eighties, McDonald's corporation created new strategies to go after the family market. Its ads anticipated and reflected changes in American family life with amazing sales results. Most children are as likely to recognize the Ronald McDonald character as they are to recognize Mickey Mouse and Joe Camel. An article in

Journal of Popular Culture chronicles how McDonald's new marketing strategies shifted emphasis from the food products to "the realm of human feeling." They worked, according to author James Helmer, to "attempt symbolically to reconstitute the family and relocate it under the golden arches." They used images of families "as a means of persuasion that ultimately portrayed McDonald's as a potential source of love and human happiness—as a place for being a family." The scene in one ad: "[A] sad little girl waits for her working mother to come home on a chilly, rainy night. Mother and daughter go to a bright, lively, warm McDonald's and order Happy Meals; little girl smiles again." The message is clear: "McDonald's heals families." Tapping into parents' and children's feelings of being overwhelmed by impossible, competing demands, McDonald's corporation strives to characterize itself as a salve to "people's basic and powerful need for someone to mend the fragments with caring."

However, despite their pro-family rhetoric, McDonald's and other food-industry conglomerates aren't doing children any favors. They are flooding children's programming with ads that "promote an unbalanced, unhealthful way of eating." A recent study found, "The diet presented on Saturday morning television is the antithesis of what is recommended for healthful eating for children." According to *Advertising Age*, "the percentage of high-fat foods advertised during Saturday morning children's TV viewing time increased from 16 percent to 41 percent of all food advertising between 1989 and 1993." Almost half of the ads that are shown during children's shows are for foods rich in fats, oils, and sweets, such as candy, soda, cookies, and potato chips. Over 10 percent are devoted solely to fast food from chains such as McDonald's, Burger King, and Pizza Hut. In one survey, researchers found two hundred and twenty-two ads for junk food during four hours of programming.

And food companies don't spend all this money on advertising for nothing. Advertising creates and perpetuates demand. "Commercial food advertisements," according to *Nutrition Today*, "especially those presenting foods of low nutritional value, have increased positive attitudes and preferences for those foods." Research suggests that children "who watch the most TV have the worst diets and the lowest levels of nutrition knowledge." Not surprisingly then, since most children watch a great deal of television, most have terrible diets. There is a strong correlation between television watching and snacking (especially on the high-fat foods being advertised), and between TV watching and what pediatricians have called an "epidemic of inactivity" among children.

The food industry's onslaught of junk-food advertising targeted at children has had dramatic negative consequences. Children are eating more saturated fat, sodium, cholesterol, and sugar than ever before. On average, American children get 50 percent of their calories from fat and sugar. Over one-quarter of American children are obese, and the numbers are steadily increasing. Obesity in children is linked to a variety of disorders in adult life including hypertension, respiratory disease, diabetes, skeletal disorders, stroke, and cardiovascular disease. In the *New York Times*, a spokesperson for the American Academy of Pediatrics was quoted as saying that "the single most important health issue for pediatricians in this country today is overweight children."

When confronted with the overwhelming evidence that

junk-food advertising is bad for children, the food industry passes the buck to parents (but not the profits). The editor of the *Marketing to Kids Report* told *Advertising Age* that it's up to parents to choose and control what their children eat. "The No. 1 responsibility lies first and foremost with the parent," the editor told the trade. "To stick advertisers with the burden of controlling kids' eating when their first mandate is to sell their product is unfair." "The fact is," another executive told the trade, "the ultimate responsibility for dealing with slick 'n' sleazy kids marketing is not with the consumer-wise child but with the parent."

Corporate location of responsibility for children's diets in the hands of parents assumes a number of not-so-self-evident circumstances: It assumes that parents are willing to be attentive and loving to their children on a daily basis; it assumes that parents, who themselves have been raised on a steady diet of manipulative advertising, will be informed and insightful enough to educate their children about the corporate agenda; and it assumes that parents will have the time and the resources to be physically and emotionally present in their children's lives. In response to an HBO special produced for children on the misleading nature of ads, one executive complained that the producers showed "a weird, parentless world." And he asked rhetorically: "Where are the parents who are saying 'No, we're not going to give you the money to buy that. You don't need that'?"

So far, our culture has not seriously challenged the industry on either its exploitation of children, or its shirking of responsibility. We have not, for example, pointed out that the industry knows very well where the parents are—at work. The food industry aggressively exploits the very lack of parental guidance it criticizes. It has made billions of dollars off the "dietary chaos" created by women in the workforce. In addition, corporations have spent millions of dollars to infiltrate public schools: a setting in which, by definition, there are no parents. "In today's classrooms," as *Newsweek* reported, "corporate logos and learning often go hand in hand. . . . [S]chool-age children are being bombarded by a growing number of blatantly commercial messages."

We also haven't dwelled on the fact that companies which market food products directly to children are by definition sidestepping and undermining parental authority. Many commercials are designed specifically to arm children to influence what food products their parents buy. The food industry exploits what some marketing consultants are disingenuously calling "child power." One consultant told the *New York Times* how things stand from a marketing perspective: "You've got a two-member earning situation or a broken home which means that the adults are just plain not there much. Children as clever as they are, can take advantage of the situation." Or put another way, "Parents are busier and feeling guiltier. So they are softer when it comes to children's requests," another marketer told *Fortune*. The article added that "kids are no dummies at exploiting these emotions."

An article in *Mediaweek*, described how one company, "conspires with kids to get their mothers to buy the products." It paraphrased the company's vice president explaining how ads need to give children the rhetoric to "sell" their parents on the food being advertised. "We know that kids are quick to pick up on ammunition to use with mom," the vice president told *Advertising Age*. In one article, a marketing consultant argued that food products targeted at children "should come across with a sense of doing it on your own, and how you don't need parents to do this." Another ad plays on parents' guilt about not being home to cook meals for their children, or to eat with them. An ad for a food product called "My Own Meals," begins, "As a busy mother like you, I worry about my children eating right."

The food industry's assault on the family epitomizes what is wrong with targeting products at children. Overall, the products that are being pitched don't have redeeming aspects. While the toy industry could argue that it provides at least a few products that children need and can benefit from, the food industry, by definition, only provides that which is unnecessary and harmful: junk food. There is no role for the processed, packaged, and fast-food industry to play in children's lives that is both positive and profitable. An increase in the child-market share for a food corporation like Kraft means that more children are eating more food that is both bad for their health, in and of itself, and takes the place of food that contributes to good health. The Committee on Communications of the American Academy of Pediatrics has found, "Because young children cannot understand the relationship between food choices and chronic, nutritional disease, advertising food products to children promotes profit rather than health." It has taken the position, "Food advertisements aimed at children should be eliminated."

However, as one article editorialized in response, "[T]he elimination of commercials pitched at kids is unlikely to happen anytime soon, if at all." To begin with, there is a great deal of money at stake. Spending on and by children is "one of the fastest-growing sectors of America's economy." In addition, the food industry, like most industries in this country, is immensely powerful, and it argues that its job is to move products as profitably as possible, not to teach children about nutrition or to encourage them to eat well. As a senior ad executive told *Advertising Age*: "We have a responsibility as marketers and we have to be concerned with [children's diets], but marketers don't make or advertise what won't sell. And I don't think it's up to marketers to lead consumers in that sense."

In fact, as any economics student knows, corporations are essentially amoral institutions, designed to make money, not to serve the public interest. As an article in *Business and Society Review* explains:

> a corporation is essentially a machine, a technological structure, an organization that follows its own principles and its own morality, and in which human morality is anomalous. . . . Corporations require that subjective information be translated into objective form, i.e., numbers. This excludes from the decision-making process all values that do not so translate. . . . Production elements that pose danger to public health or welfare . . . are translated to value-free objective concepts, such as "cost-benefit ratio" or "trade-off."

There are instances in which the profit motive and the public interest follow the same general trajectory, but they are few and far between, especially with regard to children. As the food-industry example illustrates, unbridled capitalism is an enemy of children's welfare.

For the same reasons that we can't expect corporations to safeguard the interests of children, we shouldn't be surprised when they portray their activities as a service to children and families, or when they shirk responsibility for the public interest by blaming parents. The recent spate of corporate public-relations campaigns that promote the "benevolence, generosity, and social values of corporations" are good for sales and are effective at warding off consumer-friendly government regulations. We should be alarmed, however, at the extent to which our mainstream culture has incorporated corporate propaganda into its coverage of corporate behavior affecting children.

Over the years, the mainstream press has dutifully reported on studies that document the family-unfriendly nature of most companies and the anti-child nature of most child care. Many of these articles haven't been shy about calling attention to the inadequacies of corporate culture when it comes to the well-being of families. An article in *Time*, for example, pointed out that: "Corporate America . . . may praise family life but does virtually nothing to ease it." However, these same articles that chronicle corporate America's dismal track record over the past two decades, usually wrap up the bad news by heralding an imminent turnaround in corporate attitudes and actions. They suggest that it is only a matter of time before family-friendly corporations become the norm.

A 1991 *Newsweek* article highlighted what it termed the new "social-responsibility movement" in corporate America. "Heard about 'political correctness' on campus?" it asked:

> Now the concept is flooding the boardroom as well. Faced with mounting pressure from consumers and watchdog groups, businesses are scrambling to do the right thing— in areas ranging from homelessness and poverty to ethical investing and family-leave benefits.

The article credits this dramatic shift in corporate attitudes to a recent epiphany in the business world: namely, that social responsibility is cost-effective (i.e., profitable). While the authors of the article acknowledge that "in the rush to cash in, some [companies] are merely paying lip service to do-goodism," they point out that "[c]ompanies whose words speak louder than their actions can expect to reap little from their efforts." In other words, the authors buy into a widely held belief that corporations that don't serve society will not succeed. Or, to put it another way, they believe that the phrase "corporate social responsibility" is not a contradiction in terms. They point out that the chairman of Social Ventures Network, "a group of entrepreneurs dedicated to running for-profit, socially responsible businesses," "expects ethics and corporate citizenship to become even more important to the bottom line in the next decade."

The theme that the needs of families to thrive and corporations to prosper can dovetail in the bliss of cost-effectiveness underscores most articles on "work and family" issues. "Businesses are finding that selfless deeds can enhance their image—and increase their profits," according to *Newsweek*. *Business Week* tells readers that companies "are discovering that family-friendly work environments more than pay for themselves. Flexible hours, restructured work, and unpaid leaves for emergencies actually reduce absenteeism, cut turnover, save money, and boost efficiency." In true corporate style, these articles are selling a concept that needs the hype. Authors who push the productivity of family-friendliness have to keep readers, and perhaps themselves, from thinking about the anomaly that the vast majority of companies are family-hostile and doing fine.

Like corporate advertising, contemporary television programming is bad for children and underregulated. Despite
the Children's Television Act of 1990, which sought to
increase the number of educational and informational
shows for children, children's programming "remains a national embarrassment," as an article in *Newsweek* put it: "a
brain-rotting assault of animated comic books and shriek-
ing commercials that borders on child abuse." Despite the
increasingly significant (and negative) role television plays
in children's lives, Newton N. Minow, former chairman of
the FCC and author of *Abandoned in the Wasteland: Children,
Television and the First Amendment* describes television as, "a
business attuned exclusively to the marketplace. Children
are treated as a market to be sold to advertisers at so many
dollars per thousand eyeballs." The industry develops
shows that will attract the estimated $450 million per year
in advertising revenue. Consequently, children's television is
saturated with programming elements that sell, such as violence, and animated vehicles for spin-off products like Mu-
tant Ninja Turtle pillowcases.

The TV industry's response to criticism is, predictably,
that its job is to make money, not to educate children. As an
article in *Time* reminded readers, networks "are in the business of making money, not doing good deeds." And, as any
executive can tell you, aspects of television viewing that are
good for children—educational programming, commercial-
free zones, frequent use of the "off" button—are not profitable. As a vice president of children's programming told
USA Today, "I wanted a schedule that will get the most children; that's my job. It doesn't do any good to put the most
educational do-goody show on that no one will watch.

What's the point?" The point, of course, is that if children watched educational shows instead of what amount to program-length commercials filled with aggression, or if they got bored and turned off the television, they would be better off. But that is certainly not the point for the TV industry or any of the industries that use television to reach out and touch children.

Mainstream culture is generally quiet about the corrosive effect of programming and advertising on children. The corporate exploitation of children no longer surprises, and rarely provokes outrage. It has come to be seen as an integral, and therefore unremarkable, aspect of our culture. However, we have recently begun to protest, or at least call attention to, the excessive media violence to which children are exposed. By the time the average child graduates from high school, he or she will have watched at least 18,000 simulated murders. While researchers disagree about the extent to which violent programming adversely affects children, no one has yet argued that it is good for children, or that it wouldn't be better for them to be watching something else. Yet, despite the seemingly clear-cut conclusion that children should be watching a great deal less violence on television, our culture's mainstream response has catered to the industry's perspective, and, as a result, promises to be lame and ineffective.

In 1995, President Clinton formally endorsed the so-called V-chip, which would allow parents to block the transmission of television programs that are encoded with warnings of excessive violence, sex, or other material perceived as objectionable to children. While the TV industry complained about the V-chip as it does about any attempt to curtail its profits, one could argue that the proposed technology catered much more to corporate greed than to children's welfare. The V-chip as envisioned supports the industry's two most basic drives regarding its interactions with children: to maintain the freedom to maximize profit regardless of the damage its methods and products cause, and to resist all accountability for children's well-being, shifting all responsibility to parents regardless of their ability to exercise that responsibility.

Yet, for the most part, the mainstream press embraced this proposed solution to children's exposure to media violence. According to an article in *Time*, Clinton's announcement about the V-chip ushered in "a landmark week that brought new hope to many parents." Even though the article acknowledged that the TV industry "may invoke the First Amendment" but its "more pressing concern is the bottom line," it implied that the V-chip provided a fair solution to the problem. "[I]f Americans really want to clean up trash TV," one article pronounced, "they can vote where it counts—with their channel changers." And even though legislators admitted that we need something like the V-chip in part because employed parents are so often not home, the chip was referred to again and again as "a neat solution to the problem of asserting parental control." "Networks and stations . . . must be vigilant about the content and commercialization of kids' shows," another exhorted, but "[t]he ultimate responsibility still rests with parents." One article quoted a psychologist who argued correctly but naively, "Parents should control, limit and regulate television exactly as much as they control, limit and regulate other things the child does—like taking lessons, like eating, like being outside."

In essence, the Administration and the press hailed the

new technology for how well it catered to corporate concerns. Despite its self-righteous tone, the press simply echoed corporate rhetoric. "Rather than removing or trying to tone down objectionable shows," the article in *Time* stated in support of the new technology, "it enables parents simply to keep them out of kids' reach." What the mainstream press and the Administration didn't do was consider what solution would work best for children and make that consideration the basis for evaluating proposed solutions. James Garbarino supports the United Nations Convention on the Rights of the Child's stand that children should "be shielded from the direct demands of adult economic, political, and sexual forces," and that "childhood is a protected niche in the social environment, a special time and place in the human lifecycle, having a special claim on the community." The implications for television have been pointed out by Minow. He argues that we should provide children with "a healthier television environment" that, among other things, "should meet the child's need to be protected from harm that comes from continuous exposure to violence whose primary purpose is to serve as a conveyance for commercial matter."

As a culture, we don't talk about transforming the time blocks of television most watched by children into commercial-free, violence-free, and education-full zones. We don't talk about creating a television environment in which children are safe from commercialization and violence and exposed to intellectually stimulating programming *regardless of whether or not their parents are competent, concerned, capable, or present*. In coverage of the V-chip, we did just the opposite. Several articles warned that making television a safe haven for children would be unfair to everyone else. As one put it, "If TV were to be scrubbed clean for kids, it would be a pretty barren place for adults." Again and again, it seems that when push comes to shove, despite all of our hand-wringing about children's welfare, we are much more concerned with adult privileges, such as unfettered profit and unfettered pleasure.

Despite the evidence, the free-market argument that "business has no business in anything but making money—which of itself will provide plenty of social benefits" continues to inform and guide popular culture's attitude toward corporate America. We refuse to acknowledge that the interests of underregulated free-market capitalism and those of children rarely if ever merge; and that, in fact, they are in conflict, engaged in a full-scale battle—and children are the hands-down losers. We indulge instead in wishful thinking, telling ourselves that children can adapt to raising themselves, ward off corporate marauders on their own, and even thrive in the process. One of the most popular movies of the nineties, *Home Alone*, pits eight-year-old Kevin against materialistic intruders—and Kevin wins.

Inadvertently left behind by his hurried, stressed-out family, Kevin spends several days alone in his family's house in the suburbs. Local authorities are worse than unhelpful. The family-crisis department refuses to help Kevin's mother check on him because she can't prove that he is in danger. The police department sends an officer who leaves after only knocking for a few minutes. The community isn't much better. Most neighbors are away on vacation with their own families. The supermarket cashier asks a few questions, but doesn't intervene. The local Santa listens to Kevin's request for his family back as a Christmas present, but leaves him with nothing more than a few pieces of candy. During his time alone, Kevin encounters a variety of dangers including collapsing furniture, his brother's pellet gun, and a sled that he rides down the staircase, but he remains unharmed. After initial bingeing on junk food and television, Kevin begins to assume the habits of a full-grown, mature adult. He bathes, he shops, he cleans, he prepares food, he dresses appropriately, he doesn't watch television, he prays before meals, and he spends some time in church thinking about how ungrateful he has been. He even befriends an old man and gives him advice about reconciling with his estranged son.

The movie presents Kevin's confrontation with two greedy burglars as a growing experience in which the eight-year-old faces his fears. Kevin creates a battle plan and executes it with glee. He masters household hazards, like tar, nails, broken glass, and violent television shows, transforming them into weapons to protect himself. He ends up safe in bed, after watching the bruised, battered, and empty-handed burglars driven away in a police car. Even though Kevin has been abandoned by his family and neglected by all the other adults in his community, he emerges from the experience, not only unscathed but improved. He learns to appreciate his family regardless of their flaws and to take care of himself instead of relying on his parents. For her part, his mother feels awful about forgetting him. She tells her traveling companion, a member of a polka band, that she is a "bad" parent. But he convinces her that she is being too hard on herself for leaving her eight-year-old alone at home for several days. "You want to talk about bad parents," he quips, "look at us. We're on the road forty-eight to forty-nine weeks out of the year. We hardly see our families."

The idea that children can take care of themselves in a dangerous world with little adult guidance or supervision is a fantasy. Children are adaptable and resilient, but they can't compensate for adult inadequacies or protect themselves from adult violence. While they may survive difficult childhoods, their experiences take a toll, and, unlike Kevin, they do not come out unscathed. Our children experience too much hardship and too little nurturing in their efforts to adapt to an adult-centered society. Children cannot thrive in a culture that perpetuates dysfunctional families, an inadequate social infrastructure, and an aggressive anti-family corporate sector. Adults must face their responsibilities and do their part.

Toward a Child-Centered Culture

America's attitudes toward children manifest themselves in all aspects of our culture. In the writing of this book, I chose to focus on popular culture. I wanted to demonstrate that American myths about children are pervasive. Most of us are exposed to them on a daily basis. The information that contradicts these myths is also omnipresent, interwoven with distortions and misguided assumptions in a comprehensive and insidious fashion. I hoped that a critique of popular media would give readers the tools necessary to begin to recognize the cultural contradictions and hypocrisies that surround them.

I also made a conscious decision not to discuss the role of racial prejudice, gender bias, or homophobia in children's lives. I certainly came across numerous examples of bigotry's impact on children, both direct and indirect. Prejudice against children is prejudice in its purest and most virulent form. Race, gender, and sexual orientation complicate and exacerbate children's depressed socioeconomic conditions. However, they don't completely explain them. I wanted to keep the focus of the book on the disadvantages and difficulties that all children face, the conditions that are inherent in our culture's construction of childhood, the conditions that transcend the characteristics of individual children.

I believe many children's lives are terrifying, difficult, and dangerous due mainly to their social status as nonadults. Generally speaking, the contemporary status of childhood confers distinct disadvantages on children. Being a child means being dependent on adults. Therefore, it means being extremely vulnerable to the manifestations of adult dysfunction such as violent behavior, emotional instability, sexual exploitation, and economic injustice. It means conforming to particular social constraints, or risking dire consequences. It means, often, being trapped, being mistreated, being powerless, and being miserable.

At the same time, contrary to conventional wisdom, contemporary American childhood confers few concrete advantages. Today's children are inadequately protected. Our culture's paternalistic contract with children has severely curtailed their civil rights, but it has not guaranteed their protective ones. Children are more likely to be physically and sexually victimized than adults, and less likely to enjoy life's basics such as food, shelter, and health care. In other words, children get the worst of both worlds—less power and less protection.

In order to make childhood a safer, more nurturing state, we have to recognize the universal shortcomings of our society's current construction of childhood, particularly in relation to children's unique vulnerabilities. The balkanization of children and their interests obstructs a holistic perspective. To be better advocates, we must view childhood as a disadvantaged social and political status for all people under eighteen. This perspective will force us to see the structural conditions that imperil children, to recognize the belief systems that uphold such conditions, and to avoid losing ourselves in the details of individual cases.

Our society's paternalism is rooted in the recognition that children, especially small ones, depend on adults for their survival, and in the desire to buffer children from the dangers of the adult world until they are ready to confront them. However, our paternalism has always been conditional, on both an individual and a societal level: We protect children if they fulfill our expectations. One of the reasons we deny children civil rights is that we fear they will pursue their chosen identities and their preferred lifestyles if given the opportunity, and we don't want to give up control. When children turn out differently than we would like, or worse, manifest the dysfunctions of the adults around them, we banish them from childhood, insisting that they are no longer children.

I am not suggesting that children should be allowed to ignore the laws that make civilization possible. But I am arguing that children have the same right to self-determination as adults: the same right, for example, to pursue the religion or sexual orientation of their choice. I am arguing that we should raise children to be what they want to be, not what we want them to be, and, therefore, the goal of ideal child rearing should be to provide a safe, nurturing environment with as few restrictions as are necessary to maintain it. I am arguing that children deserve safety and protection whether their behavior pleases the adults around them or not. They deserve to be protected *and* empowered.

We often deny children legal empowerment because we maintain that they don't know what is best for them, and, therefore, should not be allowed to make their own decisions. This attitude is based on a cynical view of human nature. It assumes that, left to their own devices, children will grow into social misfits. Arguably, however, our culture's collective child-rearing methods are contributing more to the development of asocial adults than children's

natures. Children are not born violent, prejudiced, or alien-
ated from others. They learn these traits from the adults
around them. They are born good, loving, and open, and
then cultivated into dysfunctional adults by their dysfunctional social environments. And then they take over the
raising of the next generation.

Effective child advocacy, therefore, depends on a fundamental respect for children: a recognition that they contain
the best that human nature has to offer and an acknowledgment that their dysfunction reflects adult shortcomings. And this respect, in turn, requires that each of us
recognizes the children we once were, the childhoods we
once endured, and the adults we have become. Examining
how we were affected by our early experiences gives us the
tools to understand other children's situations and to appreciate the impact of their circumstances on their life
choices. Our motivation to ameliorate children's conditions
will ultimately emanate from this self-exploration, because
in advocating for children we will also be advocating for
ourselves.

But the exploration that is so necessary for good advocacy is very difficult. It is easier for many of us to turn ourselves off to the trauma faced by other children than to
recognize the pain we once experienced. Good advocacy requires that we acknowledge that we ourselves were, in all
likelihood, damaged somewhat by the adults and adult
policies that raised us, and that this damage influences who
we are today. While we certainly have the potential to modify who we are, we are not working with a blank slate. We
can never fully escape our childhoods. But we can make it
possible for the next generation to have much healthier,

more enjoyable, more functional childhoods than we ever had.

My research for this book has confirmed both my greatest hopes about children's prospects in this society, and my worst fears. I see positive signs everywhere that we, as a culture, are becoming more aware of how we treat children and the ramifications of this treatment for childhood and adult society. We recognize, to some extent, that we must intervene to stop the transmission of dysfunction from one generation to the next. However, the nature and focus of our interventions concern me. We intervene in others' lives more willingly than in our own. We intervene on the side of the powerful more readily than on the side of the oppressed. We intervene frequently at the level of the individual, and rarely, if ever, at the level of the system. Unfortunately, therefore, our interventions tend to make matters worse, diluting our motivation to change, and discouraging our progressive efforts.

To me, most young people in prison, including Lyle and Erik Menendez and Amy Fisher, are political scapegoats whose imprisonment allows our society to evade truly progressive intervention. Incarceration should be reserved for people who present a threat to the safety of others. It should be used humanely with the aim of rehabilitating people for reintroduction into society. It should not be allowed to serve as an end in itself. It is not a social program. As a society, we have to put our energies and resources into growing human beings who are centered and altruistic, rather than to building prison cells for all the children we plan to fail. We can break the cycle of dysfunction in which we are all caught. However, we have to focus more of our intervention efforts on ourselves—on the way we view our own childhoods, on the way we treat the children around us, including our own, and on the social institutions that provide us with short-term gain at the long-term expense of our children's, and therefore our society's, welfare.

Notes

CHILDREN IN AN ADULT WORLD

4 A 1996 *Time*/CNN poll found
Elizabeth Gleick, "The Children's Crusade," *Time*, 3 June 1996, p. 32.

4 "Americans cherish the notion
"Suffer the Little Children," *Time*, 8 Oct. 1990, p. 41.

7 "It is meanness to exaggerate
Wendy Kaminer, *I'm Dysfunctional, You're Dysfunctional: The Recovery Movement and Other Self-Help Fashions* (New York: Vintage Books, 1993), p. xix.

7 I agree with Kaminer when
Kaminer, *I'm Dysfunctional, You're Dysfunctional*, p. 14.

CHAPTER 1

9 The notion that
Pat Wingert and Eloise Salholz, "Irreconcilable Differences," *Newsweek*, 21 Sep. 1992, p. 84.

10 In his *Commentaries*
James Kent, *Commentaries on American Law*, Part IV, Lecture XXIX, "Of Parent and Child," in Grace Abbott, *The Child and the State, Vol. I: Legal Status in the Family Apprenticeship and Child Labor; Select Documents, with Introductory Notes* (Chicago: The University of Chicago Press, 1938), p. 51.

12 Richard N. Bond, chairman
Quoted in Margaret E. Kriz, "Political Hot Potato," *National Journal*, 5 Sep. 1992, p. 2008.

12 In response to these remarks
Eleanor Clift, "Hillary Clinton's Not-So-Hidden Agenda," *Newsweek*, 21 Sep. 1992, p. 90.

13 In her 1973 article
Hillary Rodham, "Children under the Law," *Harvard Educational Review*, 43 (1973): 508.

14 As one article summarized
Kriz, "Political Hot Potato," p. 2008.

14 Fortunately, the judge
Quoted in Larry Rohter, "Florida Girl, 14, Wins Right Not to See Biological Family," *The New York Times*, 19 Aug. 1993, p. A16.

15 Kimberly was
Tony Mauro, "A Milestone for Children's Rights," *USA Today*, 19 Aug. 1993, p. 3A.

15 As the late conservative critic
Christopher Lasch, "Hillary Clinton, Child Saver," *Harper's Magazine*, Oct. 1992, p. 76.

15 Clinton moderated the implications
Rodham, "Children under the Law," p. 510.

15–16 According to Shere Hite
Shere Hite, *The Hite Report on the Family: Growing Up under Patriarchy* (New York: Grove Press, 1994), p. 360–361.

16 In a legal article
James G. Dwyer, "Parents' Religion and Children's Welfare: Debunking the Doctrine of Parents' Rights," *California Law Review*, 82 (1994): 1371.

16–17 An editorial in
"The Better Half," *National Review*, 30 Mar. 1992, p. 13.

18 As many child-
See, for example, Richard J. Gelles, "Family/Reunification/Family Preservation: Are Children Really Being Protected?" *Journal of Interpersonal Violence*, 8 (1993): 557.

18 As a result
Karen Dorros and Patricia Dorsey, "Whose Rights Are We Protecting Anyway?" *Children Today*, 18 (1989): 8.

18 This dynamic reflects
Robert Horowitz, "Tighten Standards for Termination of Parental Rights," *Children Today*, 18 (1989): 9.

18 Because emotional abuse
Dorros and Dorsey, "Whose Rights Are We Protecting Anyway?" p. 8.

19 According to a staff attorney
Martha Matthews, "The Sadness Behind the Sensational," *The Recorder*, 8 Oct. 1992, p. 8.

19 The *New York Times* declared
Anthony DePalma, "Mother Denies Abuse of Son Suing to End Parental Tie," *The New York Times*, 25 Sep. 1992, p. A20.

19 It became an opportunity
Bob Cohn, "From Chattel to Full Citizens," *Newsweek*, 21 Sep. 1992, p. 88.

20 Many children in the system
Wingert and Salholz, "Irreconcilable Differences," p. 86–87.

20 To make matters worse
Larry Rohter, "11-Year-Old Seeks Right to 'Divorce' Parents," *The New York Times*, 8 July 1992, p. A10.

20 Even though Gregory
"Gregory Needed the Divorce," *The New York Times*, 29 Sep. 1992, p. A22.

21 The *Newsweek* cover story
Wingert and Salholz, "Irreconcilable Differences," cover, *Newsweek*, 21 Sep. 1992.

21 As one advocate
Lewis Pitts, "Family Values?" *The Nation*, 21 Sep. 1992, p. 268.

21–22 What the conservatives
"A Child Asserts His Legal Rights," *Time*, 5 Oct. 1992, p. 22; William Booth, "Boy Takes Mom to Trial in Effort to 'Divorce' Her," *The Washington Post*, 24 Sep. 1992, p. A3.

22 *Newsweek* even postulated
Wingert and Salholz, "Irreconcilable Differences," p. 85.

22 The *New York Times* editorialized
"Gregory Needed the Divorce," p. A22.

22 In a particularly stark example
Quoted in Roger Rosenblatt, "Hillary's Kids: An Interview with Mrs. Clinton," *The New Republic*, 14 Dec. 1992, p. 12.

23 An editorial in the *Chicago Tribune*
"Can a Child 'Divorce' His Parents?" *The Chicago Tribune*, 20 July 1992, p. C10.

23 A *New York Times* article
Anthony DePalma, "Court Grants Boy Wish to Select His Parents," *The New York Times*, 26 Sep. 1992, p. 1.

24 As the director of Legal Services
Quoted in Lynn Smith, "What's Best for the Children?" *The Los Angeles Times*, 18 Oct. 1992, p. E1.

24–25 As an article
Smith, "What's Best for the Children?" p. E1.

25 Jane Carey, the attorney
Jane Carey, "Juvenile 'Divorce' Steals Kids' Security," *The National Law Journal*, 30 Aug. 1993, p. 17.

25 In 1994, *Ladies' Home Journal*
Katherine Barrett and Richard Green, "Know Your Children's Rights," *Ladies' Home Journal*, Sep. 1994, p. 156.

25 The backlash consists
Quoted in Peter Applebome, "An Array of Opponents Do Battle over 'Parental Rights' Legislation," *The New York Times*, 1 May 1996, p. A1.

25 The federal version
Quoted in Kim A. Lawton, "'The Right to Parent': Should It Be Fundamental?" *Christianity Today*, 29 Apr. 1996, p. 57.

26 Proponents of parental rights legislation
Quoted in Lawton, "'The Right to Parent'," p. 57.

26 They want to reassert
Nina Shokraii, "Congress Must Act to Protect Parents' Rights," *Insight on the News*, 20 May 1996, p. 29.

26 They argue that
Shokraii, "Congress Must Act," p. 29; Lawton, "'The Right to Parent'," p. 57.

26 "This is not a dispute
Quoted in Randy Frame, "Child vs. Parent," *Christianity Today*, 7 Mar. 1994, p. 42.

26–27 Regarding schools
Quoted in Lawton, "'The Right to Parent'," p. 57; Applebome, "An Array of Opponents Do Battle over 'Parental Rights' Legislation," p. A1.

27 At the same time
Lawton, "'The Right to Parent'," p. 57; Applebome, "An Array of Opponents Do Battle over 'Parental Rights' Legislation," p. A1.

27 Opponents who see
Quoted in Kelly Owen, "Parents' Group Seeks Law for More Say at Children's Schools," *The Los Angeles Times*, 7 Feb. 1995, p. A5; Mark Frankel, "Who's Hands-On, Who's Hands-Off?" *Newsweek*, 8 July 1996, p. 58; Quoted in Owen, "Parents' Group Seeks Law for More Say at Children's Schools," p. A5.

27 The primary problem
Applebome, "An Array of Opponents Do Battle over 'Parental Rights' Legislation," p. A1.

28 "If teenagers have
David Elkind, "Teens' Privacy versus Parents Rights," *Parents Magazine*, Nov. 1990, p. 236.

28 In Minnesota vs. Hodgson
Quoted in Sue Halpern, "The Fight over Teen-age Abortion," *The New York Review of Books*, 29 Mar. 1990, p. 32.

28 As a *New York Review of Books*
Halpern, "The Fight over Teen-age Abortion," p. 32.

29 Many parents
Quoted in Mike Allen, "Conservatives Lobby for Parental Rights," *The New York Times*, 15 Jan. 1996, p. A10.

29 Murray Straus, author of
Murray A. Straus, author of *Beating the Devil Out of Them: Corporal Punishment in American Families* (Lexington, MA: Lexington Books, 1994), p. 4.

29 However, the vast majority
Sally Squires, "Should Parents Spank?" *The Washington Post*, 14 Feb. 1995, p. Z7.

29 Beyond being ineffective
Straus, *Beating the Devil Out of Them*, p. 9–10.

29–30 Physical punishment may achieve
Quoted in Clare Collins, "Spanking Is Becoming the New Don't," *The New York Times*, 11 May 1995, p. C8.

30 Corporal punishment is
Christopher G. Ellison, John P. Bartkowski and Michelle L. Segal, "Conservative Protestantism and the Parental Use of Corporal Punishment," *Social Forces*, 74 (1996): 1003.

30 The Convention contains
Michael Jupp, "Symposium: Confronting the Challenge of Realizing Human Rights Now," *Howard Law Journal*, 34 (1991): 15.

30–31 It also emphasizes
Cynthia Price Cohen and Hedwin Naimark, "United Nations Convention on the Rights of the Child," *The American Psychologist*, 46 (1991): 60.

31 Conservatives are opposed
Quoted in Greg D. Erken, "Yes: Halt Social Engineering of the Nation's Families," *Insight on the News*, 15 May 1995, p. 18.

31 Conservatives are opposed to legislation
Quoted in Rochelle L. Stanfield, "Children's Issues at a Crossroads," *National Journal*, 17 Apr. 1993, p. 956.

31 A *Newsweek* story
Frankel, "Who's Hands-On, Who's Hands-Off?" p. 58.

32 For example, after several children
Betsy Carpenter, "Taking Nature's Cure," *U. S. News & World Report*, 26 June 1995, p. 54; Elizabeth Gleick, "The Call of the Wild," *Time*, 26 June 1995, p. 64.

32 One story identified
Carpenter, "Taking Nature's Cure," p. 54.

32 One mother, whose son died
Gleick, "The Call of the Wild," p. 64.

32–33 In another article, a mother
Carpenter, "Taking Nature's Cure," p. 56.

33 A sidebar on child-escort companies
"'Wake Up, You're Coming with Me,'" *U. S. News & World Report*, 26 June 1995, p. 58.

33 Many of the programs
Carpenter, "Taking Nature's Cure," p. 55.

35 In the 1995 version
Village of the Damned. Dir. John Carpenter. 1995.

CHAPTER 2

37 The idea that children
Richard J. Gelles, "Family Reunification/Family Preservation: Are Children Really Being Protected?" *Journal of Interpersonal Violence*, 8 (1993): 560.

38 As Jessica was carried
Geoffrey Cowley, "Who's Looking After the Interests of Children?" *Newsweek*, 16 Aug. 1993, p. 54; David Grogan, "Life after Jessica," *People*, 5 Sep. 1994, p. 46.

39 In her book
Robby DeBoer, *Losing Jessica*, (New York: Doubleday, 1994), p. 249.

39 A survey of reader opinions
"Were the Courts Right to Send Jessica DeBoer Back to Her Biological Parents?" *Glamour*, Jan. 1994, p. 77.

39 *People* magazine reported
"Mail," *People*, 9 Aug. 1993, p. 5.

40 Even an article that agreed
John Taylor, "Biological Imperative," *New York*, 16 Aug. 1993, p. 12.

40 A *Time* cover story announced
Nancy Gibbs, "In Whose Best Interest?" *Time*, 19 July 1993, p. 45; Cowley, "Who's Looking After the Interests of Children?" p. 54; Leslie Bennetts, "The Baby Jessica Story: Why the Court Was Wrong," *Parents Magazine*, Sep. 1993, p. 197.

40 As Elizabeth Bartholet
Elizabeth Bartholet, "Blood Parents vs. Real Parents," *The New York Times*, 13 July 1993, p. A15.

41 For example, in the context
Anita Diamant, "Is It Safe to Adopt a Child?" *McCall's*, Jan. 1994, p. 100.

41 *Time* quoted Howard Davidson
Quoted in Gibbs, "In Whose Best Interest?" p. 49.

41 It did not challenge
Quoted in Diamant, "Is It Safe to Adopt a Child?" p. 97–98.

43 As Elizabeth Bartholet
Quoted in Sam Howe Verhovek, "Couple Ordered to Return Girl to Biological Parents," *The New York Times*, 3 July 1993, p. 5.

43 Reform goals include
Elizabeth Bartholet, *Family Bonds: Adoption and the Politics of Parenting* (Boston: Houghton Mifflin, 1993), p. 77; Eric P. Salthe, "Would Abolishing the Natural Parent Preference in Custody Disputes Be in Everyone's Best Interest?" *Journal of Family Law*, 29 (1990–91): 539; Gilbert A. Holmes, "The Tie That Binds: The Constitutional Right of Children to Maintain Relationships with Parent-Like Individuals," *University of Maryland School of Law*, 53 (1994): 358.

44 For example, the *Time* cover story
Gibbs, "In Whose Best Interest?" p. 46.

44 One of the *People*
"Baby Jessica," *People*, 27 Dec. 1993, p. 69.

44 An article in *McCall's*
Diamant, "Is It Safe to Adopt a Child?" p. 98.

44 In *Newsweek*, "Jessica symbolized
Michele Ingrassia and Karen Springen, "She's Not Baby Jessica Anymore," *Newsweek*, 21 Mar. 1994, p. 60; Steven Waldman and Lincoln Caplan, "The Politics of Adoption," *Newsweek*, 21 Mar. 1994, p. 64.

44 According to *U.S. News & World Report*
Joseph P. Shapiro, "Bonds That Blood and Birth Cannot Assure," *U. S. News & World Report*, 9 Aug. 1993, p. 13.

44 In *McCall's*
Diamant, "Is It Safe to Adopt a Child?" p. 97.

44 Although a few
"Cutting the Baby in Half," *The New York Times*, 8 Aug. 1993, p. E14; Verhovek, "Couple Ordered to Return Girl to Biological Parents," p. 5.

44–45 For example, one article
Barbara Vobejda, "The Anguish of Contested Adoption: Michigan Case Cited as Example of Urgent Need for Legal Changes," *The Washington Post*, 13 Apr. 1993, p. A1.

45 And later spin-off articles
Susan Chira, "Adoption Is Getting Some Harder Looks," *The New York Times*, 25 Apr. 1993, E1; Tamar Lewin, "The Strains on the Bonds of Adoption," *The New York Times*, 8 Aug. 1993, p. 1.

45 As the Baby Jessica case
Diamant, "Is It Safe to Adopt a Child?" p. 148; Vobejda, "The Anguish of Contested Adoption," p. A1.

45 As one delegate
Quoted in "A Familiar Custody Case, a Different Decision," *The New York Times*, 29 Aug. 1993, p. 28.

46 Then, according to one article
Taylor, "Biological Imperative," p. 12.

46 Others considered Cara Clausen
Bennetts, "The Baby Jessica Story," p. 198.

46 As one article put
Isabel Wilkerson, "Custody Battle: Is Conception Parenthood?" *The New York Times*, 27 Dec. 1992, p. 20.

47 The *New York Times* stated
Don Terry, "Tug-of-War Ends As Child Goes from Home to Home," *The New York Times*, 3 Aug. 1993, p. A8. ; Verhovek, "Couple Ordered to Return Girl to Biological Parents," p. 5.

47 *People* magazine narrowed
Bill Hewitt, "Losing Jessi," *People*, 19 July 1993, p. 49–50.

47 By characterizing the Baby Jessica
Waldman and Caplan, "The Politics of Adoption," p. 65.

48 *People* wrote that
"Baby Jessica," *People*, 27 Dec. 1993, p. 69.

48 *Newsweek* proclaimed that
Michele Ingrassia, "A Bitter New Battle in the Custody Wars," *Newsweek*, 11 July 1994, p. 59.

48 *Time* wrote that the custody
Quoted in Gibbs, "In Whose Best Interest?" p. 46.

48 In the context
Susan Chira, "Adult Tugs-of-War over What's 'Best' for a Child," *The New York Times*, 7 Aug. 1994, p. 3.

48 The *New York Times* said
Chira, "Adoption Is Getting Some Harder Looks," p. E1.

48 *National Review* called
"Biology and Destiny," *National Review*, 6 Sep. 1993, p. 19.

48 And *People* stated that
Hewitt, "Losing Jessi," p. 50.

49 *People*, for example, paraphrased
Hewitt, "Losing Jessi," p. 53.

49 Coverage did not refer
Bartholet, *Family Bonds*, p. 179.

49–50 The following two examples
Terry, "Tug-of-War Ends As Child Goes from Home to Home," p. A8 (italics mine); Ingrassia and Springen, "She's Not Baby Jessica Anymore," p. 66 (italics mine).

50 The mother of
Hewitt, "Losing Jessi," p. 53.

50 A *Newsweek* article reduced
Ingrassia and Springen, "She's Not Baby Jessica Anymore," p. 64.

51 The *New York Times* quoted
Terry, "Tug-of-War Ends As Child Goes from Home to Home," p. A8.

51–52 One *Newsweek* article quotes
Ingrassia and Springen, "She's Not Baby Jessica Anymore," p. 63–64.

52 Cara told reporters
Ingrassia and Springen, "She's Not Baby Jessica Anymore," p. 64.

52 Regarding a large toy cottage
Ingrassia and Springen, "She's Not Baby Jessica Anymore," p. 62.

52 *Newsweek* wrote that
Cowley, "Who's Looking After the Interests of Children?" p. 54.

53 As Robby DeBoer later
DeBoer, *Losing Jessica*, p. 120.

53 One psychologist
Quoted in Cowley, "Who's Looking After the Interests of Children?" p. 54.

53 According to Robby DeBoer
DeBoer, *Losing Jessica*, p. 120.

54 "She's Not Baby Jessica
Ingrassia and Springen, *Newsweek*, 21 March 1994, p. 64.

54 Based only on an interview
Ingrassia and Springen, "She's Not Baby Jessica Anymore," p. 60–61.

54 The article quoted the pilot
Quoted in Ingrassia and Springen, "She's Not Baby Jessica Anymore," p. 66.

54 We wanted to believe
Ingrassia and Springen, "She's Not Baby Jessica Anymore," p. 60.

54–55 *People* magazine wrote
"Baby Jessica," *People*, 27 Dec. 1993, p. 70.

55 Coverage of the case
Losing Isaiah. Dir. Stephen Gyllenhaal. 1995.

55 In a scene from
Ingrassia and Springen, "She's Not Baby Jessica Anymore," p. 61 (italics mine).

56 On some level
Bartholet, *Family Bonds*, p. 167.

56 Studies on adoption
Bartholet, *Family Bonds*, p. 80.

56 As an article
Salthe, "Would Abolishing the Natural Parent Preference in Custody Disputes Be in Everyone's Best Interest?" p. 545.

57 As Todd explains
Parenthood. Dir. Ron Howard. 1990.

59 As Roger McIntire
Roger McIntire, "Parental Competency Tests," in Mary Ann Mason and Eileen Gambrill, eds. *Debating Children's Lives: Current Controversies on Children and Adolescents* (Thousand Oaks, CA: Sage Publications, 1994), p. 5.

59 In her book
Judith D. Schwartz, *The Mother Puzzle: A New Generation Reckons with Motherhood* (New York: Simon & Schuster, 1993), p. 12–13.

59–60 The feature film
Nine Months. Dir. Chris Columbus. 1995.

61 Article after article quoted
See, for example, "A Familiar Custody Case, a Different Decision," *The New York Times*, 29 Aug. 1993, p. 28; and Judith Gaines, "'Unique' Adoption Ruling: Both Sides Cheer Settlement That Shares Vt. Boy," *The Boston Globe*, 21 Aug. 1993, p. 1.

61 The problem with holding
Quoted in Jean Seligmann, "Stirring Up the Muddy Waters," *Newsweek*, 30 Aug. 1993, p. 58.

CHAPTER 3

63 If there is any pattern
Stephanie Coontz, *The Way We Never Were: American Families and the Nostalgia Trap* (New York: Basic Books, 1992), p. 230.

64 Articles quoted neighbors
Quoted in Robert Davis, "A Shocked S. C. Town Asks: Why?" *USA Today*, 4 Nov. 1994, p. 3A.

64–65 Polly's murder by
Elizabeth Gleick, "'America's Child,'" *People*, 20 Dec. 1993, p. 84.

65 Ted Gest wrote
Ted Gest, "Violence in America," *U. S. News & World Report*, 17 Jan. 1994, p. 22.

65 Article after article
Gleick, "'America's Child,'" p. 84.

66 "While the absolute numbers
Gest, "Violence in America," p. 22.

66–67 For example, one cover story
Gest, "Violence in America," p. 22.

67 "Missing Children
Laura Sessions Stepp, "Missing Children: The Ultimate Nightmare," *Parents Magazine*, Apr. 1994, p. 47 (italics mine).

67 Like the *Parents Magazine*
"How Parents Can Talk to Their Kids," *Newsweek*, 10 Jan. 1994, p. 50.

67–68 In contrast, *New York* magazine
Michael W. Robbins, "Sparing the Child," *New York*, 10 Dec. 1990, p. 43–44.

68 One article explained
Gest, "Violence in America," p. 22.

68–69 *Newsweek*'s Jerry Adler pontificated
Jerry Adler, "Kids Growing Up Scared," *Newsweek*, 10 Jan. 1994, p. 43 (italics mine).

69 "By the 1950s
Barbara J. Nelson, *Making an Issue of Child Abuse: Political Agenda Setting for Social Problems* (Chicago, IL: University of Chicago Press, 1984), p. 12–13, 129.

69–70 He does say
Adler, "Kids Growing Up Scared," p. 46.

70 If Smith was involved
Davis, "A Shocked S. C. Town Asks: Why?" p. 3A.

70 Smith's claim that
Rick Bragg, "Insanity Plea Expected in Boys' Drownings," *The New York Times*, 9 Nov. 1994, p. A18.

71 Coverage of the Smith case
Karen S. Peterson, "South Carolina Killings May Haunt Families Everywhere," *USA Today*, 7 Nov. 1994, p. 4D.

71 Another woman told
Peterson, "South Carolina Killings May Haunt Families Everywhere," p. 4D.

71–72 As Diane E. Eyer writes
Diane E. Eyer, *Mother-Infant Bonding: A Scientific Fiction* (New Haven, CT: Yale University Press, 1992), p. 14.

72 The popular image
Arlene Skolnick, "The Family Revisited: Themes in Recent Social Science Research," *The Journal of Interdisciplinary History*, 4 (1975): 715.

72 The social sciences
Skolnick, "The Family Revisited," p. 715.

72 "Child rearing evokes
Jane Swigart, *The Myth of the Bad Mother: The Emotional Realities of Mothering* (New York: Doubleday, 1991), p. 7.

258 · LUCIA HODGSON

72 A recent mainstream article
Nancy Gibbs, "Death and Deceit," *Time*, 14 Nov. 1994, p. 42.

73 Diane Eyer urges
Eyer, *Mother-Infant Bonding*, p. 199.

73 "Obviously, the most desirable
"How to Pick a Proper Nanny," *USA Today*, 123 (1994): 4.

74 However, the nannies-
Karen S. Schneider, "When the Bough Breaks," *People*, 24 Feb. 1992, p. 60.

74 An article about
Schneider, "When the Bough Breaks," p. 60.

74–75 In early 1990
Robin Abcarian, "Just Like Home?" *The Los Angeles Times*, 15 May 1991, p. E1.

76 Our culture's entrenched doctrine
W. Norton Grubb and Marvin Lazerson, *Broken Promises: How Americans Fail Their Children* (Chicago, IL: University of Chicago Press, 1982), p. 6.

76 "Even when the child's
Laura Oren, "The State's Failure to Protect Children and Substantive Due Process: DeShaney in Context," *North Carolina Law Review*, 68 (1990): 718–719.

77 As Cynthia Crosson Tower writes
Cynthia Crosson Tower, *Understanding Child Abuse and Neglect* (Boston, MA: Allyn and Bacon, 1993), p. 38.

77 Much abuse evades
Brian Corby, *Child Abuse: Towards a Knowledge Base* (Bristol, PA: Open University Press, 1993), p. 99.

77 The answer to the question
Richard J. Gelles and Murray A. Straus, *Intimate Violence* (New York: Simon & Schuster, 1988), p. 20.

77–78 They are, according to
Tower, *Understanding Child Abuse and Neglect*, p. 37.

78 One contemporary religious article
David R. Miller, "The Discipline Decision," *Fundamentalist Journal*, Mar. 1987, p. 65.

78 Most "severe
Bruce Bower, "Growing Up in Harm's Way," *Science News*, 25 May 1996, p. 333.

78 In families where stress
Blair Justice, Ph.D. and Rita Justice, Ph.D., *The Abusing Family* (New York: Plenum Press, 1990), p. 14.

78–79 As Gelles and Straus
Gelles and Straus, *Intimate Violence*, p. 35.

79–80 And, of course
Quoted in David Gelman, "An Emotional Moonscape," *Newsweek*, 17 May 1993, p. 53.

81 As the regional director
Melinda Beck, "'Someone Dropped the Ball,'" *Newsweek*, 17 May 1993, p. 51.

81 And so the organization
Beck, "'Someone Dropped the Ball,'" p. 51.

81 In further defense
Beck, "'Someone Dropped the Ball,'" p. 51.

81 "Every law-enforcement agent
Beck, "'Someone Dropped the Ball,'" p. 51.

81 Workers were sensitive
Quoted in Ginny Carroll and Peter Annin, "Children of the Cult," *Newsweek*, 17 May 1993, p. 50.

83 Texas law states
Quoted in Justice and Justice, *The Abusing Family*, p. 5.

83 Furthermore, the definition
Dean M. Herman, "A Statutory Proposal to Prohibit the Infliction of Violence upon Children," *Family Law Quarterly*, 19 (1985): 12.

84 A past president
Lisa C. Jones, "Why Are We Beating Our Children?" *Ebony*, Mar. 1993, p. 81–82.

84–85 Martha Minow, a professor
Martha Minow, "Perspective on Children: Coming Between Parent and Child," *The Los Angeles Times*, 28 Sep. 1992, p. B7.

85 Linda Gordon, an historian
Linda Gordon, *Heroes of Their Own Lives: The Politics and History of Family Violence* (New York, Viking Penguin, 1988), p. 3.

85 "This just don't happen
Davis, "A Shocked S. C. Town Asks: Why?" p. 3A.

85 "While the explanations
Rick Bragg, "Life of a Mother Accused of Killing Offers No Clues," *The New York Times*, 6 Nov. 1994, p. 1.

CHAPTER 4

89 [A]cceptable doublespeak
Louise Armstrong, *Rocking the Cradle of Sexual Politics: What Happened When Women Said Incest* (Reading, MA: Addison-Wesley Publishing, 1994), p. 105.

89 "Amid a plethora of concerns
Anna Quindlen, "Public & Private: The Passion to Keep Them Safe," *The New York Times,* 6 Aug. 1994, p. 19.

90 *Indictment*, the HBO version
Indictment. Dir. Mick Jackson. 1996.

91 "Had Jordan [Minnesota]
Armstrong, *Rocking the Cradle of Sexual Politics*, p. 114.

94 These editorial decisions
Debbie Nathan, "'The Teacher Hurt Me': Why Children Don't Always Tell the Truth about Sexual Abuse," *Redbook Magazine*, Apr. 1996, p. 96.

94 It prompted the press
Lawrence Wright, "Child-Care Demons," *The New Yorker*, 3 Oct. 1994, p. 5; Charles Krauthammer, "The Return of the Primitive," *Time*, 29 Jan. 1996, p. 82.

94 In the mid-1990s
Laura Shapiro, "The Lesson of Salem," *Newsweek*, 31 Aug. 1992, p. 64.

94–95 "I suspect it will be virtually
The Crucible. Dir. Nicholas Hytner. 1996; Victor Navasky, "The Demons of Salem, with Us Still," *The New York Times*, 8 Sep. 1996, p. H37.

95 The conservative publication
"The Salem Epidemic: Comparison of Ritual Child Sex Abuse Cases to Salem Witchcraft Trials," *National Review*, 3 Sep. 1990, p. 14.

95 Even Richard A. Gardner
Richard A. Gardner, *Sex Abuse Hysteria: Salem Witch Trials Revisited* (Cresskill, NJ: Creative Therapeutics, 1991), p. 7.

96 The case of Margaret Kelly Michaels
Wright, "Child-Care Demons," p. 5.

96 An article in *Harper's*
Dorothy Rabinowitz, "From the Mouths of Babes to a Jail Cell," *Harper's Magazine*, May 1990, p. 52–53.

96 Even though articles
Andrea Gross, "Who's Telling the Truth?" *Ladies' Home Journal*, June 1994, p. 76.

96 Michaels was convicted
Rabinowitz, "From the Mouths of Babes to a Jail Cell," p. 52.

96 However, her conviction
John Taylor, "Salem Revisited: Justice in a Sex-Abuse Case," *New York*, 12 Apr. 1993, p. 10.

97 Sexual abuse of children
Stephen J. Ceci and Eduardus de Bruyn, "Child Witnesses in Court: A Growing Dilemma," *Children Today*, 22 (1993): 5.

97–98 An article in *Redbook*
Debbie Nathan, "Sweet Justice: My Fight to Free Kelly Michaels," *Redbook Magazine*, June 1995, p. 85.

98 In some cases
David Finkelhor and Linda Meyer Williams with Nanci Burns, *Nursery Crimes: Sexual Abuse in Day Care* (Newbury Park, CA: Sage Publications, 1988), p. 95.

98 They are most likely
Teena Sorensen and Barbara Snow, "How Children Tell: The Process of Disclosure in Child Sexual Abuse," *Child Welfare*, 120 (1991): 13.

98 In the Michaels case
Quoted in Rabinowitz, "From the Mouths of Babes," p. 54.

99 For example, children
Sandra A. Burkhardt and Anthony F. Rotatori, *Treatment and Prevention of Childhood Sexual Abuse: A Child-Generated Model* (Washington, D.C.: Taylor & Francis, 1995), p. 145.

99 During the phase
Sorensen and Snow, "How Children Tell," p. 10.

99 For some, denial
Sorensen and Snow, "How Children Tell," p. 14.

99–100 During this part
Sorensen and Snow, "How Children Tell," p. 10.

100 One-fifth of the children
Margaret Rieser, "Recantation in Child Sexual Abuse Cases," *Child Welfare*, 120 (1991): 612; Sorensen and Snow, "How Children Tell," p. 11.

100 One writer wondered
Wright, "Child-Care Demons," p. 6.

100 This task made them
Taylor, "Salem Revisited," p. 10.

100–101 We criticized investigators
Rich Lowry, "Creating Victims," *National Review*, 5 Dec. 1994, p. 66.

101 For example, they didn't
Gina Richardson, "Understanding the Development of Children's Language Can Help Adults Communicate Better," *NRCCSA News*, May/June 1995, p. 6.

101 For example, passive
Richardson, "Understanding the Development of Children's Language Can Help Adults Communicate Better," p. 6.

101 One McMartin juror
Quoted in Tracy Wilkinson and James Rainey, "Tapes of Children Decided the Case for Most Jurors," *The Los Angeles Times*, 19 Jan. 1990, p. A1.

101–102 Abuse victims often
Finkelhor and Williams, *Nursery Crimes*, p. 103.

102 In McMartin, people
Douglas J. Besharov, "Protecting the Innocent: McMartin Pre-School Case," *National Review*, 19 Feb. 1990, p. 44.

103 The press refers
Laura Shapiro, "Rush to Judgment," *Newsweek*, 19 Apr. 1993, p. 59.

103 According to Gail S. Goodman
Gail S. Goodman, "Understanding and Improving Children's Testimony," *Children Today*, 22 (1993): 13.

103 A notable exception
Carol Tavris, "Can Children's Testimony in Sexual Abuse Cases Be Trusted?" *Vogue*, Apr. 1990, p. 284–288.

103–104 The children were asked
Tavris, "Can Children's Testimony in Sexual Abuse Cases Be Trusted?" p. 286.

104 According to Goodman
Quoted in Tavris, "Can Children's Testimony in Sexual Abuse Cases Be Trusted?" p. 286.

104 Three of the children
Goodman, "Understanding and Improving Children's Testimony," p. 13.

104 In addition, according to
Ceci and de Bruyn, "Child Witnesses in Court," p. 5.

104–105 In other words
Lowry, "Creating Victims," p. 66.

105 Second, the powerful
May Benatar, "Running Away from Sexual Abuse: Denial Revisited," *Families in Society: The Journal of Contemporary Human Services*, 76 (1995): 316.

105 The appellate court
Quoted in Taylor, "Salem Revisited," p. 10.

106 One writer commented
Taylor, "Salem Revisited," p. 10.

106 Another argued that
Lowry, "Creating Victims," p. 66.

106–107 The *Economist*, writing
"Satanic Abuse: Salem Revisited," *The Economist*, 31 Aug. 1991, p. 23.

107 "The libel that our
Wright, "Child-Care Demons," p. 6.

107 For example, a *Newsweek*
Shapiro, "Rush to Judgment," p. 54–60.

109 A study of confirmed
Charol Shakeshaft and Audrey Cohan, "Sexual Abuse of Students by School Personnel," *Phi Delta Kappan*, Mar. 1995, p. 513–520.

110 Despite our culture's anti-child
Gross, "Who's Telling the Truth?" p. 76.

110 Apparently, our society
Shapiro, "Rush to Judgment," p. 54.

110–111 We had, it turns out
Nathan, "'The Teacher Hurt Me,'" p. 96.

111 "A social attitude
Gardner, *Sex Abuse Hysteria*, p. 125.

111 In an article on allegations
Wright, "Child-Care Demons," p. 6.

111 An article in *Newsweek*
Jon Meacham, "Trials and Troubles in Happy Valley," *Newsweek*, 8 May 1995, p. 60.

112 We couldn't believe
Taylor, "Salem Revisited," p. 10.

113 For example, *Time* columnist
Margaret Carlson, "Six Years of Trial by Torture," *Time*, 29 Jan. 1990, p. 26.

113–114 Several judges have written
Quoted in Wright, "Child-Care Demons," p. 6; Quoted in Besharov, "Protecting the Innocent," p. 44.

114 *National Review* went
Lowry, "Creating Victims," p. 66.

114 We can claim
Charles S. Clark, "Child Sexual Abuse," *CQ Researcher*, 3 (1993): 39.

CHAPTER 5

117 It is hard to think
Kai Erikson, "Scandal or Scapegoating?" *The New York Times*,
1 Sep. 1996, p. 12.

118 A key element
Neil Postman, *The Disappearance of Childhood* (New York: Delacorte
Press, 1982; New York: Random House, 1994).

118–119 Instead, they identify media
Nancy Gibbs, "How Should We Teach Our Children About Sex?"
Time, 24 May 1993, p. 63.

119 In an article about
Bruno Bettelheim, "Letting Children Be Children . . . While They
Can," *The Chicago Tribune*, 13 May 1990, p. 23.

119 A *New York Times* article entitled
Lucinda Franks, "Little Big People," *The New York Times,* 10 Oct. 1993,
p. 28.

120 In his book
Mike A. Males, *The Scapegoat Generation: America's War on Adolescents* (Monroe, ME: Common Courage Press, 1996), p. 16–18.

120 Adults also play
Males, *The Scapegoat Generation*, p. 16–19, 48, 56.

121 Our culture's response
Michele Ingrassia, "Calvin's World," *Newsweek*, 11 Sep. 1995, p. 60.

121 Even when we could
Margaret Carlson, "Where Calvin Crossed the Line," *Time*,
11 Sep. 1995, p. 64.

121 *U.S. News & World Report*
Joseph P. Shapiro, "Sins of the Fathers," *U. S. News & World Report*,
14 Aug. 1995, p. 51.

121 Joe Klein wrote
Joe Klein, "The Predator Problem," *Newsweek*, 29 Apr. 1996, p. 32.

121–122 We now realize
Ruth Shalit, "Romper Room: Sexual Harassment—by Tots," *The New Republic*, 29 Mar. 1993, p. 13.

122 In reference to a new
John Leo, "What Qualifies as Sexual Harassment?" *U. S. News & World Report*, 13 Aug. 1990, p. 17.

122 Less than six years later
John Leo, "Expel Georgie Porgie Now!" *U. S News & World Report*, 14 Oct. 1996, p. 37.

122 Major magazines
Carin Rubenstein, "Educators Urged to Address Sexual Harassment in School," *The New York Times*, 10 June 1993, p. A13.

122 In other words
Felicity Barringer, "School Hallways As a Gauntlet of Sexual Taunts," *The New York Times*, 2 June 1993, p. A10.

122 Harassment was found
Barringer, "School Hallways As a Gauntlet of Sexual Taunts," p. A10.

122–123 And students of both sexes
Jane Gross, "Schools Are Newest Arena for Sex-Harassment Cases," *The New York Times*, 11 Mar. 1992, p. A1.

123 Articles did complain
John Leland, "A Kiss Isn't Just a Kiss," *Newsweek*, 21 Oct. 1996, p. 71.

123 "While some schools
Tamar Lewin, "Kissing Cases Highlight Schools' Fears of Liability for Sexual Harassment," *The New York Times*, 6 Oct. 1996, p. 10.

123 According to the survey
American Association of University Women Educational Foundation, "Hostile Hallways: The AAUW Survey on Sexual Harassment in America's Schools," June 1993, p. 10.

123 The few articles that did
See, for example, Barringer, "School Hallways As a Gauntlet of Sexual Taunts," or Gross, "Schools Are Newest Arena for Sex-Harassment Cases."

124 A study presented
Kelly Corbett, Cynthia S. Gentry, and Willie Pearson, Jr., "Sexual Harassment in High School," *Youth & Society*, 25 (1993): 97–98.

124 Another survey of college
Charol Shakeshaft and Audrey Cohan, "Sexual Abuse of Students by School Personnel," *Phi Delta Kappan*, Mar. 1995, p. 514.

125–126 Like the prosecuting attorney
Quoted in Rod Carveth, "Amy Fisher and the Ethics of 'Headline' Docudramas," *Journal of Popular Film and Television*, 21 (1993):121.

126 "Now I see a blob
Betsy Israel, "Amy Fisher's Time," *The New York Times Magazine*, 21 July 1996, p. 18.

126 "I was lonely and so scared
Israel, "Amy Fisher's Time," p. 18.

127 One magazine characterized
Jeanie Kasindorf, "Running Wild: The Amy Fisher Story," *New York*, 10 Aug. 1992, p. 29.

127 "She was their only child
Joe Treen, "Sex, Lies & Videotape," *People*, 12 Oct. 1992, p. 104.

127 In general, coverage expressed
Maria Eftimiades, "I Survived a Media Feeding Frenzy," *Inside Media*, 18 Nov. 1992, p. 1.

127 In general, we did not
Quoted in Treen, "Sex, Lies & Videotape," p. 104.

127 At the same time
William A. Henry, III, "Read All about Lolita!" *Time*, 15 June 1992, p. 62.

128 The woman who ran
Kasindorf, "Running Wild," p. 29.

128 The Nassau County district attorney
Quoted in Kasindorf, "Running Wild," p. 29.

128 The most widely quoted
Quoted in Treen, "Sex, Lies & Videotape," p. 104.

128 *The Crush*
The Crush. Dir. Alan Shapiro. 1993.

130 Woody Allen rationalized
Quoted in Walter Isaacson, "'The Heart Wants What It Wants,'" *Time*, 31 Aug. 1992, p. 59.

130 This belief pervades
Husbands and Wives. Dir. Woody Allen. 1992.

132 "The correlation between
Males, *The Scapegoat Generation*, p. 11.

132 Many young women "try
Michelle Oberman, "At Issue: Statutory Rape Laws," *ABA Journal*, 82 (1996): 86.

132–133 Many young women "may
Mike Males, "In Defense of Teenaged Mothers," *The Progressive*, 58 (1994): 22.

133 Teenage girls growing up
Judith S. Musick, *Young, Poor, and Pregnant: The Psychology of Teenage Motherhood* (New Haven, CT: Yale University Press, 1993), p. 13.

133 "The adolescent mother
Quoted in Males, *The Scapegoat Generation*, p. 92–93.

133 In a speech given
Weekly Compilation of Presidential Documents, "Remarks on Receiving the Teen Pregnancy Report," 32 (1996): 1054.

133 According to *U.S. News & World Report*
Joseph P. Shapiro, "Teenage Sex: Just Say 'Wait,'" *U.S. News & World Report*, 26 July 1993, p. 56.; Michele Ingrassia, "Virgin Cool," *Newsweek*, 17 Oct. 1994, p. 58.

134 Magazines ran stories
Katrine Ames, "Practicing the Safest Sex of All," *Newsweek*, 20 Jan. 1992, p. 52; Lance Morrow, "Fifteen Cheers for Abstinence," *Time*, 2 Oct 1995, p. 90; Philip Elmer-Dewitt, "Making the Case for Abstinence," *Time*, 24 May 1993, p. 64.

134 One survey found
Quoted in Shapiro. "Teenage Sex," p. 56.

134 As Mike A. Males points out
Males, *The Scapegoat Generation*, p. 68.

134–135 Mainstream articles tend
Shapiro. "Teenage Sex," p. 56.

135 A *Newsweek* article expressed
Joe Klein, "Learning How to Say No," *Newsweek*, 13 June 1994, p. 29.

135 Articles also criticize
Ingrassia, "Virgin Cool," p. 58.

136 The doll, designed
Susan Reed, "Wake-Up Call," *People*, 10 Oct. 1994, p. 103; "Lifelike Dolls That Can Make You Cry," *Newsweek*, 5 Dec. 1994, p. 68.

136 One article touted
Don Oldenburg, "A Real Doll, But Not So Cuddly or Cute," *The Washington Post*, 13 Sep. 1996, p. F5.

136 The doll apparently
Reed, "Wake-Up Call," p. 103; Terese Hudson, "Practice Parenting," *Hospitals & Health Networks*, 5 Sep. 1996, p. 68; Oldenburg, "A Real Doll, But Not So Cuddly or Cute," p. F5.

136 Coverage praised
Oldenburg, "A Real Doll, But Not So Cuddly or Cute," p. F5.

136 "It woke me up three times
Reed, "Wake-Up Call," p. 103.

136 Another girl was described
Oldenburg, "A Real Doll, But Not So Cuddly or Cute," p. F5.

137 Lance Morrow argued
Morrow, "Fifteen Cheers for Abstinence," p. 90.

138 It may be true
Jonathan Alter, "The Name of the Game Is Shame," *Newsweek,*
12 Dec. 1994, p. 41.; Larry D. Dorrell, "A Future at Risk: Children
Having Children," *The Clearing House,* 67 (1994): 224.

138–139 Not only do studies
Males, *The Scapegoat Generation,* p. 9.

<h2 style="text-align:center">CHAPTER 6</h2>

141 The adult temptation
Richard Rodriguez, "A Crisis of Intimacy: Who Are Our Children?" *The Los Angeles Times,* 19 Dec. 1993, p. M1.

142 Yet the public
"Are We Too Soft on Juvenile Crime?" *Glamour,* Oct. 1994, p. 167.

142 A news analysis
Jennifer Vogel, "Throw Away the Key," *Utne Reader,* July–Aug. 1994,
p. 60.

142 A 1996 *New York Times* editorial
"Wrong Approach to Teen-Age Crime," *The New York Times,*
30 June 1996, p. E14.

144 Articles predict a future epidemic
Mike A. Males, *The Scapegoat Generation: America's War on Adolescents* (Monroe, ME: Common Courage Press, 1996), p. 21.

144 In a *U. S. News & World Report* article
Ted Gest and Dorian Friedman, "The New Crime Wave," *U. S.
News & World Report,* 29 Aug. 1994, p. 26.

145 As an article entitled
Gordon Witkin and Ted Gest, "Street Crime: An Agenda for Change," *U. S. News & World Report*, 5 Oct. 1992, p. 44 (italics mine).

145 Mainstream coverage indirectly
David Gelman, "The Violence in Our Heads," *Newsweek*, 2 Aug. 1993, p. 48.

145 The American Psychological
Daniel Goleman, "Hope Seen for Curbing Youth Violence," *The New York Times*, 11 Aug. 1993, p. A10.

145 "Without adults to keep
Brent Staples, "The Littlest Killers," *The New York Times*, 6 Feb. 1996, p. A22.

145 In this context
Quoted in Tom Morganthau, "The Lull Before the Storm?" *Newsweek*, 4 Dec. 1995, p. 40.

145 An article in *Time*
Anastasia Toufexis, "Our Violent Kids," *Time*, 12 June 1989, p. 52.

146 An article entitled
Quoted in Scott Minerbrook, "A Generation of Stone Killers," *U. S. News & World Report*, 17 Jan. 1994, p. 33.

146 "As today's five-year-old
Paul J. McNulty, "Natural Born Killers?" *Policy Review*, Wntr, 1995, p. 84.

146 This logic dictates
Males, *The Scapegoat Generation*, p. 21.

146 It creates a context
Quoted in Fox Butterfield, "Republicans Challenge Notion of Separate Jails for Juveniles," *The New York Times*, 24 June 1996, p. A1.

147 As one article
Peter Katel, "The Bust in Boot Camps," *Newsweek*, 21 Feb. 1994, p. 26.

147 Sometimes articles do
Minerbrook, "A Generation of Stone Killers," p. 33.

148 For example, a short
Peter Annin, "'Superpredators Arrive," *Newsweek*, 22 Jan. 1996, p. 57.

148 Once children who
Katel, "The Bust in Boot Camps," p. 21.

148 As one reporter
Richard Lacayo, "When Kids Go Bad," *Time*, 19 Sep. 1994, p. 60.

149 As a family-court judge
Judy Sheindlin with Josh Getlin, "No Excuses," *Ladies' Home Journal*, May 1996, p. 130.

149 In other words
Quoted in Fox Butterfield, "States Revamping Youth Crime Laws," *The New York Times*, 12 May 1996, p. A1.

149 Alex Kotlowitz, author
Alex Kotlowitz, "'They Are, in Fact, Just Children,'" *USA Weekend*, 21–23 Oct. 1994, p. 4.

150 In 1992, *Time*
Anastasia Toufexis, "When Kids Kill Abusive Parents," *Time*, 23 Nov. 1992, p. 60.

150 In fear for her life
Jane Mayer, "Rejecting Gina," *The New Yorker*, 5 June 1995, p. 49.

151 Her former lawyer
Quoted in Fox Butterfield, "Woman Who Killed Mother Denied Harvard Admission," *The New York Times*, 8 Apr. 1995, p. A1.

151 And her mother's brother
Quoted in Bill Hewitt, "Poisoned Ivy," *People*, 24 Apr. 1995, p. 42.

152 According to Kathleen M. Heide
Kathleen M. Heide, "How a Legacy of Child Abuse Leads to Homicide," *Psychology Today*, Sep.–Oct. 1992, p. 66.

152 Sometimes when his father
Toufexis, "When Kids Kill Abusive Parents," p. 60.

152 Once, according to court records
Mayer, "Rejecting Gina," p. 46.

153 Prosecutor Pamela Bozanich
Quoted in Jerry Adler, "Killing as a Cry for Help," *Newsweek*, 20 Dec. 1993, p. 103; Quoted in Elizabeth Gleick, "Blood Brothers," *People*, 27 Sep. 1993, p. 32.

153 Even an article
John Taylor, "L. A. Blues," *New York*, 20 Sep. 1993, p. 43.

153 Menendez was so oppressive
Taylor, "L. A. Blues," p. 43.

153 One of the tennis
Gleick, "Blood Brothers," p. 32.

153 "When Erik's swimming
Jerry Adler, "Murder 90210: Crime Styles of the Young, Rich and Impatient?" *Newsweek*, 2 Aug. 1993, p. 60.

153 Another time
Adler, "Murder 90210," p. 60.

154 She once
"Sons Killed Parents: Why Is Only Issue," *The New York Times*, 21 July 1993, p. A8.

154 She sometimes locked
Adler, "Killing as a Cry for Help," p. 103.

154 In a routine
Seth Mydans, "Stories of Sexual Abuse Transform Murder Trial," *The New York Times*, 12 Sep. 1993, p. 30.

154 Their parents often
Gleick, "Blood Brothers," p. 32; "Sons Killed Parents," p. A8.

154 The parents kept
Mydans, "Stories of Sexual Abuse Transform Murder Trial," p. 30.

154 Jose told him
"Sons Killed Parents," p. A8.

155 According to Lyle
George J. Church, "Sons and Murderers," *Time*, 4 Oct. 1993, p. 68.

155 And he lectured
Gleick, "Blood Brothers," p. 32.

155 "Sometimes putting his
Mydans, "Stories of Sexual Abuse Transform Murder Trial," p. 30.

155 As one journalist wrote
Seth Mydans, "Killers as Victims: Defending Menendez Brothers," *The New York Times*, 19 Nov. 1993, p. A30.

156 Despite the fact
Church, "Sons and Murderers," p. 68.

156 An article in *Commentary*
Walter Berns, "Getting Away with Murder," *Commentary*, Apr. 1994, p. 25.

156 An article in the *New York Times*
Robert Reinhold, "Bevery Hills Journal: Real Life Produces Plot Fit for Movie," *The New York Times*, 14 Mar. 1990, p. A20.

156 An article in *Esquire*
Pete Hamill, "Murder on Mulholland," *Esquire*, June 1990, p. 70.

157 A *Time* article stated
Jill Smolowe, "Waiting for the Verdicts," *Time*, 20 Dec. 1993, p. 48.

157 While articles stated
Mydans, "Stories of Sexual Abuse," p. 30.

157 The prosecuting attorney's cryptic
Quoted in Stuart Goldman, "Murder as Therapy," *National Review*, 29 Nov. 1993, p. 44.

157 The trial, the author wrote
Goldman, "Murder as Therapy," p. 44.

158 According to Kathleen M. Heide
Heide, "How a Legacy of Child Abuse Leads to Homicide," p. 66.

158 She "had been flying
Mayer, "Rejecting Gina," p. 48.

159 Erik told his therapist
Quoted in Mydans, "Killers as Victims," p. A30.

159 Like a battered woman
Church, "Sons and Murderers," p. 68.

159 Three days before
"Sons Say Slayings Were Only Option," *The New York Times*, 19 Sep. 1993, p. 29.

159 A few days later
Quoted in "Sons Say Slayings Were Only Option," p. 29.

159 At that point
"Sons Say Slayings Were Only Option," p. 29; Quoted in Elizabeth Gleick, "Second Time Around," *Time*, 23 Oct. 1995, p. 90.

159–160 According to court testimony
Church, "Sons and Murderers," p. 68.

160 As a friend of Kitty's
Quoted in Gleick, "Blood Brothers," p. 32.

160 Even though victims
Berns, "Getting Away with Murder," p. 25.

160 A column in *Time*
Margaret Carlson, "That Killer Smile," *Time*, 7 Feb. 1994, p. 76.

160 Another article argued
Berns, "Getting Away with Murder," p. 25.

160 An editorial in
Brent Staples, "The Rhetoric of Victimhood," *The New York Times*, 13 Feb. 1994, p. 14.

161 The belief that they
Carlson, "That Killer Smile," p. 76.

161 "That may be the
Toufexis, "When Kids Kill Abusive Parents," p. 60.

162 Within days, however
Mayer, "Rejecting Gina," p. 47.

162 One argued that the brothers
Joe Domanick, "Family Affair," *Los Angeles*, June 1990, p. 140.

162 An article in *Time* editorialized
Nancy Gibbs, "The Hottest Show in Hollywood," *Time*, 1 Oct. 1990, p. 46.

162 Another article pointed out
Church, "Sons and Murderers," p. 68.

163 In an interview given
Quoted in John Johnson and Ronald L. Soble, "The Brothers Menendez," *The Los Angeles Times Magazine*, 22 July 1990, p. 6, 15.

163 One article quoted the priest
Quoted in Johnson and Soble, "The Brothers Menendez," p. 8.

163 A young man
Quoted in Toufexis, "When Kids Kill Abusive Parents," p. 60.

163 A *Newsweek* article argued
Adler, "Murder 90210," p. 60.

163–164 An article in *Time* magazine
Church, "Sons and Murderers," p. 68.

164 The prosecution felt
Mydans, "Stories of Sexual Abuse Transform Murder Trial," p. 30.

164 As Erik's lawyer explained
Quoted in Taylor, "L. A. Blues," p. 42.

165 One article doubted
Taylor, "L. A. Blues," p. 43.

165 "I spent my whole
Quoted in Toufexis, "When Kids Kill Abusive Parents," p. 60.

165 According to an article
Toufexis, "When Kids Kill Abusive Parents," p. 60.

165 This woman called
Mayer, "Rejecting Gina," p. 48.

166 When Lyle confided
Gleick, "Blood Brothers," p. 32.

166 "We discussed: Would
Quoted in Church, "Sons and Murderers," p. 68.

166 Yet, in addition
Quoted in Smolowe, "Waiting for the Verdicts," p. 48.

166 However, one critical article
Berns, "Getting Away with Murder," p. 25.

167 The idea that Lyle
"Not Guilty on Grounds of Being a Victim," *Glamour*, July 1994, p. 68.

167 Despite its basis
Sophfronia Scott Gregory, "Oprah! Oprah in the Court!" *Time*, 6 June 1994, p. 30.

167 Another complained that
Taylor, "L. A. Blues," p. 42.

167 The defense was criticized
Adler, "Murder 90210," p. 60.

167 The defense countered
Interview by Mary A. Fischer, "'Knock It Off, Darden,'" *GQ*, Nov. 1995, p. 192.

167 Yet many people felt
Quoted in Mydans, "Stories of Sexual Abuse Transform Murder Trial," p. 30.

167 The prosecution did not deny
Gleick, "Second Time Around" p. 90.

167 Instead, they argued
Mydans, "Stories of Sexual Abuse Transform Murder Trial," p. 30.

168 As one article noted
Domanick, "Family Affair," p. 140.

168 Another commented
Johnson and Soble, "The Brothers Menendez," p. 8.

168 While it was repeatedly
Joseph Pointdexter, "A Beverly Hills Paradise Lost," *People*, 26 Mar. 1990, p. 66.

168 As he greets
Quoted in Johnson and Soble, "The Brothers Menendez," p. 13.

168 One critic of the Menendez
Taylor, "L. A. Blues," p. 43.

169 While it's true
Leslie Abramson, "Unequal Justice," *Newsweek*, 25 July 1994, p. 25.

169 On the contrary
Carlson, "That Killer Smile," p. 76; Staples, "The Rhetoric of Victimhood," p. 14

169 The Menendez brothers
John Taylor, "Don't Blame Me: The New Culture of Victimization," *New York*, 3 June 1991, p. 28.

169–170 As Erik's attorney explained
Abramson, "Unequal Justice," p. 25.

170 An article in *Vogue*
Julia Reed, "Excuse Me," *Vogue*, May 1994, p. 105.

170 A *Time* magazine article
Carlson, "That Killer Smile," p. 76.

170 An article in *Glamour* acknowledged
"Not Guilty on Grounds of Being a Victim," p. 68.

170 An article in *Time* entitled
Gregory, "Oprah! Oprah in the Court!" p. 30.

170 As an article in the *New Yorker*
Jeffrey Toobin, "Humility and Justice: What People Do Is a Lot Clearer Than Why They Do It," *The New Yorker*, 1 Apr. 1996, p. 7.

170 According to an interview
Gregory, "Oprah! Oprah in the Court!" p. 31.

171 The commissioner of the state's
Mayer, "Rejecting Gina," p. 49.

171 While we self-righteously
"Not Guilty on Grounds of Being a Victim," p. 68.

171–172 Of all the hundreds
Gleick, "Blood Brothers," p. 32.

172 Adults are right
John Leo, "The It's-Not-My-Fault Syndrome," *U. S. News & World Report*, 18 June 1990, p. 16.

172 The author of a sarcastic
Reed, "Excuse Me," p. 104.

173 In *The Good Son*
The Good Son. Dir. Joseph Ruben. 1993.

173–174 In a critique of parental
Ellen Goodman, "The Latest Parent Trap," *The Boston Globe*, 16 May 1996, p. 25.

CHAPTER 7

177 One thing is sure
Sylvia Ann Hewlett, *When the Bough Breaks: The Cost of Neglecting Our Children* (New York: Basic Books, 1991), p. 18.

176 Within less than two weeks
Eleanor Clift, "The Murphy Brown Policy," *Newsweek*, 1 June 1992,
p. 46.

177 The ensuing "family values" debate
Dan Quayle, "Restoring Basic Values: Strengthening the Family,"
Vital Speeches of the Day, 15 June 1992, p. 517.

177 According to an article
William Schneider, "Why 'Family Values' Won't Go Away,"
National Journal, 5 Sep. 1992, p. 36.

177 "That there is something called
Katha Pollitt, "Why I Hate 'Family Values' (Let Me Count the
Ways)," *The Nation*, 20 July 1992, p. 88.

177–178 "From coast to coast
Ronald Brownstein, "Democrats Find the Right's Stuff: Family
Values," *The Los Angeles Times*, 1 Aug. 1994, p. A1.

178 The *National Center for Children in Poverty*
Judith E. Jones, "Child Poverty: A Deficit That Goes Beyond Dollars," *National Center for Children in Poverty*, 1994, p. 7.

178 Most poor children
"Number of Poor Children under Six Increased from 5 to 6 Million 1987–1992," *National Center for Children in Poverty*, 5 (1995): 1.

180 *Time*'s cover story editorialized
David Van Biema, "Abandoned to Her Fate," *Time*, 11 Dec. 1995,
p. 32.

180 A *New York Times* editorial
"Abusing the Nation's Children," *The New York Times*, 1 Jan. 1996,
p. 20.

180 And an article in *National Review*
Joyce Milton, "Suffer Little Children?" *National Review*, 26 Feb. 1996,
p. 50.

181 In general, according to
Lela B. Costin, Cynthia J. Bell, and Susan W. Downs, *Child Welfare: Policies and Practices*, 4th ed. (New York: Longman, 1991), p. 69.

182 As an article in the journal
Howard Dubowitz, Maureen Black, Raymond H. Starr, Jr., and Susan Zuravin, "A Conceptual Definition of Child Neglect," *Criminal Justice and Behavior*, 20 (1993): 22.

182 The *New York Times* called
"Keeping Families Off Foster Care," *The New York Times*, 13 Aug. 1991, p. A10.

182–183 *Newsweek* commented that
Katrine Ames, "Fostering the Family," *Newsweek*, 22 June 1992, p. 64.

183 As one reporter noted
Cathy Corman, "Fragile Families Are Guided Past Crises," *The New York Times*, 11 Nov. 1990, p. CN12.

183–184 In one scene
Corman, "Fragile Families Are Guided Past Crises," p. CN12.

185 As an editoral in
Andrew L. Shapiro, "Children in Court—the New Crusade," *The Nation*, 27 Sep. 1993, p. 301.

185 Apparently, family-preservation caseworkers
Jon Nordheimer, "Early Action Rescuing Troubled Families," *The New York Times*, 11 Apr. 1991, p. C1.; Corman, "Fragile Families Are Guided Past Crises," p. CN12.

185 One article reported
Ames, "Fostering the Family," p. 64.

185 Another argued that
J. C. Barden, "Counseling to Keep Families Together," *The New York Times*, 21 Sep. 1990, p. A12.

185–186 Even though the foster-care
Judy Mann, "An Investment in the Future," *The Washington Post*, 28 July 1993, p. E15.

186 In the context of this
Lucille Renwick, "Recession Propels Increase in Child Abuse," *The Los Angeles Times*, 20 Mar. 1994, p. 3.

186 Who could resist
Quoted in Renwick, "Recession Propels Increase in Child Abuse," p. 3.

186 A typical article explained
Celia W. Dugger, "New York City Bets Millions on Preserving Families," *The New York Times*, 19 July 1991, p. A1.

186 Another reported that caseworkers
Corman, "Fragile Families Are Guided Past Crises," p. CN12.

187 *Time* opened its description
David Van Biema, "Calcutta, Illinois," *Time*, 14 Feb. 1994, p. 30.

187 *Newsweek* felt that
Michele Ingrassia and John McCormick, "Why Leave Children with Bad Parents?" *Newsweek*, 25 Apr. 1994, p. 52.

187 To its credit, the *Newsweek* article
Ingrassia and McCormick, "Why Leave Children with Bad Parents?" p. 52.

188 The media's discussion
Dugger, "New York City Bets Millions on Preserving Families," p. A1.

188 The *New York Times* argued that
Celia W. Dugger, "Plan to Save Families Draws Child-Welfare Debate," *The New York Times*, 6 Aug. 1993, p. A1.

189 He argues that many
Richard Wexler, "Child Abuse—the Wrong Message," *Neiman Reports*, 47 (1993): 22.

189 An article in
Mann, "An Investment in the Future," p. E15.

189 Critics of family preservation
Bruce A. Boyer, Letter to the Editor, *The New York Times*, 3 July 1993, p. 18.

189 They embraced Dan Quayle's notion
Heather Mac Donald, "The Ideology of 'Family Preservation,'" *The Public Interest*, 115 (1994): 58.

190 "Left out of the analysis
Mac Donald, "The Ideology of 'Family Preservation,'" p. 59.

190 Articles acknowledge that
Dugger, "New York City Bets Millions on Preserving Families," p. A1.; "Assault on the Family," *U. S. News & World Report*, 6 Apr. 1992, p. 63.

190 As Ann Hartman
Ann Hartman, "Family Preservation under Attack," *Social Work*, 38 (1993): 511.

191 While it is certainly true
Mindy Holliday and Robin Cronin, "Families First: A Significant Step toward Family Preservation," *Families in Society: The Journal of Contemporary Human Services*, 71 (1990): 303.

191–192 Poverty, according to
David Hamburg, *Today's Children: Creating a Future for a Generation in Crisis* (New York: Times Books, 1992), p. 9–10.

192 Ideally, family preservation
Holliday and Cronin, "Families First," p. 306.

192 It may be true that
Mac Donald, " The Ideology of 'Family Preservation,'" p. 57.

193 In brief, as an article
Martha Morrison Dore, "Family Preservation and Poor Families: When 'Homebuilding' Is Not Enough," *Families in Society: The Journal of Contemporary Human Services*, 74 (1993): 549–550.

193 Even the conservative columnist
George F. Will, "Mothers Who Don't Know How," *Newsweek*, 23 Apr. 1990, p. 80.

193–194 In 1994, Will backtracked
George F. Will, "About Those 'Orphanages,'" *Newsweek*, 12 Dec. 1994, p. 88.

194 As a result, underprivileged children
Douglas J. Besharov, "How Child Abuse Programs Hurt Poor Children: The Misuse of Foster Care," *Clearinghouse Review*, 22 (1988): 222.

194 In sum, our society
Besharov, "How Child Abuse Programs Hurt Poor Children," p. 222.

196 According to George F. Will
Will, "About Those 'Orphanages,'" p. 88.

196 An editorial in *National*
"Scrooge Redivivus? Newt Gingrich's Call for Public Orphanages," *National Review*, 31 Dec. 1994, p. 14.

196 As one columnist pointed
Katha Pollitt, "Subject to Debate," *The Nation*, 13 Feb. 1995, p. 192.

197 One article explained
Tom Morganthau, "The Orphanage," *Newsweek*, 12 Dec. 1994, p. 28.

197 According to an article in *Insight*
Elena Neuman, "Caring for Kids When Parents Don't," *Insight on the News*, 6 July 1992, p. 34.

198 While they build
Quoted in Neuman, "Caring for Kids When Parents Don't," p. 34.

199 *Nation* columnist Katha Pollitt
Katha Pollitt, "The Violence of Ordinary Life," *The Nation*, 1 Jan. 1996, p. 9.

199 And Jonathan Kozol
Jonathan Kozol, "Spare Us the Cheap Grace," *Time*, 11 Dec. 1995, p. 96.

CHAPTER 8

203 [C]hildren are changing fast
Patricia Sellers, "The ABC's of Marketing to Kids," *Fortune*, 8 May 1989, p. 120.

205 "The scene," one article
Annetta Miller and Dody Tsiantar, "The Kids Play—and You Pay," *Newsweek*, 12 Nov. 1990, p. 52.

205 Another article on pay-per-use
Elizabeth Rudulph, "Old-Fashioned Play—for Pay," *Time*, 4 Nov. 1991, p. 86.

205 An article about "Kids Only"
Karen Springen, "Drop the Kid, Then Shop," *Newsweek*, 21 Jan. 1991, p. 56.

205 As one article put it
Miller and Tsiantar, "The Kids Play—and You Pay," p. 52.

205–206 The "days of shopping
Springen, "Drop the Kid, Then Shop," p. 56.

206 Another reported that
Jean Seligmann, "Mind the Kids, Hold the Starch," *Newsweek*, 11 Nov. 1991, p. 67B.

206 "As public playgrounds grow
Rudulph, "Old Fashioned Play—for Pay," p. 86.

207 "Stealth baby-sitting" is an expression
Michel Marriott, "Stealth Baby-Sitting," *Newsweek*, 14 Aug. 1995, p. 60.

207 On the one hand,
Laura Bird, "Need a Sitter? Some Parents Use Barnes & Noble," *The Wall Street Journal*, 17 Aug. 1995, p. B1.

207 Rather than questioning
Quoted in Bird, "Need a Sitter?" p. B1.

207 An article in the *Wall Street Journal*
Bird, "Need a Sitter?" p. B1.

208 The *Wall Street Journal* called
Bird, "Need a Sitter?" p. B1; Marriott, "Stealth Baby-Sitting," p. 60.

208 The *Wall Street Journal* asks
Bird, "Need a Sitter?" p. B1.

208 In an anecdote, *Newsweek*
Marriott, "Stealth Baby-Sitting," p. 60.

209 In addition, they must
Arlene Skolnick, *Embattled Paradise: The American Family in the Age of Uncertainty* (New York: Basic Books, 1991), p. 203.

209 In January 1996, *Time*
George J. Church, "Are We Better Off?" *Time*, 29 Jan. 1996, p. 36.

210 A *National Journal* article
Rochelle L. Stanfield, "Valuing the Family," *National Journal*, 4 July 1992, p. 1562.

210 Even *Business Week* acknowledged
"The Right Family Values in the Workplace," *Business Week*, 28 June 1993, p. 134.

210 We also acknowledge that
Jill Smolowe, "The Stalled Revolution," *Time*, 6 May 1996, p. 63.

210 Even though over
James E. Ellis, "What Price Child Care?" *Business Week*, 8 Feb. 1993, p. 104.

211 David Elkind, author of
David Elkind, "The Family in the Postmodern World," *National Forum*, 75 (1995): 24.

211 While infant day care
Elkind, "The Family in the Postmodern World," p. 27.

211 Finding the best environment
Andrea Atkins, "Choosing Child Care," *Better Homes and Gardens*, Sep. 1995, p. 62.

211 Despite our knowledge
Mary Loftin Grimes, "Who's Minding the Parents?" *National Forum*, 75 (1995): 4

211 As one article put it
Ellis, "What Price Child Care?" p. 104.

211–212 Given how much time
Kenneth Labich, "Can Your Career Hurt Your Kids?" *Fortune*, 20 May 1991, p. 52.

212 Roughly one-third
Barbara Vobejda, "Child-Care Centers Get Low Ratings," *The Washington Post*, 6 Feb. 1995, p. A1.

212 Overall, "Most [center] child
Rochelle L. Stanfield, "When a Penny Saved Is a Dollar Spent," *National Journal*, 29 Apr. 1995, p. 1059.

212 Another five million children
Barbara Vobejda, "6 Million of Nation's Youngest Children Face Developmental Risks," *The Washington Post*, 13 Apr. 1994, p. A3.

212 For school-age children
James Willwerth, "'Hello? I'm Home Alone,'" *Time*, 1 Mar. 1993, p. 46

212–213 According to *Time* magazine
Willwerth, "'Hello? I'm Home Alone,'" p. 46

213 They are more likely
Charlene Marmer Solomon, "Latchkey Kids," *Parents Magazine*, Mar. 1994, p. 42.

213 "As a nation
Quoted in "Study: Child Care Centers Often Dismal," *The Atlanta Journal and The Atlanta Constitution*, 6 Feb. 1995, p. A4.

213 And when it comes
Tom Engelhardt, "The Primal Screen" *Mother Jones*, May–June 1991, p. 69.

214 Due to several dramatic
Ellen Wartella, "The Commercialization of Youth: Channel One in Context," *Phi Delta Kappan*, Feb. 1995, p. 448.

214 According to a widely quoted
Christopher Power, "Getting 'Em While They're Young," *Business Week*, 9 Sep. 1991, p. 94.

214 Teens spend over
Lorne Manly, "The Teen Dream: Marketers Pursue the Growing Teenage Market," *Mediaweek*, 22 July 1991, p. 26.

214 These sales figures
Manly, "The Teen Dream," p. 26.

214 Children are touted
Power, "Getting 'Em While They're Young," p. 94.; Deborah Baldwin, "Read This: American Are Badgered Around the Clock by the Hard Sell. Is There Any Escape?" *Common Cause Magazine*, May–June 1991, p. 30.

214 Corporations have sought
Wartella, "The Commercialization of Youth," p. 448.

214 The youth market has become
Quoted in Sellers, "The ABC's of Marketing to Kids," p. 115.

214 In 1990, we invested
Baldwin, "Read This," p. 30.

214 "Visuals count
Paul Kurnit, "10 Tips from the Top Agency," *Advertising Age*, 10 Feb. 1992, p. S10.

215 When conducted with children
Betsy Spethmann, "Focus Groups Key to Reaching Kids," *Advertising Age*, 10 Feb. 1992, p. S1.

215 The most important lesson
Spethmann, "Focus Groups Key to Reaching Kids," p. S1.

215 According to James Garbarino
James Garbarino, *Raising Children in a Socially Toxic Environment* (San Francisco, CA: Jossey-Bass Publishers, 1995), p. 14.

215 "Smart marketers recognize
Quoted in Manly, "The Teen Dream," p. 26.

215 As a result, writes
Murray Raphel, "Are You Kidding?" *Direct Marketing*, July 1993, p. 38.

215 Add to the receptive
Baldwin, "Read This," p. 30.

215 The average child
Steven Pratt, "Cartoon-Fed Kids," *The Chicago Tribune*, 29 Mar. 1995, p. 3.

216 Once billions of consumer
Peter Newcomb, "Hey, Dude, Let's Consume," *Forbes*, 11 June 1990, p. 126.

216 "The kids' market is
Sellers, "The ABC's of Marketing to Kids," p. 115.

216 "With the traditional household
Junu Bryan Kim, "For Kids, It's a Fast Spinning, Real World," *Advertising Age*, 14 Feb. 1994, p. S1.

216 Fortunately for advertisers
Penelope Leach, *Children First: What Society Must Do—and Is Not Doing—for Children Today* (New York: Alfred A. Knopf, 1994), p. 23.

216–217 "Working and single parents
Power, "Getting 'Em While They're Young," p. 94.

217 Children are being forced
Spethmann, "Focus Groups Key to Reaching Kids," p. S1.

217 Targeting advertising directly
Susan Antilla, "'I Want' Now Gets," *The New York Times*, 4 Apr. 1993, p. EA17.

217 In addition, researchers
Antilla, "'I Want' Now Gets," p. EA17.

217 As one researcher told
Quoted in Antilla, "'I Want' Now Gets," p. EA17.

217 In most child-care settings
Diane Bennett, "From the Lone Ranger to Power Rangers," *Vital Speeches*, 1 Feb. 1995, p. 251.

217 Latchkey children who
Solomon, "Latchkey Kids," p. 42.

217 According to a survey
Carin Rubenstein, "Today's Kids Turn Off Fitness," *The New York Times Magazine*, 7 Oct. 1990, p. 34.

217–218 The average child
Richard Zoglin, "Is TV Ruining Our Children," *Time*, 15 Oct. 1990, p. 75–76.

218 In 1991, the president
Quoted in Fred Hift, "TV Stations Try to Toe the Line on Better Programs for Children," *The Christian Science Monitor*, 25 June 1991, p. 15.

218 "Kids have no childhood
Quoted in Hift, "TV Stations Try to Toe the Line on Better Programs for Children," p. 15.

218 An article in *Forbes*
Newcomb, "Hey, Dude, Let's Consume," p. 126.

218 With "that current American
Brian Bagot, "What's Up for Kids," *Marketing and Media Decisions*, May 1990, p. 49.

218–219 One expert predicts
Bagot, " What's Up for Kids," p. 49.

219 In addition, with
Laura Shapiro, "The Zap Generation," *Newsweek*, 26 Feb. 1990, p. 56.

219 "In their bids to
Bagot, "What's Up for Kids," p. 49.

219 "[W]ith fast-food sales
Newcomb, "Hey, Dude, Let's Consume," p. 126.

219 For example, Kraft
Alison Fahey, "'Batman' Set to Rouse Next Generation of Syndicated TV Viewers," *Advertising Age*, 10 Feb. 1992, p. S21.

219 In addition, children
Shapiro, "The Zap Generation," p. 56.

219 And perhaps most
Pratt, "Cartoon-Fed Kids," p. 3.

219–220 The food industry is
Sellers, "The ABC's of Marketing to Kids," p. 115.

220 In the "two-working-parent
Manly, "The Teen Dream," p. 26.

220 The good news
Kim, "For Kids, It's a Fast Spinning, Real World," p. S1.

220 "Mom's got to run
Bagot, "What's Up for Kids," p. 49.

220 An ad for Kid Cuisine
Bagot, "What's Up for Kids," p. 49.

220 An ad for Hormel
Shapiro, "The Zap Generation," p. 56.

220–221 An article in *Journal*
James Helmer, "Love on a Bun: How McDonald's Won the Burger Wars," *Journal of Popular Culture*, 26 (1992): 85.

221 The scene in one ad
Stephen Drucker, "Who Is the Best Restaurateur in America?" *The New York Times Magazine*, 10 Mar. 1996, p. 45.

221 Tapping into parents'
Helmer, "Love on a Bun," p. 85.

221 They are flooding
"TV Food Ads Feed Kids the Wrong Message," *Tufts University Diet and Nutrition Letter*, Jan. 1995, p. 7.

221 A recent study found
Pratt, "Cartoon-Fed Kids," p. 3.

221 According to *Advertising Age*
Emily DeNitto, "Fast-Food Ads Come under Fire," *Advertising Age*, 14 Feb. 1994, p. S14.

222 In one survey
"Study Says Kids' TV Ads Too Sweet," *The Chicago Tribune*, 4 June 1991, p. C5.

222 "Commercial food advertisements
Gina Pazzaglia Sylvester, Cheryl Achterberg and Jerome Williams, "Children's Television and Nutrition: Friends or Foes?" *Nutrition Today*, 30 (1995): 6; Rubenstein, "Today's Kids Turn Off Fitness," p. 34.

222 Research suggests that
Quoted in Pratt, "Cartoon-Fed Kids," p. 3.

222 There is a strong correlation
Sylvester, Achterberg and Williams, "Children's Television and Nutrition," p. 34.

222 In the *New York Times*
Rubenstein, "Today's Kids Turn Off Fitness," p. 34.

223 "The No. 1 responsibility
DeNitto, "Fast-Food Ads Come under Fire," p. S14.

223 "The fact is," another executive
"Kids' Ad Special Raises Some Eyebrows of Critics," *Advertising Age*, 10 Feb. 1992, p. S14.

223 In response to an HBO
"Kids' Ad Special Raises Some Eyebrows of Critics," p. S14.

224 It has made billions
Rubenstein, "Today's Kids Turn Off Fitness," p. 34.

224 "In today's classrooms
Elizabeth Gleick, "Blackboards As Billboards," *Time*, 10 June 1996, p. 68.

224 One consultant told
Quoted in Antilla, "'I Want Now Gets," p. EA17.

224 Or put another way
Sellers, "The ABC's of Marketing to Kids," p. 116.

224 An article in *Mediaweek*
Bagot, "What's Up for Kids," p. 49.

224–225 In one article
Kim, "For Kids, It's a Fast Spinning, Real World," p. S1.

225 Another ad plays
Sellers, "The ABC's of Marketing to Kids," p. 116.

225 The Committee on Communications
"TV Food Ads Feed Kids the Wrong Message," p. 7.

225 However, as one article editorialized
"TV Food Ads Feed Kids the Wrong Message," p. 7.

226 As a senior ad executive
DeNitto, "Fast-Food Ads Come under Fire," p. S14.

226 As an article in *Business*
Jerry Mander, "The Myth of the Corporate Conscience," *Business and Society Review*, 81 (1992):56.

227 The recent spate
Ann Louise Page, "We're Good Guys: Image Propaganda for Mobil Oil," *Business and Society Review*, 93 (1995): 33.

227 An article in *Time*
Nancy R. Gibbs, "Bringing Up Father," *Time*, 28 June 1993, p. 52.

227 A 1991 *Newsweek* article
Springen, "Drop the Kid, Then Shop," p. 56.

228 "Businesses are finding
Springen, "Drop the Kid, Then Shop," p. 56.

228 *Business Week* tells readers
"The Right Family Values in the Workplace," p. 134.

229 Despite the Children's Television
Harry F. Waters, "Watch What Kids Watch," *Newsweek*, 8 Jan. 1990, p. 50.

229 Despite the increasingly significant
Newton M. Minow and Craig L. LaMay, *Abandoned in the Wasteland: Children, Television and the First Amendment* (New York: Hill and Wang, 1995), p. 10.

229 The industry develops shows
Wartella, "The Commercialization of Youth," p. 448.

229 As an article in *Time* reminded
Steve Wulf, "Glued to the Tube," *Time*, 26 June 1995, p. 66.

229–230 As a vice president
Quoted in Brain Donlon, "Watching Kids' TV," *USA Today*, 16 Apr. 1991, p. D1.

231 According to an article in *Time*
Jonathan Alter, "Next: 'The Revolt of the Revolted,'" *Newsweek*, 6 Nov. 1995, p. 46.

231 And even though legislators
Ginia Bellafante, "Locking Out Violence," *Time*, 24 July 1995, p. 64.

231 "Networks and stations
Zoglin, "Is TV Ruining Our Children," p. 76.

232 "Rather than removing
Richard Zoglin, "Chips Ahoy," *Time*, 19 Feb. 1996, p. 58.

232 James Garbarino supports
Garbarino, *Raising Children in a Socially Toxic Environment*, p. 8.

232 He argues that we
Minow and LaMay, *Abandoned in the Wasteland*, p. 153.

233 As one put it
Zoglin, "Chips Ahoy," p. 59.

233 Despite the evidence
Bill Saporito, "Good for the Bottom Line," *Time*, 20 May 1996, p. 41.

233 One of the most popular
Home Alone. Dir. Chris Columbus. 1990.

LUCIA HODGSON has been involved with children's issues since 1991. She is currently director of the Gaylord Donnelley Children and Youth Studies Center at Crossroads School for Arts & Sciences in Santa Monica, California. She has served as a consultant to the Harvard Project on Schooling and Children at Harvard University, where she helped to develop a childrens' studies program as a new interdisciplinary field within the university.

Raised in Captivity has been set in the Legacy family of typefaces. Legacy reinterprets Renaissance masterpieces for digital composition. The roman is based on a type cut in Venice by Nicolas Jenson (1469). The model for the italic was cut in Paris by Claude Garamond (1539).

Typesetting by Stanton Publication Services, Inc., St. Paul. Printed by Quebecor-Fairfield on acid-free paper.

Book design by Will Powers